HUTCHINSON POCKET

Dictionary of
British History

GW00402046

Other titles in the Hutchinson Pocket series:

HUTCHINSON POCKET

Dictionary of
British History

Copyright © Helicon Publishing Ltd 1994

All rights reserved

Helicon Publishing Ltd
42 Hythe Bridge Street
Oxford OX1 2EP

Printed and bound in Great Britain by
Unwin Brothers Ltd, Old Woking, Surrey

ISBN-1-85986-008-7

British Cataloging in Publication Data

A catalogue record for this book is available
from the British Library

Acquisitions Director
Anne-Lucie Norton

Contributor
Adrian Room

Text Editor
Paul Davis

Page make-up
Ann Dixon

Production
Tony Ballsdon

Introduction

There are over 1000 entries in the *Hutchinson Pocket Dictionary of British History* covering everything from abdication crisis to Kim Philby to Fire of London to Hadrian's Wall to the Magna Carta. The aim is to provide a grounding in all the main people, periods, events, movements, landmark legislation and places over a period covering 3,500 years.

'British History' in the Pocket does include Welsh, Scottish and Irish history where the person or development is inextricably linked (as is often the case) with English history. All of these are, of course, worthy of books on their own, but it is valuable, even in a book the size of the *Pocket*, to appreciate how the histories of these countries overlap and affect each other over the centuries.

The book is not aimed at the specialist, nor is for anyone requiring detailed information within the vast subject that is British history.

Of course, history does not stop and the *Pocket* contains much of current interest and including recent events, e.g. Maastricht Treaty, the members of the current Cabinet, the 1991 population of London (the most recent available officially) are examples.

It is the intention that the *Pocket Dictionary of British History* provide a satisfying tour through several thousand years of human development as it has expressed itself in the British Isles.

A

abdication crisis in British history, the constitutional upheaval of the period 16 Nov 1936 to 10 Dec 1936, brought about by the British king Edward VIII's decision to marry Wallis Simpson, a US divorcee.

The marriage of the 'Supreme Governor' of the Church of England to a divorced person was considered unsuitable and the king was finally forced to abdicate on 10 Dec and left for voluntary exile in France. He was created Duke of Windsor and married Mrs Simpson on 3 June 1937.

Abercromby Ralph 1734–1801. Scots soldier who in 1801 commanded an expedition to the Mediterranean, charged with the liquidation of the French forces left behind by Napoleon in Egypt. He fought a brilliant action against the French at Aboukir Bay in 1801, but was mortally wounded at the battle of Alexandria a few days later.

Aberdeen George Hamilton Gordon, 4th Earl of Aberdeen 1784–1860. British Tory politician, prime minister 1852–55 when he resigned because of the criticism aroused by the miseries and mismanagement of the ◊Crimean War.

absolutism or *absolute monarchy* system of government in which the ruler or rulers have unlimited power. The principle of an absolute monarch, given a right to rule by God (see ◊divine right of kings), was extensively used in Europe during the 17th and 18th centuries.

Absolute monarchy is contrasted with limited or constitutional monarchy, in which the sovereign's powers are defined or limited.

act of Parliament in Britain, a change in the law originating in Parliament and called a statute. Before an act receives the royal assent and becomes law it is a *bill*.

An act of Parliament may be either public (of general effect), local, or private. The body of English statute law comprises all the acts passed by Parliament: the existing list opens with the Statute of Merton, passed 1235. An act (unless it is stated to be for a definite period and then to come to an end) remains on the statute book until it is repealed.

How an act of Parliament becomes law:

1 first reading of the bill The title is read out in the House of Commons (H of C) and a minister names a day for the second reading.

2 The bill is officially printed.

3 second reading A debate on the whole bill in the H of C followed by a vote on whether or not the bill should go on to the next stage.

4 committee stage A committee of MPs considers the bill in detail and makes amendments.

5 report stage The bill is referred back to the H of C which may make further amendments.

6 third reading The H of C votes whether the bill should be sent on to the House of Lords.

7 House of Lords The bill passes through much the same stages in the Lords as in the H of C. (Bills may be introduced in the Lords, in which case the H of C considers them at this stage.)

8 last amendments The H of C considers any Lords' amendments, and may make further amendments which must usually be agreed by the Lords.

9 royal assent The Queen gives her formal assent.

10 The bill becomes an act of Parliament at royal assent, although it may not come into force until a day appointed in the act.

Acton John Emerich Edward Dalberg-Acton, 1st Baron Acton 1834–1902. British historian and Liberal politician. Elected to Parliament 1859, he was a friend and adviser of Prime Minister Gladstone. Appointed professor of modern history at Cambridge in 1895, he planned and edited the Cambridge Modern History but did not live to complete more than the first two volumes.

Adams Gerry (Gerard) 1948– . Northern Ireland politician, president of Provisional Sinn Féin (the political wing of the IRA) from 1978. He was elected member of Parliament for Belfast West 1983 but declined to take up his Westminster seat, stating that he did not believe in the British government. He has been criticized for failing to denounce IRA violence. He was interned in the 1970s because of his connections with the IRA, and later released.

Addington Henry 1757–1844. British Tory politician and prime minister 1801–04, he was created Viscount Sidmouth 1805. As home secretary 1812–1822, he was responsible for much repressive legislation, including the notorious ◊Six Acts.

Addled Parliament the English Parliament that met for two months in 1614 but failed to pass a single bill before being dissolved by James I.

Adelaide 1792–1849. Queen consort of ◊William IV of England. Daughter of the Duke of Saxe-Meiningen, she married William, then Duke of Clarence, in 1818. No children of the marriage survived infancy.

Admiralty, Board of the in Britain, the controlling department of state for the Royal Navy from the reign of Henry VIII until 1964, when most of its functions – apart from that of management – passed to the Ministry of Defence. The 600-year-old office of Lord High Admiral reverted to the sovereign.

Adrian IV (Nicholas Breakspear) *c.* 1100–1159. Pope 1154–59, the only British pope. He secured the execution of Arnold of Brescia, crowned Frederick I Barbarossa as German emperor, refused Henry II's request that Ireland should be granted to the English crown in absolute ownership, and was at the height of a quarrel with the emperor when he died.

Afghan Wars three wars waged between Britain and Afghanistan to counter the threat to British India from expanding Russian influence in Afghanistan.
First Afghan War 1838–42, when the British garrison at Kabul was wiped out.
Second Afghan War 1878–80, when General Roberts captured Kabul and relieved Kandahar.
Third Afghan War 1919, when peace followed the dispatch by the UK of the first aeroplane ever seen in Kabul.

Agincourt, Battle of battle of the Hundred Years' War in which Henry V of England defeated the French on 25 Oct 1415, mainly through the overwhelming superiority of the English longbow. The French lost more than 6,000 men to about 1,600 English casualties. As a result of the battle, Henry gained France and the French princess, Catherine of Valois, as his wife. The village of Agincourt (modern *Azincourt*) is south east of Calais, in N France.

Alamein, El, Battles of in World War II, two decisive battles in the western desert, N Egypt. In the *First Battle of El Alamein* 1–27 July 1942, the British 8th Army under Auchinleck held the German and Italian forces under Rommel. In the *Second Battle of El Alamein* 23 Oct–4 Nov 1942, ◊Montgomery defeated Rommel.

Albert Prince Consort 1819–1861. Husband of British Queen Victoria from 1840; a patron of the arts, science, and industry. Albert was the second son of the Duke of Saxe-Coburg-Gotha and first cousin to Queen Victoria, whose chief adviser he became. He planned the Great Exhibition of 1851; the profit was used to buy the sites in London of all the South Kensington museums and colleges and the Royal Albert Hall, built 1871. He died of typhoid.

Albion ancient name for Britain used by the Greeks and Romans. It was mentioned by Pytheas of Massilia (4th century BC), and is probably of pre-Celtic origin, but the Romans, having in mind the white cliffs of Dover, assumed it to be derived from *albus* (white).

Alcock John William 1892–1919. British aviator. On 14 June 1919, he and Arthur Whitten Brown (1886–1948) made the first nonstop transatlantic flight, from Newfoundland to Ireland.

alderman Anglo-Saxon term for the noble governor of a shire; after the Norman Conquest the office was replaced with that of sheriff. From the 19th century aldermen were the senior members of the borough or county councils in England and Wales, elected by the other councillors, until the abolition of the office 1974; the title is still used in the City of London, and for members of a municipal corporation in certain towns in the USA.

Alexander three kings of Scotland:

Alexander I c. 1078–1124. King of Scotland from 1107, known as *the Fierce*. He ruled to the north of the rivers Forth and Clyde while his brother and successor David ruled to the south. He assisted Henry I of

England in his campaign against Wales 1114, but defended the independence of the church in Scotland. Several monasteries, including the abbeys of Inchcolm and Scone, were established by him.

Alexander II 1198–1249. King of Scotland from 1214, when he succeeded his father William the Lion. Alexander supported the English barons in their struggle with King John after ◊Magna Carta.

Alexander III 1241–1285. King of Scotland from 1249, son of Alexander II. In 1263, by military defeat of Norwegian forces, he extended his authority over the Western Isles, which had been dependent on Norway. He strengthened the power of the central Scottish government.

Alexandra 1844–1925. Queen consort of ◊Edward VII, whom she married 1863. She was the daughter of Christian IX of Denmark. An annual Alexandra Rose Day in aid of hospitals commemorates her charitable work.

Alfred *the Great* c. 848–c. 900. King of Wessex from 871. He defended England against Danish invasion, founded the first English navy, and put into operation a legal code. He encouraged the translation of works from Latin (some he translated himself), and promoted the development of the ◊Anglo-Saxon Chronicle.

Alfred was born at Wantage, Oxfordshire, the youngest son of Ethelwulf (died 858), king of the West Saxons. In 870 Alfred and his brother Ethelred fought many battles against the Danes. He gained a victory over the Danes at Ashdown 871, and succeeded Ethelred as king April 871 after a series of defeats. Five years of uneasy peace followed while the Danes were occupied in other parts of England. In 876 the Danes attacked again, and in 878 Alfred was forced to retire to the stronghold of Athelney, from where he finally emerged to win the victory of Edington, Wiltshire. By the Peace of Wedmore 878 the Danish leader Guthrum (died 890) agreed to withdraw from Wessex and from Mercia west of Watling Street. A new landing in Kent encouraged a revolt of the East Anglian Danes, which was suppressed 884–86, and after the final foreign invasion was defeated 892–96, Alfred strengthened the navy to prevent fresh incursions.

Aliens Act in the UK, an act of Parliament passed by the Conservative government 1905 to restrict the immigration of 'undesirable persons' into Britain; it was aimed at restricting Jewish immigration.

Allenby Henry Hynman, 1st Viscount Allenby 1861–1936. English field marshal. In World War I he served in France before taking command 1917–19 of the British forces in the Middle East. His defeat of the Turkish forces at Megiddo in Palestine in Sept 1918 was followed almost at once by the capitulation of Turkey. He was high commissioner in Egypt 1919–35.

Alliance, the in UK politics, a loose union 1981–87 formed by the ◊Liberal Party and ◊Social Democratic Party (SDP) for electoral purposes.

American Revolution revolt 1775–83 of the British North American colonies that resulted in the establishment of the United States of America.

It was caused by colonial opposition to British economic exploitation and by the unwillingness of the colonists to pay for a standing army. It was also fuelled by the colonists' antimonarchist sentiment and a desire to participate in the policies affecting them.

Amery Leo(pold Stennett) 1873–1955. English Conservative politician, First Lord of the Admiralty 1922–24, secretary for the colonies 1924–29, secretary for the dominions 1925–29, and secretary of state for India and Burma (now Myanmar) 1940–45.

André John 1751–1780. British army major in the American Revolution, with whom Benedict Arnold plotted the surrender of West Point. André was caught by Washington's army, tried, and hanged as a spy.

Andrew (full name Andrew Albert Christian Edward) 1960– . Prince of the UK, Duke of York, second son of Queen Elizabeth II. He married Sarah Ferguson 1986; their first daughter, Princess Beatrice, was born 1988, and their second daughter, Princess Eugenie, was born 1990. The couple separated 1992. Prince Andrew is a naval helicopter pilot.

Angell Norman 1874–1967. British writer on politics and economics. In 1910 he acquired an international reputation with his book The Great Illusion, which maintained that any war must prove ruinous to the victors as well as to the vanquished. Nobel Peace Prize 1933.

Angevin relating to the reigns of the English kings Henry II, and Richard I (also known, with the later English kings up to Richard III, as the *Plantagenets*). Angevin derives from Anjou, the region in France controlled by English kings at this time. The *Angevin Empire* comprised the territories (including England) that belonged to the Anjou dynasty.

Angle member of the Germanic tribe that invaded Britain in the 5th century; see ◊Anglo-Saxon.

Anglesey Henry William Paget 1768–1854. British cavalry leader during the Napoleonic wars. He was twice Lord Lieutenant of Ireland, and succeeded his father as earl of Uxbridge 1812. At the Battle of Waterloo he led a charge, losing.

Anglo-Irish Agreement or *Hillsborough Agreement* concord reached 1985 between the UK premier Margaret Thatcher and Irish premier Garret FitzGerald. One sign of the improved relations between the two countries was increased cooperation between police and security forces across the border with Northern Ireland.

The pact also gave the Irish Republic a greater voice in the conduct of Northern Ireland's affairs. However, the agreement was rejected by Northern Ireland Unionists as a step towards renunciation of British sovereignty. In March 1988 talks led to further strengthening of the agreement.

Anglo-Irish relations the political relations between England and Ireland. See ◊Ireland, Northern and ◊Ireland, Republic of.

Anglo-Saxon one of the several Germanic invaders (Angles, Saxons, and Jutes) who conquered much of Britain between the 5th and 7th centuries. After the conquest kingdoms were set up, which are commonly referred to as the *Heptarchy*; these were united in the early 9th century under the overlordship of Wessex. The Norman invasion 1066 brought Anglo-Saxon rule to an end.

Anglo-Saxon Chronicle history of England from the Roman invasion to the 11th century, in the form of a series of chronicles written in Old English by monks, begun in the 9th century (during the reign of King Alfred), and continuing to the 12th century.

Anne 1665–1714. Queen of Great Britain and Ireland 1702–14. She was the second daughter of James, Duke of York, who became James II, and

Anne Hyde. She succeeded William III 1702. Events of her reign include the War of the Spanish Succession, Marlborough's victories at Blenheim, Ramillies, Oudenarde, and Malplaquet, and the union of the English and Scottish parliaments 1707. Anne was succeeded by George I.

Anne (full name Anne Elizabeth Alice Louise) 1950– . Princess of the UK, second child of Queen Elizabeth II, declared Princess Royal 1987. She is an excellent horsewoman, winning a gold medal at the 1976 Olympics, and is actively involved in global charity work, especially for children.

Anne of Cleves 1515–1557. Fourth wife of ◊Henry VIII of England 1540. She was the daughter of the Duke of Cleves, and was recommended to Henry as a wife by Thomas ◊Cromwell, who wanted an alliance with German Protestantism against the Holy Roman Empire. Henry did not like her looks, had the marriage declared void after six months, pensioned her, and had Cromwell beheaded.

Anne of Denmark 1574–1619. Queen consort of James VI of Scotland (later James I of Great Britain 1603). She was the daughter of Frederick II of Denmark and Norway, and married James 1589. Anne was suspected of Catholic leanings and was notably extravagant.

Anson George, 1st Baron Anson 1697–1762. English admiral who sailed around the world 1740–44. In 1740 he commanded the squadron attacking the Spanish colonies and shipping in South America; he returned home by circumnavigating the world, with £500,000 of Spanish treasure. He carried out reforms at the Admiralty, which increased the efficiency of the British fleet and contributed to its success in the Seven Years' War (1756–63) against France.

Anti-Corn Law League in UK history, an extra-parliamentary pressure group formed 1838, led by the Liberals ◊Cobden and ◊Bright, which argued for free trade and campaigned successfully against duties on the import of foreign corn to Britain imposed by the ◊Corn Laws, which were repealed 1846.

Antonine Wall Roman line of fortification built AD 142. It was the Roman Empire's northwest frontier, between the Clyde and Forth rivers, Scotland. It was defended until c. 200.

Arch Joseph 1826–1919. English Radical member of Parliament and trade unionist, founder of the National Agricultural Union (the first of its kind) 1872. He was born in Warwickshire, the son of an agricultural labourer. Entirely self-taught, he became a Methodist preacher, and was Liberal-Labour MP for NW Norfolk.

archbishop in the Christian church, a bishop of superior rank who has authority over other bishops in his jurisdiction and often over an ecclesiastical province. The office exists in the Roman Catholic, Eastern Orthodox, and Anglican churches.

Argyll line of Scottish peers who trace their descent to the Campbells of Lochow. The earldom dates from 1457. They include:

Argyll Archibald Campbell, 5th Earl of Argyll 1530–1573. Adherent of the Scottish presbyterian John ◊Knox. A supporter of Mary Queen of Scots from 1561, he commanded her forces after her escape from Lochleven Castle 1568. He revised his position and became Lord High Chancellor of Scotland 1572.

Arras, Battle of battle of World War I, April–May 1917. It was an effective but costly British attack on German forces in support of a French offensive, which was only partially successful, on the Siegfried Line. British casualties totalled 84,000 as compared to 75,000 German casualties.

Arthur 6th century AD. Legendary British king and hero in stories of ◊Camelot and the quest for the Holy Grail. Arthur is said to have been born in Tintagel, Cornwall, and buried in Glastonbury, Somerset. He may have been a Romano-Celtic leader against pagan Saxon invaders.

Arthur Duke of Brittany 1187–1203. Grandson of Henry II of England and nephew of King ◊John, who is supposed to have had him murdered, 13 April 1203, as a rival for the crown.

Arthur Prince of Wales 1486–1502. Eldest son of Henry VII of England. He married ◊Catherine of Aragon 1501, when he was 16 and she was 15, but died the next year.

Arundel Thomas Howard, 2nd Earl of Arundel 1586–1646. English politician and patron of the arts. The Arundel Marbles, part of his collection of Italian sculptures, were given to Oxford University in 1667 by his grandson.

Archbishops of Canterbury from 1414 to present day.

1414	Henry Chichele (1362–1414)
1443	John Stafford (?–1452)
1452	John Kemp (c. 1380–1454)
1454	Thomas Bourchier (c. 1410–1486)
1486	John Morton (c. 1429–1500)
1501	Henry Deane (?–1503)
1503	William Warham (1450–1532)
1533	Thomas Cranmer (1489–1556)
1556	Reginald Pole (1500–1558)
1559	Matthew Parker (1504–1575)
1576	Edmund Grindal (c. 1519–1583)
1583	John Whitgift (c. 1530–1604)
1604	Richard Bancroft (1544–1610)
1611	George Abbot (1562–1633)
1633	William Laud (1573–1645)
1660	William Juxon (1582–1663)
1663	Gilbert Sheldon (1598–1677)
1678	William Sancroft (1617–1693)
1691	John Tillotson (1630–1694)
1695	Thomas Tenison (1636–1715)
1716	William Wake (1657–1737)
1737	John Potter (c. 1674–1747)
1747	Thomas Herring (1693–1757)
1757	Matthew Hutton (1693–1758)
1758	Thomas Secker (1693–1768)
1768	Hon. Frederick Cornwallis (1713–1783)
1783	John Moore (1730–1805)
1805	Charles Manners-Sutton (1755–1828)
1828	William Howley (1766–1848)
1848	John Bird Sumner (1780–1862)
1862	Charles Longley (1794–1868)
1868	Archibald Campbell Tait (1811–1882)
1883	Edward White Benson (1829–1896)
1896	Frederick Temple (1821–1902)
1903	Randall Thomas Davidson (1848–1930)
1928	Cosmo Gordon Lang (1864–1945)
1942	William Temple (1881–1944)
1945	Geoffrey Fisher (1887–1972)
1961	Arthur Ramsey (1904–1988)
1974	Donald Coggan (1909–)
1980	Robert Runcie (1921–)
1991	George Carey (1935–)

Ascham Roger c. 1515–1568. English scholar and royal tutor, author of The Scholemaster 1570 on the art of education.

Ashdown Paddy (Jeremy John Durham) 1941–   . English politician, leader of the merged Social and Liberal Democrats from 1988. He served in the Royal Marines as a commando, leading a Special Boat Section in Borneo, and was a member of the Diplomatic Service 1971–76. He became a Liberal member of Parliament 1983. His constituency is Yeovil, Somerset.

Ashmole Elias 1617–1692. English antiquary, whose collection forms the basis of the Ashmolean Museum, Oxford, England.

Asquith Herbert Henry, 1st Earl of Oxford and Asquith 1852–1928. British Liberal politician, prime minister 1908–16. As chancellor of the Exchequer he introduced old-age pensions 1908. He limited the powers of the House of Lords and attempted to give Ireland Home Rule.

Astor prominent US and British family. *John Jacob Astor* (1763–1848) was a US millionaire. His great-grandson *Waldorf Astor*, 2nd Viscount Astor (1879–1952), was Conservative member of Parliament for Plymouth 1910–19, when he succeeded to the peerage. He was chief proprietor of the British Observer newspaper. His US-born wife Nancy Witcher Langhorne (1879–1964), *Lady Astor*, was the first woman member of Parliament to take a seat in the House of Commons 1919, when she succeeded her husband for the constituency of Plymouth. Government policy was said to be decided at Cliveden, their country home.

Athelstan c. 895–939. King of the Mercians and West Saxons. Son of Edward the Elder and grandson of Alfred the Great, he was crowned king 925 at Kingston upon Thames. He subdued parts of Cornwall and Wales, and defeated the Welsh, Scots, and Danes at Brunanburh 937.

Atlantic, Battle of the German campaign during World War I to prevent merchant shipping from delivering food supplies from the USA to the Allies, chiefly the UK. By 1917, some 875,000 tons of shipping had been lost. The odds were only turned by the belated use of naval *convoys* and *depth charges* to deter submarine attack.

Atlantic Charter declaration issued during World War II by the British prime minister Winston Churchill and the US president

Franklin Roosevelt after meetings Aug 1941. It stressed their countries' broad strategy and war aims and was largely a propaganda exercise to demonstrate public solidarity among the Allies.

attainder, bill of legislative device that allowed the English Parliament to declare guilt and impose a punishment on an individual without bringing the matter before the courts. Such bills were used intermittently from the Wars of the Roses until 1798. Some acts of attainder were also passed by US colonial legislators during the American Revolution to deal with 'loyalists' who continued to support the English crown.

Atterbury Francis 1662–1732. English bishop and Jacobite politician. In 1687 he was appointed a royal chaplain by William III. Under Queen Anne he received rapid promotion, becoming bishop of Rochester 1713. His Jacobite sympathies prevented his further rise, and in 1722 he was sent to the Tower of London and subsequently banished. He was a friend of the writers Alexander Pope and Jonathan Swift.

Attlee Clement (Richard), 1st Earl 1883–1967. British Labour politician. In the coalition government during World War II he was Lord Privy Seal 1940–42, dominions secretary 1942–43, and Lord President of the Council 1943–45, as well as deputy prime minister from 1942. As prime minister 1945–51 he introduced a sweeping programme of nationalization and a whole new system of social services.

Auchinleck Sir Claude John Eyre 1884–1981. British commander in World War II. He won the First Battle of El ◊Alamein 1942 in N Egypt. In 1943 he became commander in chief in India and founded the modern Indian and Pakistani armies. In 1946 he was promoted to field marshal; he retired 1947.

Auckland George Eden, 1st Earl of Auckland 1784–1849. British Tory politician after whom Auckland, New Zealand, is named. He became a member of Parliament 1810, and 1835-41 was governor general of India.

Augustine, St ?–605. first archbishop of Canterbury, England. He was sent from Rome to convert England to Christianity by Pope Gregory I. He landed at Ebbsfleet in Kent 597 and soon after baptized Ethelbert, King of Kent, along with many of his subjects. He was consecrated bishop of the English at Arles in the same year, and appointed archbishop 601, establishing his see at Canterbury. Feast day 26 May.

Auld Alliance alliance between Scotland and France that lasted from the end of the 13th century until 1560, when Protestantism displaced Catholicism as the dominant faith in Scotland.

Austrian Succession, War of the war 1740–48 between Austria (supported by England and Holland) and Prussia (supported by France and Spain).

1740 The Holy Roman emperor Charles VI died and the succession of his daughter Maria Theresa was disputed by a number of European powers. Frederick the Great of Prussia seized Silesia from Austria.

1743 At ◊Dettingen an army of British, Austrians, and Hanoverians under the command of George II was victorious over the French.

1745 An Austro-English army was defeated at ◊Fontenoy but British naval superiority was confirmed, and there were gains in the Americas and India.

1748 The war was ended by the Treaty of Aix-la- Chapelle.

Avebury Europe's largest stone circle (diameter 412 m/1,352 ft), in Wiltshire, England. It was probably constructed in the Neolithic period 3,500 years ago, and is linked with nearby Silbury Hill. The village of Avebury was built within the circle, and many of the stones were used for building material.

Avebury John Lubbock, 1st Baron Avebury 1834–1913. British banker. A Liberal (from 1886 Liberal Unionist) member of Parliament 1870-1900, he was responsible for the Bank Holidays Act 1871 introducing statutory public holidays.

B

Babington Anthony 1561–1586. English traitor who hatched a plot to assassinate Elizabeth I and replace her with ◊Mary Queen of Scots; its discovery led to Mary's execution and his own.

Back to Basics phrase used by British prime minister John Major during his keynote address to the Conservative Party conference in Oct 1993, in which he argued for a return to 'traditional British values'. It was subsequently adopted as a slogan by the Conservative Party, some members of which emphasized the morality aspect. In the following months, a series of sexual indiscretions by Conservative politicians and corrupt practices by Conservative-run councils and government departments caused deep embarrassment to the party.

Bacon Francis 1561–1626. English politician, philosopher, and essayist. He became Lord Chancellor 1618, and the same year confessed to bribe-taking, was fined £40,000 (which was later remitted by the king), and spent four days in the Tower of London. His works include Essays 1597, characterized by pith and brevity; The Advancement of Learning 1605, a seminal work discussing scientific method; the Novum Organum 1620, in which he redefined the task of natural science, seeing it as a means of empirical discovery and a method of increasing human power over nature; and The New Atlantis 1626, describing a utopian state in which scientific knowledge is systematically sought and exploited.

Bagehot Walter 1826–1877. British writer and economist, author of The English Constitution 1867, a classic analysis of the British political system. He was editor of The Economist magazine 1860-77.

Balaclava, Battle of in the Crimean War, an engagement on 25 Oct 1854, near a town in Ukraine, 10 km/6 mi SE of Sevastopol. It was the scene of the ill-timed ***Charge of the Light Brigade*** of British cavalry against the Russian entrenched artillery. Of the 673 soldiers who took part, there were 272 casualties. *Balaclava helmets* were knitted hoods worn here by soldiers in the bitter weather.

Baldwin Stanley, 1st Earl Baldwin of Bewdley 1867–1947. British Conservative politician, prime minister 1923–24, 1924–29, and 1935–37; he weathered the general strike 1926, secured complete adult suffrage 1928, and handled the ◊abdication crisis of Edward VIII 1936, but failed to prepare Britain for World War II.

Balfour Arthur James, 1st Earl of Balfour 1848–1930.

British Conservative politician, prime minister 1902–05 and foreign secretary 1916–19, when he issued the Balfour Declaration 1917 and was involved in peace negotiations after World War I, signing the Treaty of Versailles.

Balfour Declaration letter, dated 2 Nov 1917, from the British foreign secretary A J Balfour to Lord Rothschild (chair, British Zionist Federation) stating: 'HM government view with favour the establishment in Palestine of a national home for the Jewish people.' It helped form the basis for the foundation of Israel 1948.

Baliol (or *Balliol*) John de c. 1250–1314. King of Scotland 1292–96. As an heir to the Scottish throne on the death of Margaret, the Maid of Norway, his cause was supported by the English king, Edward I, against 12 other claimants. Having paid homage to Edward, Baliol was proclaimed king but soon rebelled and gave up the kingdom when English forces attacked Scotland.

Ball John died 1381. English priest, one of the leaders of the ◊Peasants' Revolt 1381, known as 'the mad priest of Kent'. A follower of John Wycliffe and a believer in social equality, he was imprisoned for disagreeing with the archbishop of Canterbury. During the revolt he was released from prison, and when in Blackheath, London, incited people against the ruling classes by preaching from the text 'When Adam delved and Eve span, who was then the gentleman?' When the revolt collapsed he escaped but was captured near Coventry and executed.

Balmoral Castle residence of the British royal family in Scotland on the river Dee, 10.5 km/61/2 mi NE of Braemar, Grampian region. The castle, built of granite in the Scottish baronial style, is dominated by a square tower and circular turret rising 30 m/100 ft. It was rebuilt 1853–55 by Prince Albert, who bought the estate in 1852.

Bannockburn, Battle of battle on 24 June 1314 in which ◊Robert (I) the Bruce of Scotland defeated the English under Edward II, who had come to relieve the besieged Stirling Castle. Named after the town of Bannockburn, S of Stirling, central Scotland.

Barebones Parliament English assembly called by Oliver ◊Cromwell to replace the 'Rump Parliament' July 1653. It consisted of 140 members nominated by the army and derived its name from one of its members, Praise-God Barbon. Although they attempted to pass sensible legislation (civil marriage; registration of births, deaths, and marriages; custody of lunatics), its members' attempts to abolish tithes, patronage, and the court of chancery, and to codify the law, led to the resignation of the moderates and its dissolution Dec 1653.

Barnet, Battle of in the English Wars of the ◊Roses, the defeat of Lancaster by York on 14 April 1471 in Barnet (now in N London).

baron rank in the ◊peerage of the UK, above a baronet and below a viscount.

baron any member of the higher nobility, a direct vassal (feudal servant) of the king, not bearing other titles such as duke or count. The term originally meant the vassal of a lord, but acquired its present meaning in the 12th century.

baronage collective title for all the landed nobility of medieval England, including earls and other important tenants-in-chief as well as the barons.

baronet British order of chivalry below the rank of baron, but above that of knight, created 1611 by James I to finance the settlement of Ulster. It is a hereditary honour, although women cannot succeed to a baronetcy. A baronet does not have a seat in the House of Lords but is entitled to the style *Sir* before his name. The sale of baronetcies was made illegal 1937.

Barons' Wars civil wars in England:
1215–17 between King John and his barons, over his failure to honour Magna Carta; *1264–67* between Henry III (and the future GEdward I) and his barons (led by Simon de Montfort);

1264 14 May *Battle of Lewes* at which Henry III was defeated and captured.
1265 4 Aug Simon de Montfort was defeated by Edward at Evesham and killed.

barrow burial mound, usually composed of earth but sometimes of stones, examples of which are found in many parts of the world. The two main types are *long*, dating from the New Stone Age, or Neolithic, and *round*, dating from the later Mesolithic peoples of the early Bronze Age.

Bayeux Tapestry linen hanging made about 1067–70 which gives a vivid pictorial record of the invasion of England by William I (the Conqueror) 1066. It is an embroidery rather than a true tapestry, sewn with woollen threads in blue, green, red, and yellow, 70 m/231 ft long and 50 cm/20 in wide, and containing 72 separate scenes with descriptive wording in Latin. It is exhibited at the museum of Bayeux in Normandy, France.

Beaconsfield, Earl of. Title taken by Benjamin ◊Disraeli, prime minister of Britain 1868 and 1874–80.

Beaker people people thought to be of Iberian origin who spread out over Europe from the 3rd millennium BC. They were skilled in metalworking, and are identified by their use of distinctive earthenware beakers with various designs, of which the bell-beaker type was widely distributed throughout Europe. They favoured inhumation (burial of the intact body), often round barrows, or secondary burials in some form of chamber tomb. A beaker accompanied each burial, possibly to hold a drink for the deceased on their final journey.

Beaton David 1494–1546. Scottish nationalist cardinal and politician, adviser to James V. Under Mary Queen of Scots, he was opposed to the alliance with England and persecuted reformers such as George Wishart, who was condemned to the stake; he was killed by Wishart's friends.

Beatty David, 1st Earl 1871–1936. British admiral in World War I. He commanded the cruiser squadron 1912–16 and bore the brunt of the Battle of Jutland.

Beaufort Henry 1375–1447. English priest, bishop of Lincoln from 1398, of Winchester from 1405. As chancellor of England, he supported his half- brother Henry IV and made enormous personal loans to

Henry V to finance war against France. As a guardian of Henry VI from 1421, he was in effective control of the country until 1426. In the same year he was created a cardinal. In 1431 he crowned Henry VI as king of France in Paris.

Beaufort Margaret, Countess of Richmond and Derby 1443–1509. English noblewoman. She married Edmund Tudor, Earl of Richmond 1455. Their son, ◊Henry VII, claimed the English throne through his mother's descent from ◊John of Gaunt.

Beaverbrook (William) Max(well) Aitken, 1st Baron Beaverbrook 1879–1964. British financier, newspaper proprietor, and politician, born in Canada. He bought a majority interest in the Daily Express 1919, founded the Sunday Express 1921, and bought the London Evening Standard 1929. He served in Lloyd George's World War I cabinet and Churchill's World War II cabinet.

Becket St Thomas à 1118–1170. English priest and politician. He was chancellor to ◊Henry II 1155–62, when he was appointed archbishop of Canterbury. The interests of the church soon conflicted with those of the crown and Becket was assassinated; he was canonized 1172.

Bede c. 673–735. English theologian and historian, known as *the Venerable Bede*, active in Durham and Northumbria. He wrote many scientific, theological, and historical works. His Historia Ecclesiastica Gentis Anglorum/Ecclesiastical History of the English People 731 is a seminal source for early English history.

Beloff Max 1913– . British historian. From 1974 to 1979 he was principal of the University College at Buckingham, the UK's first independent institution at university level.

Benbow John 1653–1702. English admiral, hero of several battles with France. He ran away to sea as a boy, and from 1689 served in the navy. He fought at the battles of Beachy Head 1690 and La Hogue 1692, and died of wounds received in a fight with the French off Jamaica.

Benn Tony (Anthony Wedgwood) 1925– . British Labour politician, formerly the leading figure on the party's left wing. He was minister of technology 1966–70 and of industry 1974–75, but his campaign against entry to the European Community led to his transfer to the Department of Energy 1975–79. A skilled parliamentary orator, he unsuccessfully contested the Labour Party leadership 1988.

Bentinck Lord William Cavendish 1774–1839. British colonial administrator, first governor general of India 1828–35. He acted against the ancient Indian rituals of thuggee and suttee, and established English as the medium of instruction.

Bentinck Lord William George Frederic Cavendish 1802–1848. (known as Lord George Bentinck) English nobleman and politician, son of the 4th Duke of Portland. He was a leading opponent of the repeal of the ◊Corn Laws 1848 but after the repeal helped defeat ◊Peel's government. He was best known as a racehorse owner.

Bentham Jeremy 1748–1832. English philosopher, legal and social reformer, and founder of utilitarianism. The essence of his moral philosophy is found in the pronouncement of his Principles of Morals and Legislation (written 1780, published 1789): that the object of all legislation should be 'the greatest happiness for the greatest number'.

Berkeley Sir William 1606–1677. British colonial administrator in North America, governor of the colony of Virginia 1641–77. Siding with the Royalists during the English Civil War, he was removed from the governorship by Oliver Cromwell 1652. He was reappointed 1660 by Charles II after the Restoration of the monarchy. However, growing opposition to him in the colony culminated in Bacon's Rebellion 1676 and in 1677 Berkeley was removed from office for his brutal repression of that uprising.

Berwick James Fitzjames, Duke of Berwick 1670–1734. French marshal, illegitimate son of the Duke of York (afterwards James II of England) and Arabella Churchill (1648–1730), sister of the great duke of Marlborough, his enemy in battle. He was made duke of Berwick in 1687. After the revolution of 1688 he served under his father in Ireland, joined the French army, fought against William III and Marlborough, and in 1707 defeated the English at Almansa in Spain. He was killed at the siege of Philippsburg.

Bevan Aneurin (Nye) 1897–1960. British Labour politician. Son of a Welsh miner, and himself a miner at 13, he became member of Parliament for Ebbw Vale 1929–60. As minister of health 1945-51, he inaugurated the National Health Service (NHS); he was minister of labour Jan–April 1951, when he resigned (with Harold Wilson) on the introduction of NHS charges and led a Bevanite faction against the government. In 1956 he became chief Labour spokesperson on foreign affairs, and deputy leader of the Labour party 1959. He was an outstanding speaker.

Beveridge William Henry, 1st Baron Beveridge 1879–1963. British economist. A civil servant, he acted as Lloyd George's lieutenant in the social legislation of the Liberal government before World War I. The *Beveridge Report* 1942 formed the basis of the welfare state in Britain.

Beveridge Report, the popular name of Social Insurance and Allied Services, a report written by William Beveridge 1942 that formed the basis for the social reform legislation of the Labour Government of 1945–50.

Also known as the Report on Social Security it identified five 'giants': illness, ignorance, disease, squalor and want. It proposed a scheme of social insurance from 'the cradle to the grave', and recommended a national health service, social insurance and assistance, family allowances, and full-employment policies.

Bevin Ernest 1881–1951. British Labour politician. Chief creator of the Transport and General Workers' Union, he was its general secretary from 1921 to 1940, when he entered the war cabinet as minister of labour and national service. He organized the 'Bevin boys', chosen by ballot to work in the coal mines as war service, and was foreign secretary in the Labour government 1945–51.

Bill of Rights in Britain, an act of Parliament 1689 which established it as the primary governing body of the country. The Bill of Rights embodied the Declarations of Rights which contained the conditions on which William and Mary were offered the throne. It made provisions limiting ꝑroyal prerogative with respect to legislation, executive power, money levies, courts, and the army and stipulated Parliament's consent to many government functions.

Birkenhead Frederick Edwin Smith, 1st Earl of Birkenhead 1872–1930. British Conservative politician. A flamboyant character, known as 'FE', he joined with Edward Carson in organizing armed resistance in Ulster to Irish Home Rule. He was Lord Chancellor 1919–22 and a much criticized secretary for India 1924–28.

bishop priest next in rank to an archbishop in the Roman Catholic, Eastern Orthodox, Anglican or episcopal churches. A bishop has charge of a district called a *diocese*.

Black and Tans nickname of a special auxiliary force of the Royal Irish Constabulary employed by the British 1920–21 to combat the Sinn Féiners (Irish nationalists) in Ireland; the name derives from the colours of the uniforms, khaki with black hats and belts.

Black Prince nickname of ◊Edward, Prince of Wales, eldest son of Edward III of England.

Blake Robert 1599–1657. British admiral of the Parliamentary forces during the English ◊Civil War. Appointed 'general-at-sea' 1649, he destroyed Prince Rupert's privateering fleet off Cartagena, Spain, in the following year. In 1652 he won several engagements against the Dutch navy. In 1654 he bombarded Tunis, the stronghold of the Barbary corsairs, and in 1657 captured the Spanish treasure fleet in Santa Cruz.

Blenheim, Battle of battle on 13 Aug 1704 in which Allied troops under ◊Marlborough defeated the French and Bavarian armies near the Bavarian village of Blenheim (now in Germany) on the left bank of the Danube.

Bligh William 1754–1817. English sailor who accompanied Captain James ◊Cook on his second voyage around the world 1772–74, and in 1787 commanded HMS Bounty on an expedition to the Pacific. On the return voyage the crew mutinied 1789, and Bligh was cast adrift in a boat with 18 men. He was appointed governor of New South Wales 1805, where his discipline again provoked a mutiny 1808 (the Rum Rebellion). He returned to Britain, and was made an admiral 1811.

Blitzkrieg (German 'lightning war') swift military campaign, as used by Germany at the beginning of World War II 1939–41. The abbreviated *Blitz* was applied to the attempted saturation bombing of London by the German air force between Sept 1940 and May 1941.

Blood Thomas 1618–1680. Irish adventurer, known as Colonel Blood, who attempted to steal the crown jewels from the Tower of London, England, 1671.

Bloody Assizes courts held by judges of the High Court in the west of England under the Lord Chief Justice, Judge ◊Jeffreys, after ◊Monmouth's rebellion 1685. Over 300 rebels were executed and many more flogged or imprisoned.

Bloody Sunday dispersion by the police of a meeting in Trafalgar Square Sunday 13 Nov 1887, with over 100 casualties. The meeting was organised by the Social Democratic Federation to demand the release from prison of the Irish nationalist William O'Brien.

Blount Charles, Earl of Devonshire, 8th Baron Mountjoy 1562–1606. English soldier, a friend of the 2nd Earl of ◊Essex. Blount accompanied him and ◊Raleigh on their unsuccessful expedition to the Azores 1597. He became Lord Deputy of Ireland 1600 and quelled the revolt led by the Irish chief Hugh O'Neill, 2nd Earl of Tyrone, when the Irish failed in their attempt to reach a Spanish force that had arrived at Kinsale 1601. He subdued most of Ireland and was created earl 1603.

Blunt Anthony 1907–1983. British art historian and double agent. As a Cambridge lecturer, he recruited for the Soviet secret service and, as a member of the British Secret Service 1940–45, passed information to the USSR. In 1951 he assisted the defection to the USSR of the British agents Guy ◊Burgess and Donald Maclean (1913–1983). He was the author of many respected works on French and Italian art. Unmasked 1964, he was given immunity after his confession.

Boadicea alternative spelling of British queen ◊Boudicca.

Bodley Thomas 1545–1613. English scholar and diplomat, after whom the Bodleian Library in Oxford is named. After retiring from Queen Elizabeth I's service 1597, he restored the university's library, which was opened as the Bodleian Library 1602.

Boer War the second of the ◊South African Wars 1899–1902, waged between Dutch settlers in South Africa and the British.

Boleyn Anne 1507–1536. Queen of England 1533-36. Henry VIII broke with the pope in order to divorce his first wife and marry Anne. She was married to him 1533 and gave birth to the future Queen Elizabeth I in the same year. Accused of adultery and incest with her half-brother (a charge invented by Thomas ◊Cromwell), she was beheaded.

Bolingbroke title of Henry of Bolingbroke, ◊Henry IV of England.

Bolingbroke Henry St John, Viscount Bolingbroke 1678–1751. British Tory politician and political philosopher. He was foreign secretary 1710-14 and a Jacobite conspirator. His books, such as Idea of a Patriot King 1738 and The Dissertation upon Parties 1735, laid the foundations for 19th-century Toryism.

Bonar Law British Conservative politician; see ◊Law, Andrew Bonar.

Bondfield Margaret Grace 1873–1953. British socialist who became a trade-union organizer to improve working conditions for women. She was a Labour member of Parliament 1923-24 and 1926-31, and was the first woman to enter the cabinet – as minister of labour 1929-31.

Bonham Carter Violet, Lady Asquith of Yarnbury 1887–1969. British peeress, president of the Liberal party 1945–47.

Bonnie Prince Charlie Scottish name for ◊Charles Edward Stuart, pretender to the throne.

Boothby Robert John Graham, Baron Boothby 1900–1986. Scottish politician. He became a Unionist member of Parliament 1924 and was parliamentary private secretary to Churchill 1926–29. He advocated Britain's entry into the European Community, and was a powerful speaker.

Boscawen Edward 1711–1761. English admiral who served against the French in the mid-18th- century wars, including the War of Austrian Succession and the Seven Years' War. He led expeditions to the East Indies 1748–50 and served as lord of the Admiralty from 1751, vice admiral from 1755, and admiral from 1758. To his men he was known as 'Old Dreadnought'.

Bosworth, Battle of last battle of the Wars of the ◊Roses, fought on 22 Aug 1485. Richard III, the Yorkist king, was defeated and slain by Henry of Richmond, who became Henry VII. The battlefield is near the town of Market Bosworth, 19 km/12 mi W of Leicester, England.

Bothwell James Hepburn, 4th Earl of Bothwell c. 1536–1578. Scottish nobleman, third husband of ◊Mary Queen of Scots, 1567–70, alleged to have arranged the explosion that killed Darnley, her previous husband, 1567.

Boudicca Queen of the Iceni (native Britons), often referred to by the Latin form *Boadicea*. Her husband, King Prasutagus, had been a tributary of the Romans, but on his death AD 60 the territory of the Iceni was violently annexed. Boudicca was scourged and her daughters raped. Boudicca raised the whole of SE England in revolt, and before the main Roman armies could return from campaigning in Wales she burned Londinium (London), Verulamium (St Albans), and Camulodunum (Colchester). Later the Romans under governor Suetonius Paulinus defeated the British between London and Chester; they were virtually annihilated and Boudicca poisoned herself.

Bounty, Mutiny on the naval mutiny in the Pacific 1789 against British captain William ◊Bligh.

Boycott Charles Cunningham 1832–1897. English land agent in County Mayo, Ireland, who strongly opposed the demands for agrarian reform by the Irish Land League 1879–81, with the result that the peasants refused to work for him; hence the word *boycott*.

Boyne, Battle of the battle fought 1 July 1690 in E Ireland, in which James II was defeated by William III and fled to France. It was the decisive battle of the War of English Succession, confirming a Protestant monarch. It took its name from the river Boyne which rises in County Kildare and flows 110 km/69 mi NE to the Irish Sea.

Bradlaugh Charles 1833–1891. British freethinker and radical politician. In 1880 he was elected Liberal member of Parliament for Northampton, but was not allowed to take his seat until 1886 because, as an atheist, he (unsuccessfully) claimed the right to affirm instead of taking the oath. He was associated with the feminist Annie Besant.

Breda, Treaty of 1667 treaty that ended the Second Anglo-Dutch War (1664–67). By the terms of the treaty, England gained New Amsterdam, which was renamed New York.

Bright John 1811–1889. British Liberal politician, a campaigner for free trade, peace, and social reform. A Quaker millowner, he was among the founders of the Anti-Corn Law League in 1839, and was largely instrumental in securing the passage of the Reform Bill of 1867.

Britain island off the NW coast of Europe, one of the British Isles. It comprises England, Scotland, and Wales (together officially known as

◊Great Britain), and is part of the ◊United Kingdom. The name is derived from the Roman name Britannia, which in turn is derived from the ancient Celtic name of the inhabitants, *Bryttas*.

Britain, ancient period in the British Isles (excluding Ireland) extending through prehistory to the Roman occupation (1st century AD). Settled agricultural life evolved in Britain during the 3rd millennium BC. Neolithic society reached its peak in southern England, where it was capable of producing the great stone circles of Avebury and Stonehenge early in the 2nd millennium BC. It was succeeded in central southern Britain by the Early Bronze Age Wessex culture, with strong trade links across Europe. The Iron Age culture of the Celts was predominant in the last few centuries BC, and the Belgae (of mixed Germanic and Celtic stock) were partially Romanized in the century between the first Roman invasion of Britain under Julius Caesar (54 BC) and the Roman conquest (AD 43). For later history, see ◊England, history; ◊Roman Britain; ◊Scotland, history; ◊Wales, history; and ◊United Kingdom.

At the end of the last Ice Age, Britain had a cave-dwelling population of Palaeolithic hunter-gatherers, whose culture was called Creswellian, after Creswell Crags, Derbyshire, where remains of flint tools were found. Throughout prehistory successive waves of migrants from continental Europe accelerated or introduced cultural innovations. Important Neolithic remains include: the stone houses of Skara Brae, Orkney; so-called causewayed camps in which hilltops such as Windmill Hill, Wiltshire, were enclosed by concentric fortifications of ditches and banks; the first stages of the construction of the ritual monuments known as henges (for example, Stonehenge, Woodhenge); and the flint mines at Grimes Graves, Norfolk. Burial of the dead was in elongated earth mounds (long barrows).

The ◊Beaker people probably introduced copper working to the British Isles. The aristocratic society of the Bronze Age Wessex culture of southern England is characterized by its circular burial mounds (round barrows); the dead were either buried or cremated, and cremated remains were placed in pottery urns. Later invaders were the ◊Celts, a warrior aristocracy with an Iron Age technology; they introduced horse-drawn chariots, had their own distinctive art forms, and occupied fortified hilltops. The Belgae, who buried the ashes of their dead in richly furnished flat graves, were responsible for the earliest British sites large and complex enough to be called towns; settled in southern Britain, the Belgae resisted the Romans from centres such as Maiden Castle, Dorset.

Britain, Battle of World War II air battle between German and British air forces over Britain lasting 10 July–31 Oct 1940.

British Broadcasting Corporation (BBC) the UK state-owned broadcasting network. It operates television and national and local radio stations, and is financed almost wholly by the sale of television viewing licences; it is not allowed to carry advertisements. Overseas radio broadcasts (World Service) have a government subsidy.

British East India Company see ◊East India Company.

British Empire various territories all over the world conquered or colonized by Britain from about 1600, most now independent or ruled by other powers; the British Empire was at its largest at the end of World War I, with over 25% of the world's population and area. The ◊Commonwealth is composed of former and remaining territories of the British Empire.

British Empire, Order of the British order of chivalry, instituted by George V in 1917. There are military and civil divisions, and the ranks are GBE, Knight Grand Cross or Dame Grand Cross; KBE, Knight Commander; DBE, Dame Commander; CBE, Commander; OBE, Officer; MBE, Member.

British India Line shipping line founded 1856 as the Calcutta and Burmah Steam Navigation Company. By 1869 it had 50 ships, and by 1893 100.

British Museum largest museum of the UK. Founded in 1753, it opened in London in 1759. Rapid additions led to the constuction of the present buildings (1823–47). In 1881 the Natural History Museum was transferred to South Kensington.

British National Party (BNP) extreme right-wing political party. Initially a small but violent offshoot of the ◊National Front, it has now taken the latter's place as the leading far-right party in the UK, achieving

British Empire

current name	colonial names and history	colonized	independent
India	British East India Company	18th century–1858	1947
Pakistan	British East India Company	18th century–1858	1947
Myanmar	Burma	1866	1948
Sri Lanka	Portuguese, Dutch 1602–1796; Ceylon 1802–1972	16th century	1948
Ghana	Gold Coast; British Togoland integrated 1956	1618	1957
Nigeria		1861	1960
Cyprus	Turkish to 1878, then British rule	1878	1960
Sierra Leone	British protectorate	1788	1961
Tanzania	German E Africa to 1921; British mandate fromLeague of Nations/ UN as Tanganyika	19th century	1961
Jamaica	Spanish to 1655	16th century	1962
Trinidad & Tobago	Spanish 1532–1797; British 1797–1962	1532	1962
Uganda	British protectorate	1894	1962
Kenya	British colony from 1920	1895	1963
Malaysia	British interests from 1786; Federation of Malaya 1957–63	1874	1963
Malawi	British protectorate of Nyasaland 1907–53; Federation of Rhodesia & Nyasaland 1953–64	1891	1964
Malta	French 1798–1814	1798	1964
Zambia	N Rhodesia - British protectorate; Federation of Rhodesia & Nyasaland 1953–64	1924	1964
The Gambia		1888	1965
Singapore	Federation of Malaya 1963–65	1858	1965
Guyana	Dutch to 1796; British Guiana 1796–1966	1620	1966
Botswana 1966	Bechuanaland - British protectorate	1885	
Lesotho	Basutoland	1868	1966
Bangladesh	British East India Company 18th century–1858; British India 1858–1947; E Pakistan 1947–71	18th century	1971
Zimbabwe	S Rhodesia from 1923; UDI under Ian Smith 1965–79	1895	1980
Belize	British Honduras	17th century	1981

national prominence 1993 when Derek Beackon became the first BNP councillor in by-elections for the Tower Hamlets council. The party is heavily implicated in the rise in racial violence in the area and near its Bexhill headquarters.

Brooke James 1803–1868. British administrator who became rajah of Sarawak, on Borneo, 1841. In 1838 he headed a private expedition to Borneo, where he helped to suppress a revolt, for which the sultan gave him the title. Brooke became known as the 'the white rajah'.

Brookeborough Basil Brooke, Viscount Brookeborough 1888–1973. Unionist politician of Northern Ireland. He entered Parliament in 1929, held ministerial posts 1933–45, and was prime minister of Northern Ireland 1943–63. He was a staunch advocate of strong links with Britain.

Brougham Henry Peter, 1st Baron Brougham and Vaux 1778–1868. British Whig politician and lawyer. From 1811 he was chief adviser to the Princess of Wales (afterwards Queen Caroline), and in 1820 he defeated the attempt of George IV to divorce her. He was Lord Chancellor 1830–34, supporting the Reform Bill.

Brown George, Baron George-Brown 1914–1985. British Labour politician. He entered Parliament in 1945, was briefly minister of works 1951, and contested the leadership of the party on the death of Gaitskell, but was defeated by Harold Wilson. He was secretary for economic affairs 1964–66 and foreign secretary 1966–68. He was created a life peer 1970.

Brown John 1825–1883. Scottish servant and confidant of Queen Victoria from 1858.

Bruce Robert de, 5th Lord of Annandale 1210–1295. Scottish noble, one of the unsuccessful claimants to the throne at the death of Alexander II 1290. His grandson was ◊Robert (I) the Bruce.

Bruce Robert. King of Scotland; see ◊Robert I the Bruce.

Brummell Beau (George Bryan) 1778–1840. British dandy and leader of fashion. He introduced long trousers as conventional day and evening wear for men. A friend of the Prince of Wales, the future George IV, he later quarrelled with him. Gambling losses drove him in 1816 to exile in France, where he died in an asylum.

Brussels, Treaty of pact of economic, political, cultural, and military alliance established 17 March 1948, for 50 years, by the UK, France, and the Benelux countries, joined by West Germany and Italy 1955. It was the forerunner of the North Atlantic Treaty Organization and the European Community.

Bryce James, 1st Viscount Bryce 1838–1922. British Liberal politician, professor of civil law at Oxford University 1870–93. He entered Parliament 1880, holding office under Gladstone and Rosebery. He was author of The American Commonwealth 1888, ambassador to Washington 1907–13, and improved US-Canadian relations.

Buchan John, Baron Tweedsmuir 1875–1940. Scottish politician and author. Called to the Bar 1901, he was Conservative member of Parliament for the Scottish universities 1927–35, and governor general of Canada 1934–40. His adventure stories, today criticized for their anti-semitism, include *The Thirty-Nine Steps* 1915, *Greenmantle* 1916, and *The Three Hostages* 1924.

Buckingham George Villiers, 1st Duke of Buckingham 1592–1628. English courtier, adviser to James I and later Charles I. After Charles's accession, Buckingham attempted to form a Protestant coalition in Europe, which led to war with France, but he failed to relieve the Protestants (◊Huguenots) besieged in La Rochelle 1627. This added to his unpopularity with Parliament, and he was assassinated.

Buckingham George Villiers, 2nd Duke of Buckingham 1628–1687. English politician, a member of the ◊Cabal under Charles II. A dissolute son of the first duke, he was brought up with the royal children. His play *The Rehearsal* satirized the style of the poet Dryden, who portrayed him as Zimri in Absalom and Achitophel.

Bull John. Imaginary figure supposedly personifying England.

Buller Redvers Henry 1839–1908. British commander against the Boers in the South African War 1899–1902. He was defeated at Colenso and Spion Kop, but relieved Ladysmith; he was superseded by Lord Roberts.

Bunker Hill, Battle of the first significant engagement in the American Revolution, 17 June 1775, near a small hill in Charlestown (now part of Boston), Massachusetts, USA; the battle actually took place on Breed's Hill. Although the colonists were defeated they were able to retreat to Boston and suffered fewer casualties than the British.

Burgess Guy (Francis de Moncy) 1910–1963. British spy, a diplomat recruited by the USSR as an agent. He was linked with Kim ◊Philby, Donald Maclean (1913–1983), and Anthony ◊Blunt.

Burgh Hubert de died 1243. English ◊justiciar and regent of England. He began his career in the administration of Richard I, and was promoted to the justiciarship by King John; he remained in that position under Henry III from 1216 until his dismissal. He was a supporter of King John against the barons, and ended French intervention in England by his defeat of the French fleet in the Strait of Dover 1217. He reorganized royal administration and the Common Law.

Burghley William Cecil, Baron Burghley 1520–1598. English politician, chief adviser to Elizabeth I as secretary of state from 1558 and Lord High Treasurer from 1572. He was largely responsible for the religious settlement of 1559, and took a leading role in the events preceding the execution of Mary Queen of Scots 1587.

Burke Edmund 1729–1797. British Whig politician and political theorist, born in Dublin, Ireland. In Parliament from 1765, he opposed the government's attempts to coerce the American colonists, for example in *Thoughts on the Present Discontents* 1770, and supported the emancipation of Ireland, but denounced the French Revolution, for example in *Reflections on the Revolution in France* 1790.

Burke wrote *A Philosophical Inquiry into the Origin of our Ideas on the Sublime and Beautiful* 1756, on aesthetics. He was paymaster of the forces in Rockingham's government 1782 and in the Fox–North coalition 1783, and after the collapse of the latter spent the rest of his career in opposition. He attacked Warren Hastings' misgovernment in India and promoted his impeachment. Burke defended his inconsistency in supporting the American but not the French Revolution in his *Appeal from the New to the Old Whigs* 1791 and *Letter to a Noble Lord* 1796, and attacked the suggestion of peace with France in *Letters on a Regicide Peace* 1795–97. He retired 1794. He was a skilled orator and is regarded by British Conservatives as the greatest of their political theorists.

Burke John 1787–1848. First publisher, in 1826, of ◊*Burke's Peerage*.

Burke's Peerage popular name of the *Genealogical and Heraldic*

History of the Peerage, Baronetage, and Knightage of the United Kingdom, first issued by John Burke 1826. The most recent edition was 1970.

Burns John 1858–1943. British labour leader, sentenced to six weeks' imprisonment for his part in the Trafalgar Square demonstration on 'Bloody Sunday' 13 Nov 1887, and leader of the strike in 1889 securing the 'dockers' tanner' (wage of 6d per hour). An Independent Labour member of Parliament 1892–1918, he was the first working-class person to be a member of the cabinet, as president of the Local Government Board 1906–14.

Bute John Stuart, 3rd Earl of Bute 1713–1792. British Tory politician, prime minister 1762–63. On the accession of George III in 1760, he became the chief instrument in the king's policy for breaking the power of the Whigs and establishing the personal rule of the monarch through Parliament.

Butler Richard Austen ('Rab'), Baron Butler 1902–1982. British Conservative politician. As minister of education 1941–45, he was responsible for the 1944 Education Act; he was chancellor of the Exchequer 1951–55, Lord Privy Seal 1955–59, and foreign minister 1963–64. As a candidate for the prime ministership, he was defeated by Harold Macmillan in 1957 (under whom he was home secretary 1957–62), and by Alec Douglas-Home in 1963.

Buxar, Battle of battle 1764 at Buxar, in Bihar, NE India, in which the British ◊East India Company secured dominance of N India. It defeated the triple forces of the Mogul emperor Shah Alam II (reigned 1759–1806); Mir Qasim, the recently dispossessed governor of Bengal; and Shuja-ud Daula, governor of the Ganges valley province of Oudh and *wazir* (chief minister) to the emperor.

Byng George, Viscount Torrington 1663–1733. British admiral. He captured Gibraltar 1704, commanded the fleet that prevented an invasion of England by the 'Old Pretender' James Francis Edward Stuart 1708, and destroyed the Spanish fleet at Messina 1718. John Byng was his fourth son.

Byng John 1704–1757. British admiral. Byng failed in the attempt to relieve Fort St Philip when in 1756 the island of Minorca was invaded by France. He was court-martialled and shot. The French writer Voltaire ironically commented that it was done 'to encourage the others'.

C

Cabal, the group of politicians, the English king Charles II's counsellors 1667–73, whose initials made up the word by coincidence – Clifford (Thomas Clifford 1630–1673), Ashley (Anthony Ashley Cooper, 1st Earl of ◊Shaftesbury), ◊Buckingham (George Villiers, 2nd Duke of Buckingham), Arlington (Henry Bennett, 1st Earl of Arlington 1618–1685), and ◊Lauderdale (John Maitland, Duke of Lauderdale).

cabinet in politics, the group of ministers holding a country's highest executive offices who decide government policy. In Britain the cabinet system originated under the Stuarts. Under William III it became customary for the king to select his ministers from the party with a parliamentary majority. The US cabinet, unlike the British, does not initiate legislation, and its members, appointed by the president, must not be members of Congress.

Cade Jack died 1450. English rebel. He was a prosperous landowner, but led a revolt 1450 in Kent against the high taxes and court corruption of Henry VI and demanded the recall from Ireland of Richard, Duke of York. The rebels defeated the royal forces at Sevenoaks and occupied London. After being promised reforms and pardon they dispersed, but Cade was hunted down and killed.

Cadwalader 7th century. Welsh hero. The son of Cadwallon, king of Gwynedd, N Wales, he defeated and killed ◊Edwin of Northumbria in 633. About a year later he was killed in battle.

Cadwallon 6th century. King of Gwynedd, N Wales, father of Cadwalader.

Calabria, Battle of World War II battle in 1940 in the Mediterranean Sea between Australian and British naval ships and the Italian fleet, which withdrew.

British cabinet

Prime Minister	John Major
Lord President and Leader of the House of Commons	Antony Newton
Secretary of State for Foreign and Commonwealth Affairs	Douglas Hurd
Chancellor of the Exchequer	Kenneth Clarke
Home Secretary	Michael Howard
Secretary of State for Trade and Industry	Michael Heseltine
Secretary of State for Defence	Malcolm Rifkind
Secretary of State for Scotland	Ian Lang
Secretary of State for Wales	John Redwood
Secretary of State for Northern Ireland	Sir Patrick Mayhew
Secretary of State for the Environment	John Gummer
Secretary of State for Employment	David Hunt
Secretary of State for Health	Virginia Bottomley
Secretary of State for Social Security	Peter Lilley
Secretary of State for Education	John Patten
Secretary of State for Transport	John MacGregor
Secretary of State for National Heritage	Peter Brooke
Secretary of State for Agriculture, Fisheries, and Food	Gillian Shephard
Chief Secretary to the Treasury	Michael Portillo
Chancellor of the Duchy of Lancaster	William Waldegrave
Lord Privy Seal and Leader of the House of Lords	Lord Wakeham
Lord Chancellor	Lord MacKay of Clashfern

Callaghan (Leonard) James, Baron Callaghan 1912– .British Labour politician. As Chancellor of the Exchequer 1964–67, he introduced corporation and capital- gains taxes, and resigned following devaluation. He was home secretary 1967–70 and prime minister 1976–79 in a period of increasing economic stress.

Cambridge University English university, one of the earliest in Europe, probably founded in the 12th century, though the earliest of the existing colleges, Peterhouse, was not founded until about 1284. In 1990, there were 10,000 undergraduates and 3,000 postgraduate students.

Camden William 1551–1623. English antiquary. He published his topographical survey Britannia 1586, and was headmaster of Westminster School from 1593. The *Camden Society* (1838) commemorates his work.

Camelot legendary seat of King ◊Arthur.

Campaign for Nuclear Disarmament (CND) nonparty- political British organization advocating the abolition of nuclear weapons worldwide. CND seeks unilateral British initiatives to help start the multilateral process and end the arms race. It was founded 1958.

Campbell Colin, 1st Baron Clyde 1792–1863. British field marshal. He commanded the Highland Brigade at ◊Balaclava in the Crimean War and, as commander in chief during the Indian Mutiny, raised the siege of Lucknow and captured Cawnpore.

Campbell-Bannerman Henry 1836–1908. British Liberal politician, prime minister 1905–08. It was during his term of office that the South African colonies achieved self-government, and the Trades Disputes Act 1906 was passed.

Canning Charles John, 1st Earl 1812–1862. British administrator, first viceroy of India from 1858. As governor general of India from 1856, he suppressed the Indian Mutiny with a fair but firm hand which earned him the nickname 'Clemency Canning'. He was the son of George Canning.

Canning George 1770–1827. British Tory politician, foreign secretary 1807–10 and 1822–27, and prime minister 1827 in coalition with the Whigs. He was largely responsible, during the Napoleonic Wars, for the seizure of the Danish fleet and British intervention in the Spanish peninsula.

Canning Sir Stratford, 1st Viscount Stratford de Redcliffe 1786–1880. British nobleman and diplomat. He negotiated the treaty of Bucharest between Russia and Turkey 1812 and helped establish a federal government in Switzerland 1815. He was minister to the United States 1820–23 and ambassador in Constantinople 1825–28, 1831, and 1842–58. He was made a viscount 1852.

Canterbury historic cathedral city in Kent, England, on the river Stour, 100 km/62 mi SE of London; population (1984) 39,000. In 597 King Ethelbert welcomed ◊Augustine's mission to England here, and the city has since been the metropolis of the Anglican Communion and seat of the archbishop of Canterbury.

Canute c. 995–1035. King of England from 1016, Denmark from 1018, and Norway from 1028. Having invaded England 1013 with his father, Sweyn, king of Denmark, he was acclaimed king on his father's death 1014 by his ◊Viking army. Canute defeated ◊Edmund II Ironside at Assandun (Ashingdon), Essex, 1016, and became king of all England on Edmund's death. He succeeded his brother Harold as king of Denmark 1018, compelled King Malcolm to pay homage by invading Scotland about 1027, and conquered Norway 1028. He was succeeded by his illegitimate son Harold I.

Caractacus died c. AD 54. British chieftain who headed resistance to the Romans in SE England AD 43–51, but was defeated on the Welsh border. Shown in Claudius's triumphal procession, he was released in tribute to his courage and died in Rome.

Caradon Baron. Title of Hugh ◊Foot, British Labour politician.

Cardwell Edward, Viscount Cardwell 1813–1886. British Liberal politician. He entered Parliament as a supporter of the Conservative prime minister ◊Peel 1842, and was secretary for war under Gladstone 1868–74, when he carried out many reforms, including the abolition of the purchase of military commissions and promotions.

Carlyle Thomas 1795–1881. Scottish essayist and social historian. His works include *Sartor Resartus* 1833–34, describing his loss of Christian belief; *The French Revolution* 1837; the pamphlet *Chartism* 1839, attacking the doctrine of *laissez-faire*, *Past and Present* 1843, the notable *Letters and Speeches of Cromwell* 1845, and the miniature life of his friend John Sterling 1851. His prose style was idiosyncratic, encompassing grand, thunderous rhetoric and deliberate obscurity.

Caroline of Brunswick 1768–1821. Queen of George IV of Great Britain, who unsuccessfully attempted to divorce her on his accession to the throne 1820.

Carr Edward Hallett 1892–1982. English historian, author of A History of Soviet Russia, which he began in 1944, completing the 14th and final volume in 1977. His interest in the subject was inspired by the view that Western capitalism was fatally flawed and that it would eventually have to be replaced by a planned economy and a greater attention to mass democracy.

Carson Edward Henry, Baron Carson 1854–1935. Irish politician and lawyer who played a decisive part in the trial of the writer Oscar Wilde. In the years before World War I he led the movement in Ulster to resist Irish ◊Home Rule by force of arms if need be.

Casement Roger David 1864–1916. Irish nationalist. While in the British consular service, he exposed the ruthless exploitation of the people of the Belgian Congo and Peru, for which he was knighted 1911 (degraded 1916). He was hanged for treason by the British for his involvement in the Irish nationalist cause.

Cassivelaunus chieftain of the British tribe, the Catuvellauni, who led the British resistance to the Romans under Caesar 54 BC.

Castle Barbara, Baroness Castle (born Betts) 1911–   . British Labour politician, a cabinet minister in the Labour governments of the 1960s and 1970s. She led the Labour group in the European Parliament 1979–89.

Castlemaine Lady (born Barbara Villiers) 1641–1709. Mistress of Charles II of England 1660–70 and mother of his son, the Duke of Grafton (1663–1690).

Castlereagh Robert Stewart, Viscount Castlereagh 1769–1822. British Tory politician. As chief secretary for Ireland 1797–1801, he suppressed the rebellion of 1798 and helped the younger Pitt secure the union of England, Scotland, and Ireland 1801. As foreign secretary 1812–22, he coordinated European opposition to Napoleon and represented Britain at the Congress of Vienna 1814–15.

Cat and Mouse Act popular name for the *Prisoners, Temporary Discharge for Health, Act* 1913; an attempt by the UK Liberal government under Herbert Asquith to reduce embarrassment caused by the incarceration of ◊suffragettes accused of violent offences against property.

Catesby Robert 1573–1605. English conspirator and leader of the ◊Gunpowder Plot 1605. He took part in the uprising of the 2nd Earl of ◊Essex 1601 and was an accomplice in the Rye Plot 1603 to capture ◊James I and force religious concessions from him. He was killed resisting arrest following the failure of the Gunpowder Plot to blow up parliament.

Catherine of Aragon 1485–1536. First queen of Henry VIII of England, 1509–33, and mother of Mary I. Catherine had married Henry's elder brother Prince Arthur 1501 and on his death 1502 was betrothed to Henry, marrying him on his accession. She failed to produce a male heir and Henry divorced her without papal approval, thus creating the basis for the English ◊Reformation.

Catherine of Braganza 1638–1705. Queen of Charles II of England 1662–85. Her childlessness and practice of her Catholic faith were unpopular, but Charles resisted pressure for divorce. She returned to Lisbon 1692 after his death.

Catherine of Valois 1401–1437. Queen of Henry V of England, whom she married 1420; the mother of Henry VI. After the death of Henry V, she secretly married Owen Tudor (*c.* 1400–1461) about 1425, and their son Edmund Tudor became the father of Henry VII.

Catholic Emancipation in British history, acts of Parliament passed 1780–1829 to relieve Roman Catholics of civil and political restrictions imposed from the time of Henry VIII and the ◊Reformation.

Cato Street Conspiracy in British history, unsuccessful plot hatched in Cato Street, London, to murder the Tory foreign secretary Robert Castlereagh and all his ministers on 20 Feb 1820. The leader, the Radical Arthur Thistlewood (1770–1820), who intended to set up a provisional government, was hanged with four others.

cavalier horseman of noble birth, but mainly used to describe a male supporter of Charles I in the English Civil War (Cavalier), typically with courtly dress and long hair (as distinct from a Roundhead); also a supporter of Charles II after the Restoration.

Cavell Edith Louisa 1865–1915. English matron of a Red Cross hospital in Brussels, Belgium, in World War I, who helped Allied soldiers escape to the Dutch frontier. She was court- martialled by the Germans and condemned to death.

Cavendish Frederick Charles, Lord Cavendish 1836–1882. British administrator, second son of the 7th Duke of Devonshire. He was appointed chief secretary to the lord lieutenant of Ireland in 1882. On the evening of his arrival in Dublin he was murdered in Phoenix Park with Thomas Burke, the permanent Irish undersecretary, by members of the Irish Invincibles, a group of Irish Fenian extremists founded 1881.

Cavendish Spencer. See ◊Hartington, Spencer Compton Cavendish, British politician.

Cecil Robert, 1st Earl of Salisbury 1563–1612.
Secretary of state to Elizabeth I of England, succeeding his father, Lord Burghley; he was afterwards chief minister to James I (James VI of Scotland) whose accession to the English throne he secured. He discovered the ◊Gunpowder Plot, the conspiracy to blow up the King and Parliament 1605. James I created him Earl of Salisbury 1605.

Celt member of an Indo-European people that originated in Alpine Europe and spread to the Iberian peninsula and beyond. They were ironworkers and farmers. In the 1st century BC they were defeated by the Roman Empire and by Germanic tribes and confined largely to Britain, Ireland, and N France.

ceorl freeman of the lowest class in Anglo-Saxon England.

Cerdic Saxon king of Wessex. He is said to have come to Britain about AD 495, landing near Southampton. He defeated the British in Hampshire and founded Wessex about AD 500, conquering the Isle of Wight about AD 530.

Chamberlain (Arthur) Neville 1869–1940. British Conservative politician, son of Joseph Chamberlain. He was prime minister 1937–40; his policy of appeasement toward the fascist dictators Mussolini and Hitler (with whom he concluded the ◊Munich Agreement 1938) failed to prevent the outbreak of World War II. He resigned 1940 following the defeat of the British forces in Norway.

Chamberlain (Joseph) Austen 1863–1937. British Conservative politician, elder son of Joseph Chamberlain; as foreign secretary 1924-29 he negotiated the Pact of ◊Locarno, for which he won the Nobel Peace Prize 1925, and signed the ◊Kellogg–Briand pact to outlaw war 1928.

Chamberlain Joseph 1836–1914. British politician, reformist mayor of and member of Parliament for Birmingham; in 1886, he resigned from the cabinet over Gladstone's policy of home rule for Ireland, and led the revolt of the Liberal-Unionists.

Chancellor, Lord UK state official, originally the royal secretary, today a member of the cabinet, whose office ends with a change of government. The Lord Chancellor acts as Speaker of the House of Lords, may preside over the Court of Appeal, and is head of the judiciary.

chancellor of the Exchequer in the UK, senior cabinet minister responsible for the national economy. The office, established under Henry III, originally entailed keeping the Exchequer seal.

Channel Islands group of islands in the English Channel, off the northwest coast of France; they are a possession of the British crown. They comprise the islands of Jersey, Guernsey, Alderney, Great and Little Sark, with the lesser Herm, Brechou, Jethou, and Lihou.

Channel Tunnel tunnel built beneath the English Channel, linking Britain with mainland Europe. It comprises twin rail tunnels, 50 km/31 mi long and 7.3 m/24 ft in diameter, located 40 m/130 ft beneath the seabed. Specially designed shuttle trains carrying cars and lorries will run between terminals at Folkestone, Kent, and Sangatte, W of Calais, France. It was begun 1986 and is scheduled to be operational 1994. The French and English sections were linked Dec 1990.

Charge of the Light Brigade disastrous attack by the British Light Brigade of cavalry against the Russian entrenched artillery on 25 Oct 1854 during the Crimean War at the Battle of ◊Balaclava.

Charles two kings of Britain:

Charles I 1600–1649. King of Great Britain and Ireland from 1625, son of James I of England (James VI of Scotland). He accepted the ◊petition of right 1628 but then dissolved Parliament and ruled without a parliament 1629–40. His advisers were ◊Strafford and ◊Laud, who persecuted the Puritans and provoked the Scots to revolt. The ◊Short Parliament, summoned 1640, refused funds, and the ◊Long Parliament later that year rebelled. Charles declared war on Parliament 1642 but surrendered 1646 and was beheaded 1649. He was the father of Charles II.

Charles was born at Dunfermline, and became heir to the throne on the death of his brother Henry 1612. He married Henrietta Maria, daughter of Henry IV of France. When he succeeded his father, friction with Parliament began at once. The parliaments of 1625 and 1626 were dissolved, and that of 1628 refused supplies until Charles had accepted

Channel Tunnel: chronology

1751	French farmer Nicolas Desmaret suggested a fixed link across the English Channel.
1802	French mining engineer Albert Mathieu-Favier proposed to Napoleon I a Channel tunnel through which horse-drawn carriages might travel. Discussions with British politicians ceased 1803 when war broke out between the two countries.
1834	Aim de Gamond of France suggested the construction of a submerged tube across the Channel.
1842	De la Haye of Liverpool designed an underwater tube, the sections of which would be bolted together underwater by workers without diving apparatus.
1851	Hector Horeau proposed a tunnel that would slope down towards the middle of the Channel and up thereafter, so that the carriages would be propelled downhill by their own weight and for a short distance uphill, after which compressed air would take over as the motive power.
1857	A joint committee of British and French scientists approved the aim of constructing a Channel tunnel.
1875	Channel-tunnel bills were passed by the British and French parliaments.
1876	An Anglo-French protocol was signed laying down the basis of a treaty governing construction of a tunnel.
1878	Borings began from the French and British sides of the Channel.
1882	British government forced abandonment of the project after public opinion, fearing invasion by the French, turned against the tunnel.
1904	Signing of the Entente Cordiale between France and the UK enabled plans to be reconsidered. Albert Sartiaux and Francis Fox proposed a twin-tunnel scheme.
1907	A new Channel-tunnel bill was defeated in the British parliament.
1930	A Channel-tunnel bill narrowly failed in British parliament.
1930–40	British prime minister Winston Churchill and the French government supported the digging of a tunnel.
1955	Defence objections to a tunnel were lifted in the UK by prime minister Harold Macmillan.
1957	Channel Tunnel Study Group established.
1961	Study Group plans for a double-bore tunnel presented to British government.
1964	Ernest Marples, Minister of Transport, and his French counterpart gave go-ahead for construction.
1967	British government invited tunnel-building proposals from private interests.
1973	Anglo-French treaty on trial borings signed.
1974	New tunnel bill introduced in British Parliament but was not passed before election called by Harold Wilson.
1975	British government cancelled project because of escalating costs.
1981	Anglo-French summit agreed to investigation of possible tunnel.

1982	Intergovernmental study group on tunnel established.
1984	Construction of tunnel agreed in principle at Anglo-French summit.
1986	Anglo-French treaty signed; design submitted by a consortium called the Channel Tunnel Group accepted.
1987	Legislation completed, Anglo-French treaty ratified; construction started in Nov.
1990	First breakthrough of service tunnel took place Dec.
1991	Breakthrough of first rail tunnel in May; the second rail tunnel was completed in June.
1994	Tunnel scheduled to be operational.

the Petition of Right. In 1629 it attacked Charles's illegal taxation and support of the Arminians in the church, whereupon he dissolved Parliament and imprisoned its leaders. For 11 years he ruled without a parliament, the Eleven Years' Tyranny, raising money by expedients, such as ◊ship money, that alienated the nation, while the ◊Star Chamber suppressed opposition by persecuting the Puritans. When Charles attempted 1637 to force a prayer book on the English model on Presbyterian Scotland he found himself confronted with a nation in arms. The Short Parliament, which met April 1640, refused to grant money until grievances were redressed, and was speedily dissolved. The Scots then advanced into England and forced their own terms on Charles. The Long Parliament met 3 Nov 1640 and declared extra-parliamentary taxation illegal, abolished the Star Chamber and other prerogative courts, and voted that Parliament could not be dissolved without its own consent. Laud and other ministers were imprisoned, and Strafford condemned to death. After the failure of his attempt to arrest the parliamentary leaders 4 Jan 1642, Charles, confident that he had substantial support among those who felt that Parliament was becoming too radical and zealous, withdrew from London, and on 22 Aug declared war on Parliament by raising his standard at Nottingham (see English ◊Civil War). Charles's defeat at Naseby June 1645 ended all hopes of victory; in May 1646 he surrendered at Newark to the Scots, who handed him over to Parliament Jan 1647. In June the army seized him and carried him off to Hampton Court. While the army leaders strove to find a settlement, Charles secretly intrigued for a Scottish invasion. In Nov he escaped, but was recaptured and held at Carisbrooke Castle; a Scottish invasion followed 1648, and was shattered by ◊Cromwell at Preston. In Jan 1649 the House of Commons set up a high court of justice, which tried Charles and condemned him to death. He was beheaded 30 Jan before the Banqueting House in Whitehall.

Charles II 1630–1685. King of Great Britain and Ireland from 1660, when Parliament accepted the restoration of the monarchy after the collapse of Cromwell's Commonwealth; son of Charles I. His chief minister Clarendon, who arranged his marriage 1662 with Catherine of Braganza, was replaced 1667 with the ◊Cabal of advisers. His plans to restore Catholicism in Britain led to war with the Netherlands 1672–74 in support of Louis XIV of France and a break with Parliament, which he dissolved 1681. He was succeeded by James II.

Charles was born in St James's Palace, London; during the Civil War he lived with his father at Oxford 1642–45, and after the victory of Cromwell's Parliamentary forces withdrew to France. Accepting the ◊Covenanters' offer to make him king, he landed in Scotland 1650, and was crowned at Scone 1 Jan 1651. An attempt to invade England was ended 3 Sept by Cromwell's victory at Worcester. Charles escaped, and for nine years he wandered through France, Germany, Flanders, Spain, and Holland until the opening of negotiations by George Monk (1608–1670) 1660. In April Charles issued the Declaration of Breda, promising a general amnesty and freedom of conscience. Parliament accepted the Declaration and he was proclaimed king 8 May 1660, landed at Dover on 26 May, and entered London three days later. Charles wanted to make himself absolute, and favoured Catholicism for his subjects as most consistent with absolute monarchy. The disasters of the Dutch war furnished an excuse for banishing Clarendon 1667, and he was replaced by the Cabal of Clifford and Arlington, both secret Catholics, and ◊Buckingham, Ashley (Lord ◊Shaftesbury), and ◊Lauderdale, who had links with the ◊Dissenters. In 1670 Charles signed the Secret Treaty of Dover, the full details of which were known only to Clifford and Arlington, whereby he promised Louis XIV of France he would declare himself a Catholic, re-establish Catholicism in England, and support Louis's projected war against the Dutch; in return

Louis was to finance Charles and in the event of resistance to supply him with troops. War with the Netherlands followed 1672, and at the same time Charles issued the Declaration of Indulgence, suspending all penal laws against Catholics and Dissenters. In 1673, Parliament forced Charles to withdraw the Indulgence and accept a Test Act excluding all Catholics from office, and in 1674 to end the Dutch war. The Test Act broke up the Cabal, while Shaftesbury, who had learned the truth about the treaty, assumed the leadership of the opposition. ◊Danby, the new chief minister, built up a court party in the Commons by bribery, while subsidies from Louis relieved Charles from dependence on Parliament. In 1678 Titus ◊Oates's announcement of a 'popish plot' released a general panic, which Shaftesbury exploited to introduce his Exclusion Bill, excluding James, Duke of York, from the succession as a Catholic; instead he hoped to substitute Charles's illegitimate son ◊Monmouth. In 1681 Parliament was summoned at Oxford, which had been the Royalist headquarters during the Civil War. The Whigs attended armed, but when Shaftesbury rejected a last compromise, Charles dissolved Parliament and the Whigs fled in terror. Charles now ruled without a parliament, financed by Louis XIV. When the Whigs plotted a revolt, their leaders were executed, while Shaftesbury and Monmouth fled to the Netherlands. Charles was a patron of the arts and science. His mistresses included Lady ◊Castlemaine, Nell ◊Gwyn, Lady Portsmouth, and Lucy ◊Walter.

Charles Edward Stuart the *Young Pretender* or *Bonnie Prince Charlie* 1720–1788. British prince, grandson of James II and son of James, the Old Pretender. In the Jacobite rebellion 1745 Charles won the support of the Scottish Highlanders; his army invaded England to claim the throne but was beaten back by the duke of ◊Cumberland and routed at ◊Culloden 1746. Charles went into exile.

Chartism radical British democratic movement, mainly of the working classes, which flourished around 1838-48. It derived its name from the People's Charter, a six-point programme comprising universal male suffrage, equal electoral districts, secret ballot, annual parliaments, and abolition of the property qualification for, and payment of, members of Parliament. Greater prosperity, lack of organization, and rivalry in the leadership led to its demise.

Chesterfield Philip Dormer Stanhope, 4th Earl of Chesterfield 1694–1773. English politician and writer. He was the author of *Letters to his Son* 1774, which gave voluminous instruction on aristocratic manners and morals. A member of the literary circle of Swift, Pope, and Bolingbroke, he incurred the wrath of Dr Samuel Johnson by failing to carry out an offer of patronage.

Childers (Robert) Erskine 1870–1922. British civil servant and, from 1921, Irish Sinn Féin politician, author of the spy novel The Riddle of the Sands 1903. He was executed as a Republican terrorist.

Christian Socialism a 19th-century movement stressing the social principles of the Bible and opposed to the untrammelled workings of *laissez-faire* capitalism. Its founders, all members of the Church of England were Frederick Denison Maurice (1805-1872), Charles Kingsley (1819–1875), and the novelist Thomas Hughes (1822–1896).

Church of England established form of Christianity in England, a member of the Anglican Communion. It was dissociated from the Roman Catholic Church 1534. There were approximately 1,100,000 regular worshippers in 1988.

Church of Scotland established form of Christianity in Scotland, first recognized by the state 1560. It is based on the Protestant doctrines of the reformer Calvin and governed on Presbyterian lines. The Church went through several periods of episcopacy in the 17th century, and those who adhered to episcopacy after 1690 formed the Episcopal Church of Scotland, an autonomous church in communion with the Church of England. In 1843, there was a split in the Church of Scotland (the Disruption), in which almost a third of its ministers and members left and formed the Free Church of Scotland. Its membership 1988 was about 850,000.

Churchill Randolph (Henry Spencer) 1849–1895. British Conservative politician, chancellor of the Exchequer and leader of the House of Commons 1886; father of Winston Churchill.

Churchill Winston (Leonard Spencer) 1874–1965. British Conservative politician, prime minister 1940–45 and 1951–55. In Parliament from 1900, as a Liberal until 1923, he held a number of ministerial offices, including First Lord of the Admiralty 1911-15 and chancellor of the Exchequer 1924-29. Absent from the cabinet in the 1930s, he returned Sept 1939 to lead a coalition government 1940–45, negotiating with Allied leaders in World War II to achieve the unconditional surrender of Germany 1945; he led a Conservative government 1951–55. He received the Nobel Prize for Literature 1953.

He was born at Blenheim Palace, the elder son of Lord Randolph Churchill. During the Boer War he was a war correspondent and made a dramatic escape from imprisonment in Pretoria. In 1900 he was elected Conservative member of Parliament for Oldham, but he disagreed with Chamberlain's tariff-reform policy and joined the Liberals. Asquith made him president of the Board of Trade 1908, where he introduced legislation for the establishment of labour exchanges. He became home secretary 1910. In 1911 Asquith appointed him First Lord of the Admiralty. In 1915–16 he served in the trenches in France, but then resumed his parliamentary duties and was minister of munitions under Lloyd George 1917, when he was concerned with the development of the tank. After the armistice he was secretary for war 1918–21 and then as colonial secretary played a leading part in the establishment of the Irish Free State. During the postwar years he was active in support of the Whites (anti-Bolsheviks) in Russia.

In 1922–24 Churchill was out of Parliament. He left the Liberals 1923, and was returned for Epping as a Conservative 1924. Baldwin made him chancellor of the Exchequer, and he brought about Britain's return to the gold standard and was prominent in the defeat of the General Strike 1926. In 1929–39 he was out of office as he disagreed with the Conservatives on India, rearmament, and Chamberlain's policy of appeasement.

On the first day of World War II he went back to his old post at the Admiralty. In May 1940 he was called to the premiership as head of an all- party administration and made a much quoted 'blood, toil, tears, and sweat' speech to the House of Commons. He had a close relationship with US president Roosevelt, and in Aug 1941 concluded the ◊Atlantic Charter with him. He travelled to Washington, Casablanca, Cairo, Moscow, and Tehran, meeting the other leaders of the Allied war effort. He met Stalin and Roosevelt in the Crimea Feb 1945 and agreed on the final plans for victory. On 8 May he announced the unconditional surrender of Germany.

The coalition was dissolved 23 May 1945, and Churchill formed a caretaker government drawn mainly from the Conservatives. Defeated in the general election July, he became leader of the opposition until the election Oct 1951, in which he again became prime minister. In April 1955 he resigned. His home from 1922, Chartwell in Kent, is a museum. His books include a six-volume history of World War II (1948–54) and a four-volume History of the English-Speaking Peoples (1956–58).

Cinque Ports group of ports in S England, originally five, Sandwich, Dover, Hythe, Romney, and Hastings, later including Rye, Winchelsea, and others. Probably founded in Roman times, they rose to importance after the Norman conquest and until the end of the 15th century were bound to supply the ships and men necessary against invasion.

Citizens' Advice Bureau (CAB) UK organization established 1939 to provide information and advice to the public on any subject, such as personal problems, financial, house purchase, or consumer rights. If required, the bureau will act on behalf of citizens, drawing on its own sources of legal and other experts. There are more than 900 bureaux located all over the UK.

citizenship status as a member of a state. In most countries citizenship may be acquired either by birth or by naturalization. The status confers rights such as voting and the protection of the law and also imposes responsibilities such as military service, in some countries.

civil rights rights of the individual citizen. In many countries they are specified (as in the Bill of Rights of the US constitution) and guaranteed by law to ensure equal treatment for all citizens. In the USA, the struggle to obtain civil rights for former slaves and their descendants, both through legislation and in practice, has been a major theme since the Civil War.

civil service body of administrative staff appointed to carry out the policy of a government. Members of the UK civil service may not take an active part in politics, and do not change with the government.

Civil War, English the conflict between King Charles I and the Royalists (Cavaliers) on one side and the Parliamentarians (also called

English Civil War 1625–49: chronology

1625	James I died, succeeded by Charles I, whose first parliament was dissolved after refusing to grant him tonnage and poundage (taxation revenues) for life.
1627	'Five Knights' case in which men who refused to pay a forced loan were imprisoned.
1628	Coke, Wentworth, and Eliot presented the Petition of Right, requesting the king not to tax without parliamentary consent, not to billet soldiers in private homes, and not to impose martial law on civilians. Charles accepted this as the price of parliamentary taxation to pay for war with Spain and France. Duke of Buckingham assassinated.
1629	Parliament dissolved following disagreement over religious policy, tonnage and poundage, beginning Charles' 'Eleven Years' Tyranny'. War with France ended.
1630	End of war with Spain.
1632	Strafford made lord deputy in Ireland.
1633	Laud became archibishop of Canterbury. Savage punishment of puritan Willian Prynne for his satirical pamphlet 'Histriomastix'.
1634	Ship money first collected in London.
1634–37	Laud attempted to enforce ecclesiastical discipline by metropolitan visits.
1637	Conviction of John Hampden for refusal to pay ship money infringed Petition of Right.
1638	Covenanters in Scotland protested at introduction of Laudian Prayer Book into the Kirk.
1639	First Bishops' War. Charles sent army to Scotland after its renunciation of episcopacy. Agreement reached without fighting.
1640	Short Parliament April–May voted taxes for the suppression of the Scots, but dissolved to forestall petition against Scottish war. Second Bishops' War ended in defeat for English at Newburn-on-Tyne. Scots received pension and held Northumberland and Durham in Treaty of Ripon. Long Parliament called, passing the Triennial Act and abolishing the Star Chamber. High Commission and Councils of the North and of Wales set up.
1641	Strafford executed. English and Scots massacred at Ulster. Grand Remonstrance passed appealing to mass opinion against episcopacy and the royal prerogative. Irish Catholic nobility massacred.
1642 Jan	Charles left Westminster after an unsuccessful attempt to arrest five members of the Commons united both Houses of Parliament and the City against him.
Feb	Bishop's Exclusion Bill passed, barring clergy from secular office and the Lords.
May–June	Irish rebels established supreme council. Militia Ordinance passed, assuming sovereign powers for parliament. Nineteen Propositions rejected by Charles.

Aug	Charles raised his standard at Nottingham. Outbreak of first Civil War.
Oct	General Assembly of the Confederate Catholics met at Kilkenny. Battle of Edgehill inconclusive.
1643	Irish truce left rebels in control of more of Ireland. Solemn League and Covenant, alliance between English Parliamentarians and Scots, pledged to establish Presbyterianism in England and Ireland, and to provide a Scottish army. Scots intervened in Civil War.
1643–49	Westminster Assembly attempted to draw up Calvinist religious settlement.
1644	Committee of Both Kingdoms to coordinate Scottish and Parliamentarians' military activities established. Royalists decisively beaten at Marston Moor.
1645	Laud executed. New Model Army created. Charles pulled out of Uxbridge negotiations on a new constitutional position. Cromwell and the New Model Army destroyed Royalist forces at Naseby.
1646	Charles fled to Scotland. Oxford surrendered to parliament. End of first Civil War.
1647 May	Charles agreed with parliament to accept Presbyterianism and to surrender control of the militia.
June–Aug	Army seized Charles and resolved not to disband without satisfactory terms. Army presented Heads of Proposals to Charles.
Oct–Dec	Army debated Levellers' Agreement of the People at Putney. Charles escaped to the Isle of Wight, and reached agreement withthe Scots by Treaty of Newport.
1648 Jan	Vote of No Addresses passed by Long Parliament declaring an end to negotiations with Charles.
Aug	Cromwell defeated Scots at Preston. Second Civil War began.
Nov–Dec	Army demanded trial of Charles I. Pride's Purge of parliament transfered power to the Rump of independent MPs.
1649 Jan–Feb	Charles tried and executed. Rump elected Council of State as its executive.
May	Rump declared England a Commonwealth. Cromwell landed in Dublin.
Sept–Oct	Massacres of garrisons at Drogheda and Wexford by Cromwell.

Roundheads) under Oliver ◊Cromwell on the other. Their differences centred on the king's unconstitutional acts but became a struggle over the relative powers of crown and Parliament. Hostilities began 1642 and a series of Royalist defeats (Marston Moor 1644, Naseby 1645) culminated in Charles's capture 1647 and execution 1649. The war continued until the final defeat of Royalist forces at Worcester 1651. Cromwell became Protector (ruler) from 1651 until his death 1658.

Clarendon Edward Hyde, 1st Earl of Clarendon 1609–1674. English politician and historian, chief adviser to Charles II 1651–67. A member of Parliament 1640, he joined the Royalist side 1641. The *Clarendon Code* 1661–65, a series of acts passed by the government, was directed at Nonconformists (or Dissenters) and was designed to secure the supremacy of the Church of England.

Clarendon George William Frederick Villiers, 4th Earl of Clarendon 1800–1870. British Liberal diplomat, lord lieutenant of Ireland 1847–52, foreign secretary 1853–58, 1865–66, and 1868–70.

Clarendon, Constitutions of in English history, a series of resolutions agreed by a council summoned by Henry II at Clarendon in Wiltshire 1164. The Constitutions aimed at limiting the secular power of the clergy, and were abandoned after the murder of Thomas à Becket. They form an early English legal document of great historical value.

Clarke Kenneth (Harry) 1940– . British Conservative politician, member of parliament from 1970, a cabinet minister from 1985, education secretary 1990–92, and home secretary 1992–93. He succeeded Norman Lamont as chancellor of the Exchequer May 1993.

Clarkson Thomas 1760–1846. British philanthropist. From 1785 he devoted himself to a campaign against slavery. He was one of the founders of the Anti-Slavery Society 1823 and was largely responsible for the abolition of slavery in British colonies 1833.

Claudius (Tiberius Claudius Drusus Nero Germanicus) 10 BC–AD 54. Nephew of Tiberius, made Roman emperor by his troops AD 41, after the murder of his nephew Caligula. Claudius was a scholar, historian, and able administrator. During his reign the Roman empire was considerably extended, and in 43 he took part in the invasion of Britain.

Claverhouse John Graham, Viscount Dundee 1649–1689. Scottish soldier. Appointed by Charles II to suppress the ◊Covenanters from 1677, he was routed at Drumclog 1679, but three weeks later won the battle of Bothwell Bridge, by which the rebellion was crushed. Until 1688 he was engaged in continued persecution and became known as 'Bloody Clavers', regarded by the Scottish people as a figure of evil. His army then joined the first Jacobite rebellion and defeated the loyalist forces in the pass of Killiecrankie, where he was mortally wounded.

Clive Robert, Baron Clive of Plassey 1725–1774. British soldier and administrator who established British rule in India by victories over French troops at Arcot 1751 and over the nawab of Bengal at Plassey 1757. He was governor of Bengal 1757–60 and 1765–66. On his return to Britain in 1766, his wealth led to allegations that he had abused his power. Although acquitted, he committed suicide.

closed shop a place of work, such as a factory or an office, where all workers within a section must belong to a single officially recognized ◊trade union. Closed-shop agreements are negotiated between trade unions and management.

Trade unions favour closed shops because 100% union membership gives them greater industrial power. Management can find it convenient because they can deal with workers as a group (collective bargaining) rather than having to negotiate with individual workers. The closed shop was condemned by the European Court of Human Rights 1981. In the USA the closed shop was made illegal by the Taft-Hartley Act 1947, passed by Congress over Truman's veto.

CND abbreviation for ◊*Campaign for Nuclear Disarmament*.

Cnut alternative spelling of ◊Canute.

coastguard governmental organization whose members patrol a nation's seacoast to prevent smuggling, assist distressed vessels, watch for oil slicks, and so on.

Cobbett William 1763–1835. English Radical politician and journalist, who published the weekly Political Register 1802-35. He spent much time in North America. His crusading essays on the conditions of the rural poor were collected as Rural Rides 1830.

Cobden Richard 1804–1865. British Liberal politician and economist, co-founder with John Bright of the Anti-Corn Law League 1839. A member of Parliament from 1841, he opposed class and religious privileges and believed in disarmament and free trade.

A typical early Victorian radical, he believed in the abolition of privileges, a minimum of government interference, and the securing of international peace through free trade and by disarmament and arbitration. He opposed trade unionism and most of the factory legislation of his time, because he regarded them as opposed to liberty of contract.

His opposition to the Crimean War made him unpopular. He was largely responsible for the commercial treaty with France in 1860.

Coke Edward 1552–1634. Lord Chief Justice of England 1613–17. He was a defender of common law against royal prerogative; against Charles I he drew up the ◊Petition of Right 1628, which defines and protects Parliament's liberties.

Collier Jeremy 1650–1726. British Anglican cleric, a ◊Nonjuror, who was outlawed 1696 for granting absolution on the scaffold to two men who had tried to assassinate William III. His Short View of the Immorality and Profaneness of the English Stage 1698 was aimed at the dramatists William Congreve and John Vanbrugh.

Collingwood Cuthbert, Baron Collingwood 1748–1810. British admiral who served with Horatio Nelson in the West Indies against France and blockaded French ports 1803–05; after Nelson's death he took command at the Battle of Trafalgar.

Collins Michael 1890–1922. Irish nationalist. He was a Sinn Féin leader, a founder and director of intelligence of the Irish Republican Army 1919, minister for finance in the provisional government of the Irish Free State 1922 (see ◊Ireland, Republic of), commander of the Free State forces in the civil war, and for ten days head of state before being killed by Irishmen opposed to the partition treaty with Britain.

Combination Acts laws passed in Britain 1799 and 1800 making trade unionism illegal, introduced after the French Revolution for fear that the unions would become centres of political agitation. The unions continued to exist, but claimed to be friendly societies or went underground, until the acts were repealed 1824, largely owing to the radical Francis Place.

Commons, House of the lower but more powerful of the two parts of the British and Canadian ◊parliaments.

commonwealth body politic founded on law for the common 'weal' or good. Political philosophers of the 17th century, such as Thomas Hobbes and John Locke, used the term to mean an organized political community. In Britain it was specifically applied to the regime (*the Commonwealth*) of Oliver ◊Cromwell 1649–60.

Commonwealth Immigration Acts successive acts to regulate the entry into the UK of British subjects from the Commonwealth. The Commonwealth Immigration Act, passed by the Conservative government 1962, ruled that Commonwealth immigrants entering Britain must have employment or be able to offer required skills. Further restrictions have been added.

Commonwealth of Nations formerly known as the British Commonwealth of Nations, voluntary association of 50 states that have been or still are ruled by Britain (see ◊British Empire). Independent states are full 'members of the Commonwealth', while dependent territories, such as colonies and protectorates, rank as 'Commonwealth countries'. Small self-governing countries, such as Nauru, may have special status. The Commonwealth is founded more on tradition and sentiment than political or economic factors. Queen Elizabeth II is the formal head but not the ruler of member states. The Commonwealth secretariat, headed from Oct 1989 by Nigerian Emeka Anyaoko as secretary general, is based in London.

Commonwealth, the (British) voluntary association of 50 countries and their dependencies that once formed part of the ◊British Empire and are now independent sovereign states. They are all regarded as 'full members of the Commonwealth'. Additionally, there are some 20 territories that are not completely sovereign and remain dependencies of the UK or another of the fully sovereign members, and are regarded as 'Commonwealth countries'. Heads of government meet every two years, apart from those of Nauru and Tuvalu; however, Nauru and Tuvalu have the right to participate in all functional activities. The Commonwealth has no charter or constitution, and is founded more on tradition and sentiment than on political or economic factors.

community charge in the UK, a charge (commonly known as the ◊poll tax) levied by local authorities; it was replaced 1993 by a council tax.

Companion of Honour British order of chivalry, founded by George V 1917. It is of one class only, and carries no title, but Companions append 'CH' to their names. The number is limited to 65 and the award is made to both men and women.

Connell James 1850–1929. Irish socialist who wrote the British Labour Party anthem 'The Red Flag' during the 1889 London strike.

Conservative Party UK political party, one of the two historic British parties; the name replaced *Tory* in general use from 1830 onwards. Traditionally the party of landed interests, it broadened its political base under Benjamin Disraeli's leadership in the 19th century. The present Conservative Party's free-market capitalism is supported by the world of finance and the management of industry.

conservatism approach to government favouring the maintenance of existing institutions and identified with a number of Western political parties, such as the British Conservative, US Republican, German Christian Democratic, and Australian Liberal parties. It tends to be explicitly nondoctrinaire and pragmatic but generally emphasizes free-enterprise capitalism, minimal government intervention in the economy, rigid law and order, and the importance of national traditions.

constitution body of fundamental laws of a state, laying down the system of government and defining the relations of the legislature, executive, and judiciary to each other and to the citizens. Since the French Revolution almost all countries (the UK is an exception) have adopted written constitutions; that of the USA (1787) is the oldest.

Cook James 1728–1779. British naval explorer. After surveying the St Lawrence 1759, he made three voyages: 1768–71 to Tahiti, New Zealand, and Australia; 1772–75 to the South Pacific; and 1776–79 to the South and North Pacific, attempting to find the Northwest Passage and charting the Siberian coast. He was killed in Hawaii.

Cook Robin Finlayson 1946–   . English Labour politician. A member of the moderate-left Tribune Group, he entered Parliament 1974 and became a leading member of Labour's shadow cabinet, specializing in health matters. When John Smith assumed the party leadership July 1992, Cook remained in the shadow cabinet as spokesman for trade and industry.

Cooper Alfred Duff Chancellor of the Duchy of Lancaster, sent to Singapore August 1941 to report on preparations for a Japanese attack. He had a notorious row with Shenton Thomas, Governor of Straits

Settlements, and both Cooper and Thomas bear responsibility for the appalling lack of preparation for the Japanese invasion.

Cooperative Party political party founded in Britain 1917 by the cooperative movement to maintain its principles in parliamentary and local government. A written constitution was adopted 1938. The party had strong links with the Labour Party; from 1946 Cooperative Party candidates stood in elections as Cooperative and Labour Candidates and, after the 1959 general election, agreement was reached to limit the party's candidates to 30.

Copenhagen, Battle of naval victory 2 April 1801 by a British fleet under Sir Hyde Parker (1739–1807) and ◊Nelson over the Danish fleet. Nelson put his telescope to his blind eye and refused to see Parker's signal for withdrawal.

Corn Laws in Britain until 1846, laws used to regulate the export or import of cereals in order to maintain an adequate supply for consumers and a secure price for producers. For centuries the Corn Laws formed an integral part of the mercantile system in England; they were repealed because they became an unwarranted tax on food and a hindrance to British exports.

Although mentioned as early as the 12th century, the Corn Laws only became significant in the late 18th century. After the Napoleonic wars, with mounting pressure from a growing urban population, the laws aroused strong opposition because of their tendency to drive up prices. They were modified 1828 and 1842 and, partly as a result of the Irish potato famine, repealed by prime minister Robert Peel 1846.

Cornwallis Charles, 1st Marquess 1738–1805. British general in the American Revolution until 1781, when his defeat at Yorktown led to final surrender and ended the war. He then served twice as governor general of India and once as viceroy of Ireland.

corresponding society in British history, one of the first independent organizations for the working classes, advocating annual parliaments and universal male suffrage. The London Corresponding Society was founded 1792 by politicians Thomas Hardy (1752–1832) and John Horne Tooke (1736–1812). It later established branches in

Scotland and the provinces. Many of its activities had to be held in secret and government fears about the spread of revolutionary doctrines led to its banning 1799.

Cosgrave William Thomas 1880–1965. Irish politician. He took part in the ♢Easter Rising 1916 and sat in the Sinn Féin cabinet of 1919–21. Head of the Free State government 1922–33, he founded and led the Fine Gael opposition 1933–44. His eldest son is Liam Cosgrave.

Cotton Robert Bruce 1571–1631. English antiquary. At his home in Westminster he built up a fine collection of manuscripts and coins, many of which had come from the despoiled monasteries. His son *Thomas Cotton* (1594– 1662) added to the library. The collection is now in the British Museum.

council tax method of raising revenue for local government in Britain. It replaced the community charge, or ♢poll tax, from April 1993. The tax is based on property values but takes some account of the number of people occupying each property.

county administrative unit of a country or state. In the UK it is nowadays synonymous with 'shire', although historically the two had different origins. Many of the English counties can be traced back to Saxon times. The Republic of Ireland has 26 geographical and 27 administrative counties.

county council in the UK, a unit of local government whose responsibilities include broad planning policy, highways, education, personal social services, and libraries; police, fire, and traffic control; and refuse disposal.

county palatine in medieval England, a county whose lord held particular rights, in lieu of the king, such as pardoning treasons and murders. Under William I there were four counties palatine: Chester, Durham, Kent, and Shropshire.

courtesy title in the UK, any title given to the progeny of members of the peerage. For example, the eldest son of a duke, marquess, or earl may bear one of his father's lesser titles; thus the Duke of Marlborough's son is the Marquess of Blandford. They are not peers and do not sit in the House of Lords.

Court of the Lord Lyon Scottish heraldic authority composed of one king of arms, three heralds, and three pursuivants who specialize in genealogical work. It embodies the High Sennachie of Scotland's Celtic kings.

Covenanter in Scottish history, one of the Presbyterian Christians who swore to uphold their forms of worship in a National Covenant, signed 28 Feb 1638, when Charles I attempted to introduce a liturgy on the English model into Scotland.

Craig James 1871–1940. Ulster Unionist politician, the first prime minister of Northern Ireland 1921–40. Craig became a member of Parliament 1906, and was a highly effective organizer of Unionist resistance to Home Rule. As prime minister he carried out systematic discrimination against the Catholic minority, abolishing proportional representation 1929 and redrawing constituency boundaries to ensure Protestant majorities.

Cranmer Thomas 1489–1556. English cleric, archbishop of Canterbury from 1533. A Protestant convert, he helped to shape the doctrines of the Church of England under Edward VI. He was responsible for the issue of the Prayer Books of 1549 and 1552, and supported the succession of Lady Jane Grey 1553.

Crécy, Battle of first major battle of the Hundred Years' War 1346. Philip VI of France was defeated by Edward III of England at the village of Crécy-en-Ponthieu, now in Somme *département*, France, 18 km/11 mi NE of Abbeville.

Creevey Thomas 1768–1838. British Whig politician and diarist whose lively letters and journals give information on early 19th-century society and politics. He was a member of Parliament and opposed the slave trade.

Crichton James c. 1560–1582. Scottish scholar, known as 'the Admirable Crichton' because of his extraordinary gifts as a poet, scholar, and linguist. He was also an athlete and fencer. According to one account he was killed at Mantua in a street brawl by his pupil, a son of the Duke of Mantua, who resented Crichton's popularity.

Crimean War war 1853–56 between Russia and the allied powers of England, France, Turkey, and Sardinia. The war arose from British and French mistrust of Russia's ambitions in the Balkans. It began with an allied Anglo-French expedition to the Crimea to attack the Russian Black Sea city of Sevastopol. The battles of the river Alma, Balaclava (including the charge of the Light Brigade), and Inkerman 1854 led to a siege which, owing to military mismanagement, lasted for a year until Sept 1855. The war was ended by the Treaty of Paris 1856. The scandal surrounding French and British losses through disease led to the organization of proper military nursing services by Florence Nightingale.

Crippen Hawley Harvey 1861–1910. US murderer of his wife, variety artist Belle Elmore. He buried her remains in the cellar of his London home and tried to escape to the USA with his mistress Ethel le Neve (dressed as a boy). He was arrested on board ship following a radio message, the first criminal captured 'by radio', and was hanged.

Cripps (Richard) Stafford 1889–1952. British Labour politician, expelled from the Labour Party 1939–45 for supporting a 'Popular Front' against Chamberlain's appeasement policy. He was ambassador to Moscow 1940–42, minister of aircraft production 1942–45, and chancellor of the Exchequer 1947–50.

Crockford William 1775–1844. British gambler, founder in 1827 of Crockford's Club in St James's Street, which became the fashionable place for London society to gamble.

croft small farm in the Highlands of Scotland, traditionally farming common land cooperatively; the 1886 Crofters Act gave security of tenure to crofters. Today, although grazing land is still shared, arable land is typically enclosed.

Cromwell Oliver 1599–1658. English general and politician, Puritan leader of the Parliamentary side in the ◊Civil War. He raised cavalry forces (later called *Ironsides*) which aided the victories at Edgehill 1642 and ◊Marston Moor 1644, and organized the New Model Army, which he led (with General Fairfax) to victory at Naseby 1645. He declared Britain a republic ('the Commonwealth') 1649, following the execution of Charles I. As Lord Protector (ruler) from 1653, Cromwell established religious toleration and raised Britain's prestige in Europe on the basis of an alliance with France against Spain.

Cromwell was born at Huntingdon, NW of Cambridge, son of a small landowner. He entered Parliament 1629 and became active in events leading to the Civil War. Failing to secure a constitutional settlement with Charles I 1646–48, he defeated the 1648 Scottish invasion at Preston. A special commission, of which Cromwell was a member, tried the king and condemned him to death, and a republic, known as 'the Commonwealth', was set up.

The ◊Levellers demanded radical reforms, but he executed their leaders 1649. He used terror to crush Irish clan resistance 1649–50, and defeated the Scots (who had acknowledged Charles II) at Dunbar 1650 and Worcester 1651. In 1653, having forcibly expelled the corrupt 'Rump' Parliament, he summoned a convention ('Barebone's Parliament'), soon dissolved as too radical, and under a constitution (Instrument of Government) drawn up by the army leaders, became Protector (king in all but name). The parliament of 1654–55 was dissolved as uncooperative, and after a period of military dictatorship, his last parliament offered him the crown; he refused because he feared the army's republicanism.

Cromwell Richard 1626–1712. Son of Oliver Cromwell, he succeeded his father as Lord Protector but resigned May 1659, having been forced to abdicate by the army. He lived in exile after the Restoration until 1680, when he returned.

Cromwell Thomas, Earl of Essex c. 1485–1540. English politician who drafted the legislation making the Church of England independent of Rome. Originally in Lord Chancellor Wolsey's service, he became secretary to Henry VIII 1534 and the real director of government policy; he was executed for treason.

Crossman Richard (Howard Stafford) 1907–1974. British Labour politician. He was minister of housing and local government 1964–66 and of health and social security 1968–70. His posthumous Crossman Papers 1975 revealed confidential cabinet discussions.

crown official headdress worn by a king or queen. The modern crown originated with the diadem, an embroidered fillet worn by Eastern rulers, for which a golden band was later substituted. A laurel crown was granted by the Greeks to a victor in the games, and by the Romans to a triumphant general. Crowns came into use among the Byzantine emperors and the European kings after the fall of the Western Empire.

crown colony any British colony that is under the direct legislative control of the crown and does not possess its own system of representative government. Crown colonies are administered by a crown-appointed governor or by elected or nominated legislative and executive councils with an official majority. Usually the crown retains rights of veto and of direct legislation by orders in council.

Crown Estate title (from 1956) of land in UK formerly owned by the monarch but handed to Parliament by George III in 1760 in exchange for an annual payment (called the civil list). The Crown Estate owns valuable sites in central London, and 268,400 acres in England and Scotland.

crown jewels or *regalia* symbols of royal authority. The British set (except for the Ampulla and the Anointing Spoon) were broken up at the time of Oliver Cromwell, and now date from the Restoration. In 1671 Colonel ◊Blood attempted to steal them, but was captured, then pardoned and pensioned by Charles II. They are kept in the Tower of London in the Crown Jewel House (1967).

crusade European war against non-Christians and heretics, sanctioned by the pope; in particular, the Crusades, a series of wars 1096–1291 undertaken by European rulers to recover Palestine from the Muslims. Motivated by religious zeal, the desire for land, and the trading ambitions of the major Italian cities, the Crusades were varied in their aims and effects.

Crystal Palace glass and iron building designed by Joseph Paxton, housing the Great Exhibition of 1851 in Hyde Park, London. It was later rebuilt in modified form at Sydenham Hill 1854 but burned down 1936.

Culloden, Battle of defeat 1746 of the ◊Jacobite rebel army of the British prince ◊Charles Edward Stuart by the Duke of Cumberland on a stretch of moorland in Inverness-shire, Scotland. This battle effectively ended the military challenge of the Jacobite rebellion.

Cumberland William Augustus, Duke of Cumberland 1721–1765. British general who ended the Jacobite rising in Scotland with the Battle of Culloden 1746; his brutal repression of the Highlanders earned him the nickname of 'Butcher'.

Cunedda Wledig early 5th century AD. British chieftain. He came with his sons and followers from Scotland to NW Wales to defend Britain against barbarian invaders from Ireland. He laid the foundations of the kingdom of Gwynedd, which was named after him.

Curragh 'Mutiny' demand March 1914 by the British general Hubert Gough and his officers, stationed at Curragh, Ireland, that they should not be asked to take part in forcing Protestant Ulster to participate in Home Rule. They were subsequently allowed to return to duty, and after World War I the solution of partition was adopted.

Curzon George Nathaniel, 1st Marquess Curzon of Kedleston 1859–1925. British Conservative politician, viceroy of India 1899–1905. During World War I, he was a member of the cabinet 1916–19. As foreign secretary 1919–24, he set up a British protectorate over Persia.

Cutty Sark British sailing ship, built 1869, one of the tea clippers that used to compete in the 19th century to bring their cargoes fastest from China to Britain.

Cymbeline or *Cunobelin* 1st century AD. King of the Catuvellauni AD 5–40, who fought unsuccessfully against the Roman invasion of Britain. His capital was at Colchester.

D

Dalhousie James Andrew Broun Ramsay, 1st Marquess and 10th Earl of Dalhousie 1812–1860. British administrator, governor general of India 1848–56. In the second Sikh War he annexed the Punjab 1849, and, after the second Burmese War, Lower Burma 1853. He reformed the Indian army and civil service and furthered social and economic progress.

Dalton Hugh, Baron Dalton 1887–1962. British Labour politician and economist. Chancellor of the Exchequer from 1945, he oversaw nationalization of the Bank of England, but resigned 1947 after making a disclosure to a lobby correspondent before a budget speech.

Dame in the UK honours system, the title of a woman who has been awarded the Order of the Bath, Order of St Michael and St George, Royal Victorian Order, or Order of the British Empire. It is also in law the legal title of the wife or widow of a knight or baronet, placed before her name.

Danby Thomas Osborne, Earl of Danby 1631–1712.

British Tory politician. He entered Parliament 1665, acted as Charles II's chief minister 1673–78 and was created earl of Danby 1674, but was imprisoned in the Tower of London 1678–84. In 1688 he signed the invitation to William of Orange to take the throne. Danby was again chief minister 1690–95, and in 1694 was created Duke of Leeds.

danegeld in English history, a tax imposed from 991 by Anglo-Saxon kings to pay tribute to the Vikings. After the Norman Conquest the tax continued to be levied until 1162, and the Normans used it to finance military operations.

Danelaw 11th-century name for the area of N and E England settled by the Vikings in the 9th century. It occupied about half of England, from the river Tees to the river Thames. Within its bounds, Danish law, customs, and language prevailed. Its linguistic influence is still apparent.

Darling Grace 1815–1842. British heroine. She was the daughter of a lighthouse keeper on the Farne Islands, off Northumberland. On 7 Sept 1838 the Forfarshire was wrecked, and Grace Darling and her father rowed through a storm to the wreck, saving nine lives. She was awarded a medal for her bravery.

Darnley Henry Stewart or Stuart, Lord Darnley 1545–1567. British aristocrat, second husband of Mary Queen of Scots from 1565, and father of James I of England (James VI of Scotland). On the advice of her secretary, David ◊Rizzio, Mary refused Darnley the crown matrimonial; in revenge, Darnley led a band of nobles who murdered Rizzio in Mary's presence. Darnley was assassinated 1567.

David two kings of Scotland:

David I 1084–1153. King of Scotland from 1124. The youngest son of Malcolm III Canmore and St ◊Margaret, he was brought up in the English court of Henry I, and in 1113 married ◊Matilda, widow of the 1st earl of Northampton. He invaded England 1138 in support of Queen Matilda, but was defeated at Northallerton in the Battle of the Standard, and again 1141.

David II 1324–1371. King of Scotland from 1329, son of ◊Robert I the Bruce◊. David was married at the age of four to Joanna, daughter of Edward II of England. In 1346 David invaded England, was captured at the battle of Neville's Cross, and imprisoned for 11 years.

Davitt Michael 1846–1906. Irish nationalist. He joined the Fenians (forerunners of the Irish Republican Army) 1865, and was imprisoned for treason 1870–77. After his release, he and the politician Charles Parnell founded the ◊Land League 1879. Davitt was jailed several times for land-reform agitation. He was a member of Parliament 1895–99, advocating the reconciliation of extreme and constitutional nationalism.

DBE abbreviation for *Dame Commander of the Order of the British Empire*.

Debrett Peerage 1753–1822. Directory of the British peerage, first published in 1802 by John Debrett (*c* 1750–1822) under the title

Peerage of England, Scotland and Ireland, but based on earlier compilations. Debrett aimed to avoid spurious geneologies and confine himself to authenticated facts.

Declaration of Rights in Britain, the statement issued by the Convention Parliament Feb 1689, laying down the conditions under which the crown was to be offered to ◊William III and Mary. Its clauses were later incorporated in the ◊Bill of Rights.

Defence of the Realm Act act granting emergency powers to the British government Aug 1914. The Act, popularly known as DORA, was revised several times in World War I and allowed the government to requisition raw materials, control labour, and censor cables and foreign correspondence. It was superseded by the Emergency Powers Act 1920.

Defender of the Faith one of the titles of the English sovereign, conferred on Henry VIII 1521 by Pope Leo X in recognition of the king's treatise against the Protestant Martin Luther. It appears on coins in the abbreviated form *F.D.* (Latin *Fidei Defensor*).

Derby Edward (George Geoffrey Smith) Stanley, 14th Earl of Derby 1799–1869. British politician, prime minister 1852, 1858-59, and 1866-68. Originally a Whig, he became secretary for the colonies 1830, and introduced the bill for the abolition of slavery. He joined the Tories 1834, and the split in the Tory Party over Robert Peel's free-trade policy gave Derby the leadership for 20 years.

Derby Edward George Villiers Stanley, 17th Earl of Derby 1865–1948. British Conservative politician, member of Parliament from 1892. He was secretary of war 1916–18 and 1922–24, and ambassador to France 1918–20.

deselection in Britain, removal or withholding of a sitting member of Parliament's official status as a candidate for a forthcoming election. The term came into use in the 1980s with the efforts of many local Labour parties to revoke the candidature of MPs viewed as too rightwing.

de Valera Éamon 1882–1975. Irish nationalist politician, prime minister of the Irish Free State/Eire/Republic of Ireland 1932–48, 1951–54, and 1957–59, and president 1959–73. Repeatedly imprisoned, he participated in the ◊Easter Rising 1916 and was leader of the nationalist ◊Sinn Féin party 1917–26, when he formed the republican ◊Fianna Fáil party; he directed negotiations with Britain 1921 but refused to accept the partition of Ireland until 1937.

devolution delegation of authority and duties; in the later 20th century, the movement to decentralize governmental power, as in the UK where a bill for the creation of Scottish and Welsh assemblies was introduced 1976 (rejected by referendums in Scotland and Wales 1979).

Devonshire William Cavendish, 7th Duke of Devonshire 1808–1891. British aristocrat whose development of Eastbourne, Sussex, England, was an early example of town planning.

Devonshire, 8th Duke of see ◊Hartington, Spencer Compton Cavendish, British politician.

Diana Princess of Wales 1961– . The daughter of the 8th Earl Spencer, she married Prince Charles in St Paul's Cathedral, London 1981, the first English bride of a royal heir since 1659. She is descended from the only sovereigns from whom Prince Charles is not descended, Charles II and James II.

Digger or *True Leveller* member of an English 17th-century radical sect that attempted to seize and share out common land. The Diggers became prominent April 1649 when, headed by Gerrard Winstanley (c. 1609–1660), they set up communal colonies near Cobham, Surrey, and elsewhere. These colonies were attacked by mobs and, being pacifists, the Diggers made no resistance. The support they attracted alarmed the government and they were dispersed 1650. Their ideas influenced the early ◊Quakers.

Dilke Charles Wentworth 1843–1911. British Liberal politician, member of Parliament 1868–86 and 1892–1911. A Radical, he supported a minimum wage and legalization of trade unions.

Diplock court in Northern Ireland, a type of court established 1972 by the British government under Lord Diplock (1907–1985) to try offences linked with guerrilla violence. The right to jury trial was suspended and the court consisted of a single judge, because potential jurors were allegedly being intimidated and were unwilling to serve.

Despite widespread criticism, the Diplock courts have remained in operation.

disclaimed peerage in the UK, the Peerage Act (1963) allows a peerage to be disclaimed for life provided that it is renounced within one year of the succession, and that the peer has not applied for a writ of summons to attend the House of Lords.

Disraeli Benjamin, Earl of Beaconsfield 1804–1881. British Conservative politician and novelist. Elected to Parliament 1837, he was chancellor of the Exchequer under Lord ◊Derby 1852, 1858–59, and 1866–68, and prime minister 1868 and 1874–80. His imperialist policies brought India directly under the crown, and he was personally responsible for purchasing control of the Suez Canal. The central Conservative Party organization is his creation. His popular, political novels reflect an interest in social reform and include Coningsby 1844 and Sybil 1845.

After a period in a solicitor's office, Disraeli wrote the novels Vivian Grey 1826, Contarini Fleming 1832, and others, and the pamphlet Vindication of the English Constitution 1835. Entering Parliament in 1837 after four unsuccessful attempts, he was laughed at as a dandy, but when his maiden speech was shouted down, he said: 'The time will come when you will hear me.'

Excluded from Peel's government of 1841-46, Disraeli formed his Young England group to keep a critical eye on Peel's Conservatism. Its ideas were expounded in the novel trilogy Coningsby, Sybil, and Tancred 1847. When Peel decided in 1846 to repeal the Corn Laws, Disraeli opposed the measure in a series of witty and effective speeches; Peel's government fell soon after, and Disraeli gradually came to be recognized as the leader of the Conservative Party in the Commons.

During the next 20 years the Conservatives formed short-lived minority governments in 1852, 1858-59, and 1866-68, with Lord Derby as prime minister and Disraeli as chancellor of the Exchequer and leader of the Commons. In 1852 Disraeli first proposed discrimination in income tax between earned and unearned income, but without success. The 1858-59 government legalized the admission of Jews to Parliament, and transferred the government of India from the East India

Company to the crown. In 1866 the Conservatives took office after defeating a Liberal Reform Bill, and then attempted to secure the credit of widening the franchise by the Reform Bill of 1867. On Lord Derby's retirement in 1868 Disraeli became prime minister, but a few months later he was defeated by Gladstone in a general election. During the six years of opposition that followed he published another novel, Lothair 1870, and established Conservative Central Office, the prototype of modern party organizations.

In 1874 Disraeli took office for the second time, with a majority of 100. Some useful reform measures were carried, such as the Artisans' Dwelling Act, which empowered local authorities to undertake slum clearance, but the outstanding feature of the government's policy was its imperialism. It was Disraeli's personal initiative that purchased from the Khedive of Egypt a controlling interest in the Suez Canal, conferred on the Queen the title of Empress of India, and sent the Prince of Wales on the first royal tour of that country. He accepted an earldom 1876. The Bulgarian revolt of 1876 and the subsequent Russo-Turkish War of 1877-78 provoked one of many political duels between Disraeli and Gladstone, the Liberal leader, and was concluded by the Congress of Berlin 1878, where Disraeli was the principal British delegate and brought home 'peace with honour' and Cyprus. The government was defeated in 1880, and a year later Disraeli died.

Dissenter former name for a Protestant refusing to conform to the established Christian church. For example, Baptists, Presbyterians, and Independents (now known as Congregationalists) were Dissenters.

Dissolution of the Monasteries closure of the monasteries of England and Wales 1536–40 and confiscation of their property by ◊Henry VIII. The operation was organised by Thomas ◊Cromwell and affected about 800 monastic houses with the aim of boosting royal income. Most of the property was later sold off to the gentry.

divine right of kings Christian political doctrine that hereditary monarchy is the system approved by God, hereditary right cannot be forfeited, monarchs are accountable to God alone for their actions, and rebellion against the lawful sovereign is therefore blasphemous.

Dogger Bank submerged sandbank in the North Sea, about 115 km/70 mi off the coast of Yorkshire, England. In places the water is only 11 m/36 ft deep, but the general depth is 18–36 m/60–120 ft; it is a well-known fishing ground.

dole popular name for unemployment benefit and unemployment assistance, the weekly payments to unemployed workers under the National Insurance Act. Modern unemployment benefits are based on the principles embodied in the National Insurance Act 1946.

Domesday Book record of the survey of England carried out 1086 by officials of William the Conqueror in order to assess land tax and other dues, ascertain the value of the crown lands, and enable the king to estimate the power of his vassal barons. The name is derived from the belief that its judgement was as final as that of Doomsday.

Donald III Bane ('fair') c. 1031–c. 1100. King of Scotland. He came to the throne 1093 after seizing it on the death of his brother ◊Malcolm III. He was dethroned 1094 by Malcolm's brother, ◊Duncan II. He regained power 1094 but was defeated and captured 1097 by another brother, Edgar, who had him blinded and imprisoned until his death.

Douglas-Home Alec (Alexander Frederick), Baron Home of the Hirsel 1903– . British Conservative politician. He was foreign secretary 1960–63, and succeeded Harold Macmillan as prime minister 1963. He renounced his peerage (as 14th Earl of Home) to fight (and lose) the general election 1964, and resigned as party leader 1965. He was again foreign secretary 1970–74, when he received a life peerage. The playwright William Douglas-Home was his brother.

dowager the style given to the widow of a peer or baronet.

Drake Francis c. 1545–1596. English buccaneer and explorer. Having enriched himself as a pirate against Spanish interests in the Caribbean 1567–72, he was sponsored by Elizabeth I for an expedition to the Pacific, sailing round the world 1577–80 in the Golden Hind, robbing Spanish ships as he went. This was the second circumnavigation of the globe (the first was by the Portuguese explorer Ferdinand Magellan). Drake also helped to defeat the Spanish Armada 1588 as a vice admiral in the Revenge.

Drake was born in Devon and apprenticed to the master of a coasting vessel, who left him the ship at his death. He accompanied his relative, the navigator John Hawkins, 1567 and 1572 to plunder the Caribbean, and returned to England 1573 with considerable booty. After serving in Ireland as a volunteer, he suggested to Queen Elizabeth I an expedition to the Pacific, and Dec 1577 he sailed in the Pelican with four other ships and 166 men towards South America. In Aug 1578 the fleet passed through the Straits of Magellan and was then blown south to Cape Horn. The ships became separated and returned to England, all but the Pelican, now renamed the Golden Hind. Drake sailed north along the coast of Chile and Peru, robbing Spanish ships as far north as California, and then, in 1579, headed southwest across the Pacific. He rounded the South African Cape June 1580, and reached England Sept 1580. Thus the second voyage around the world, and the first made by an English person, was completed in a little under three years. When the Spanish ambassador demanded Drake's punishment, the Queen knighted him on the deck of the Golden Hind at Deptford, London.

In 1581 Drake was chosen mayor of Plymouth, in which capacity he brought fresh water into the city by constructing leats from Dartmoor. In 1584–85 he represented the town of Bosinney in Parliament. In a raid on Cadiz 1587 he burned 10,000 tons of shipping, 'singed the King of Spain's beard', and delayed the invasion of England by the Spanish Armada for a year. He was stationed off the French island of Ushant 1588 to intercept the Armada, but was driven back to England by unfavourable winds. During the fight in the Channel he served as a vice admiral in the Revenge. Drake sailed on his last expedition to the West Indies with Hawkins 1595, capturing Nombre de Dios on the north coast of Panama but failing to seize Panama City. In Jan 1596 he died of dysentry off the town of Puerto Bello (now Portobello), Panama.

Dreadnought class of battleships built for the British navy after 1905 and far superior in speed and armaments to anything then afloat. The first modern battleship to be built, it was the basis of battleship design for more than 50 years. The first Dreadnought was launched 1906, with armaments consisting entirely of big guns.

Druidism religion of the Celtic peoples of the pre-Christian British Isles and Gaul. The word is derived from Greek *drus* 'oak'. The Druids regarded this tree as sacred; one of their chief rites was the cutting of mistletoe from it with a golden sickle. They taught the immortality of the soul and a reincarnation doctrine, and were expert in astronomy. The

Druids are thought to have offered human sacrifices. Druidism was stamped out in Gaul after the Roman conquest. In Britain their stronghold was Anglesey, Wales, until they were driven out by the Roman governor Agricola. They existed in Scotland and Ireland until the coming of the Christian missionaries. What are often termed Druidic monuments – cromlechs and stone circles – are of New Stone Age (Neolithic) origin, though they may later have been used for religious purposes by the Druids. A possible example of a human sacrifice by Druids is Lindow Man, whose body was found in a bog in Cheshire 1984.

DSO abbreviation for *Distinguished Service Order*, British military medal.

Dudley Lord Guildford English nobleman, fourth son of the Duke of Northumberland. He was married by his father to Lady Jane ◊Grey 1553, against her wishes, in an attempt to prevent the succession of ◊Mary I to the throne. The plot failed, and he and his wife were executed.

duke highest title in the English peerage. It originated in England 1337, when Edward III created his son Edward, Duke of Cornwall.

Duncan I King of Scotland. He succeeded his grandfather, Malcolm II, as king 1034, but was defeated and killed by ◊Macbeth. He is the Duncan in Shakespeare's play *Macbeth* 1605.

Duncan II King of Scotland, son of ◊Malcolm III and grandson of ◊Duncan I. He gained English and Norman help to drive out his uncle ◊Donald III 1094. He ruled for a few months before being killed by agents of Donald, who then regained power.

Duncan-Sandys Duncan (Edwin) British politician; see ◊Sandys, Duncan Edwin.

Dundas Henry, 1st Viscount Melville 1742–1811. Scottish Conservative politician. In 1791 he became home secretary and, with revolution raging in France, carried through the prosecution of the English and Scottish radicals. After holding other high cabinet posts, he was impeached 1806 for corruption and, although acquitted on the main charge, held no further office.

Durham John George Lambton, 1st Earl of Durham 1792–1840. British politician. Appointed Lord Privy Seal 1830, he drew up the first

Reform Bill 1832, and as governor general of Canada briefly in 1837 drafted the Durham Report which led to the union of Upper and Lower Canada.

Duval Claude 1643–1670. English criminal. He was born in Normandy and turned highwayman after coming to England at the Restoration. He was known for his gallantry. Duval was hanged at Tyburn, London.

E

earl in the British peerage, the third title in order of rank, coming between marquess and viscount; it is the oldest of British titles, being of Scandinavian origin. An earl's wife is a countess.

Easter Rising or *Easter Rebellion* in Irish history, a republican insurrection that began on Easter Monday, April 1916, in Dublin. It was inspired by the Irish Republican Brotherhood (IRB) in an unsuccessful attempt to overthrow British rule in Ireland. It was led by Patrick Pearce of the IRB and James Connolly of Sinn Féin.

Arms from Germany intended for the IRB were intercepted but the rising proceeded regardless with the seizure of the Post Office and other buildings in Dublin by 1,500 volunteers. The rebellion was crushed by the British Army within five days, both sides suffering major losses: 220 civilians, 64 rebels, and 134 members of the Crown Forces were killed during the uprising. Pearce, Connolly, and about a dozen rebel leaders were subsequently executed in Kilmainham Jail. Others, including éamon de Valera, were spared due to US public opinion, to be given amnesty June 1917.

East India Company (British) commercial company 1600–1858 chartered by Queen Elizabeth I and given a monopoly of trade between England and the Far East. In the 18th century, the company became, in effect, the ruler of a large part of India, and a form of dual control by the company and a committee responsible to Parliament in London was introduced by Pitt's India Act 1784. The end of the monopoly of China trade came 1834, and after the ◊Indian Mutiny (also known as the Sepoy Rebellion) 1857 the crown took complete control of the government of British India; the India Act 1858 abolished the company.

EC abbreviation for ◊*European Community*.

Edinburgh, Duke of title of Prince ◊Philip of the UK.

Edward (full name Edward Antony Richard Louis) 1964– . Prince of the UK, third son of Queen Elizabeth II. He is seventh in line to the throne after Charles, Charles's two sons, Andrew, and Andrew's two daughters.

EEC abbreviation for *European Economic Community*; see ◊European Community.

Eden Anthony, 1st Earl of Avon 1897–1977. British Conservative politician, foreign secretary 1935–38, 1940–45, and 1951–55; prime minister 1955–57, when he resigned after the failure of the Anglo-French military intervention in the ◊Suez Crisis.

Edgar known as the *Atheling* ('of royal blood') c. 1050–c. 1130. English prince, born in Hungary. Grandson of Edmund Ironside, he was supplanted as heir to Edward the Confessor by William the Conqueror. He led two rebellions against William 1068 and 1069, but made peace 1074.

Edgar the Peaceful 944–975. King of all England from 959. He was the younger son of Edmund I, and strove successfully to unite English and Danes as fellow subjects.

Edgehill, Battle of first battle of the English Civil War. It took place 1642, on a ridge in S Warwickshire, between Royalists under Charles I and Parliamentarians under the Earl of Essex. The result was indecisive.

Edington, Battle of battle May 878 at which Alfred the Great, King of Wessex, defeated the Danish forces of ◊Guthrum. The site is at Edington, 6km/4 mi east of Westbury, Wiltshire; the chalk white horse on the downs nearby is said to commemorate the victory, The battle was a decisive one for Alfred, and forced the Danes to retire from ◊Wessex into East Anglia,

Edmund (II) Ironside c. 989–1016. King of England 1016, the son of Ethelred II the Unready. He led the resistance to ◊Canute's invasion 1015, and on Ethelred's death 1016 was chosen king by the citizens of London, whereas the Witan (the king's council) elected Canute. In the struggle for the throne, Edmund was defeated by Canute at Assandun (Ashingdon), Essex, and they divided the kingdom between them; when Edmund died the same year, Canute ruled the whole kingdom.

Edmund, St c. 840–870. King of East Anglia from 855. In 870 he was defeated and captured by the Danes at Hoxne, Suffolk, and martyred on refusing to renounce Christianity. He was canonized and his shrine at Bury St Edmunds became a place of pilgrimage.

Edric the Forester or *Edric the Wild* 11th century. English chieftain on the Welsh border who revolted against William the Conqueror 1067, around what is today Herefordshire, burning Shrewsbury. He was subsequently reconciled with William, and fought with him against the Scots 1072. Later writings describe him as a legendary figure.

Edward (called *the Black Prince*) 1330–1376. Prince of Wales, eldest son of Edward III of England. The epithet (probably posthumous) may refer to his black armour. During the Hundred Years' War he fought at the Battle of Crécy 1346 and captured the French king at Poitiers 1356. He ruled Aquitaine 1360–71; during the revolt that eventually ousted him, he caused the massacre of Limoges 1370.

Edward eight kings of England or the UK:

Edward I 1239–1307. King of England from 1272, son of Henry III. Edward led the royal forces against Simon de Montfort in the ◊Barons' War 1264–67, and was on a crusade when he succeeded to the throne. He established English rule over all Wales 1282–84, and secured recognition of his overlordship from the Scottish king, although the Scots (under Wallace and Bruce) fiercely resisted actual conquest. In his reign Parliament took its approximate modern form with the ◊Model Parliament 1295. He was succeeded by his son Edward II.

Edward II 1284–1327. King of England from 1307, son of Edward I. Born at Caernarvon Castle, he was created the first Prince of Wales 1301. His invasion of Scotland 1314 to suppress revolt resulted in defeat at ◊Bannockburn. He was deposed 1327 by his wife Isabella (1292–1358), daughter of Philip IV of France, and her lover Roger de ◊Mortimer, and murdered in Berkeley Castle, Gloucestershire. He was succeeded by his son Edward III.

Edward III 1312–1377. King of England from 1327, son of Edward II. He assumed the government 1330 from his mother, through whom in 1337 he laid claim to the French throne and thus began the ◊Hundred Years' War. He was succeeded by his grandson Richard II.

Edward IV 1442–1483. King of England 1461–70 and from 1471. He was the son of Richard, Duke of York, and succeeded Henry VI in the Wars of the ◊Roses, temporarily losing the throne to Henry when Edward fell out with his adviser ◊Warwick, but regaining it at the Battle of Barnet 1471. He was succeeded by his son Edward V.

Edward V 1470–1483. King of England 1483. Son of Edward IV, he was deposed three months after his accession in favour of his uncle (◊Richard III), and is traditionally believed to have been murdered (with his brother) in the Tower of London on Richard's orders.

Edward VI 1537–1553. King of England from 1547, son of Henry VIII and Jane Seymour. The government was entrusted to his uncle the Duke of Somerset (who fell from power 1549), and then to the Earl of Warwick, later created Duke of Northumberland. He was succeeded by his sister, Mary I.

Edward VII 1841–1910. King of Great Britain and Ireland from 1901. As Prince of Wales he was a prominent social figure, but his mother Queen Victoria considered him too frivolous to take part in political life. In 1860 he made the first tour of Canada and the USA ever undertaken by a British prince.

Edward VIII 1894–1972. King of Great Britain and Northern Ireland Jan–Dec 1936, when he renounced the throne to marry Wallis Warfield Simpson (see ◊abdication crisis). He was created Duke of Windsor and was governor of the Bahamas 1940–45, subsequently settling in France.

Edward the Confessor c. 1003–1066. King of England from 1042, the son of Ethelred II. He lived in Normandy until shortly before his accession. During his reign power was held by Earl ◊Godwin and his son ◊Harold, while the king devoted himself to religion, including the rebuilding of Westminster Abbey (consecrated 1065), where he is buried. His childlessness led ultimately to the Norman Conquest 1066. He was canonized 1161.

Edward the Elder c. 870–924. King of the West Saxons. He succeeded his father ◊Alfred the Great 899. He reconquered SE England and the Midlands from the Danes, uniting ◊Wessex and ◊Mercia with the help of his sister, Athelflad. By the time Edward died, his kingdom was the most powerful in the British Isles. He was succeeded by his son ◊Athelstan.

Edward the Martyr c. 963–978. King of England from 975. Son of King Edgar, he was murdered at Corfe Castle, Dorset, probably at his stepmother Aelfthryth's instigation (she wished to secure the crown for her son, Ethelred). He was canoi ized 1001.

Edwin c. 585–633. King of Northumbria from 617. He captured and fortified Edinburgh and was killed in battle with Penda of Mercia 632.

Edwy King of England, son of Edmund I. He succeeded his uncle Edred as king 955 and drove Edred's chief adviser St Dunstan, then virtually ruler, into exile 955. On the revolt of the Mercians and Northumbrians 957, who chose his brother ◊Edgar as king, he was left to rule ◊Wessex and Kent 957–959.

Egbert died 839. King of the West Saxons from 802, the son of Ealhmund, an under-king of Kent. By 829 he had united England for the first time under one king.

Eldon John Scott, 1st Earl of Eldon 1751–1838. English politician, born in Newcastle. He became a member of Parliament 1782, solicitor-general 1788, attorney-general 1793, and Lord Chancellor 1801–05 and 1807–27. During his period the rules of the Lord Chancellor's court governing the use of the injunction and precedent in equity finally became fixed.

Eleanor of Aquitaine c. 1122–1204. Queen of France 1137–51 as wife of Louis VII, and of England from 1154 as wife of Henry II. Henry imprisoned her 1174–89 for supporting their sons, the future Richard I and King John, in revolt against him.

Eleanor of Castile c. 1245–1290. Queen of Edward I of England, the daughter of Ferdinand III of Castile. She married Prince Edward 1254, and accompanied him on his crusade 1270. She died at Harby, Nottinghamshire, and Edward erected stone crosses in towns where her body rested on the funeral journey to London. A few *Eleanor Crosses* are still standing, for example at Northampton.

Eliot John 1592–1632. English politician, born in Cornwall. He became a member of Parliament 1614, and with the Earl of

Buckingham's patronage was made a vice-admiral 1619. In 1626 he was imprisoned in the Tower of London for demanding Buckingham's impeachment. In 1628 he was a formidable supporter of the ◊petition of right opposing Charles I, and with other parliamentary leaders was again imprisoned in the Tower of London 1629, where he died.

Elizabeth the *Queen Mother* 1900–   . Wife of King George VI of England. She was born Lady Elizabeth Angela Marguerite Bowes-Lyon, and on 26 April 1923 she married Albert, Duke of York, who became King George VI in 1936. Their children are Queen Elizabeth II and Princess Margaret.

Elizabeth two queens of England or the UK:

Elizabeth I 1533–1603. Queen of England 1558–1603, the daughter of Henry VIII and Anne Boleyn. Through her Religious Settlement of 1559 she enforced the Protestant religion by law. She had ◊Mary Queen of Scots, executed 1587. Her conflict with Roman Catholic Spain led to the defeat of the ◊Spanish Armada 1588. The Elizabethan age was expansionist in commerce and geographical exploration, and arts and literature flourished. The rulers of many European states made unsuccessful bids to marry Elizabeth, and she used these bids to strengthen her power. She was succeeded by James I.

Elizabeth was born at Greenwich, London, 7 Sept 1533. She was well educated in several languages. During her Roman Catholic half-sister Mary's reign, Elizabeth's Protestant sympathies brought her under suspicion, and she lived in seclusion at Hatfield, Hertfordshire, until on Mary's death she became queen. Her first task was to bring about a broad religious settlement.

Parliament made many unsuccessful attempts to persuade Elizabeth to marry or settle the succession. She found courtship a useful political weapon, and she maintained friendships with, among others, the courtiers ◊Leicester, Sir Walter ◊Raleigh, and ◊Essex. She was known as the Virgin Queen.

The arrival in England 1568 of Mary Queen of Scots and her imprisonment by Elizabeth caused a political crisis, and a rebellion of the feudal nobility of the north followed 1569. Friction between English and Spanish sailors hastened the breach with Spain. When the Dutch rebelled against Spanish tyranny Elizabeth secretly encouraged them; Philip II retaliated by aiding Catholic conspiracies against her. This undeclared war continued for many years, until the landing of an English army in the Netherlands 1585 and Mary's execution 1587, brought it into the open. Philip's Armada (the fleet sent to invade England 1588) met with total disaster.

The war with Spain continued with varying fortunes to the end of the reign, while events at home foreshadowed the conflicts of the 17th century. Among the Puritans discontent was developing with Elizabeth's religious settlement, and several were imprisoned or executed. Parliament showed a new independence, and in 1601 forced Elizabeth to retreat on the question of the crown granting manufacturing and trading monopolies. Yet her prestige remained unabated, as was shown by the failure of Essex's rebellion 1601.

Elizabeth II 1926– . Queen of Great Britain and Northern Ireland from 1952, the elder daughter of George VI. She married her third cousin, Philip, the Duke of Edinburgh, 1947. They have four children: Charles, Anne, Andrew, and Edward.

Princess Elizabeth Alexandra Mary was born in London 21 April 1926; she was educated privately, and assumed official duties at 16. During World War II she served in the Auxiliary Territorial Service, and by an amendment to the Regency Act she became a state counsellor on her 18th birthday. On the death of George VI in 1952 she succeeded to the throne while in Kenya with her husband and was crowned on 2 June 1953.

Elton Geoffrey Rudolph 1921– . Czechoslovakian-born British historian. During World War II he worked in intelligence before teaching at Cambridge University from 1949 and becoming Regius Professor of History in 1983. His reputation was made through his study of the Tudor monarchs of England and the 'Tudor revolution' in government in the 1530s. He has since written a series of books on this and related subjects, the most well-known being *England under the Tudors* and *The Practice of History*.

Elyot Thomas 1490–1546. English diplomat and scholar. In 1531 he published *The Governour*, the first treatise on education in English.

Elizabeth II: line of succession

Charles, Prince of Wales, eldest son of Elizabeth II (1948–   )
Prince William, eldest son of Charles (1982–   )
Prince Henry (Harry), second son of Charles (1984–   )
Andrew, Duke of York, second son of Elizabeth II (1960–   )
Princess Beatrice, eldest daughter of Andrew (1988–   )
Princess Eugenie, second daughter of Andrew (1990–   )
Prince Edward, youngest son of Elizabeth II (1964–   )
Anne, Princess Royal, daughter of Elizabeth II (1950–   )
Peter Phillips, son of Anne (1977–   )
Zara Phillips, daughter of Anne (1981–   )
Princess Margaret, sister of Elizabeth II (1930–   )
Viscount Linley, son of Margaret (1961–   )
Lady Sarah Armstrong-Jones, daughter of Margaret (1964–   )
Richard, Duke of Gloucester, son of brother of George VI (father of Elizabeth II) (1944–   )
Alexander, Earl of Ulster, son of Gloucester (1974–   )
Lady Davina Windsor, eldest daughter of Gloucester (1977–   )
Lady Rose Windsor, youngest daughter of Gloucester (1980–   )
Edward, Duke of Kent, son of brother of George VI (1935–   )
Edward, Baron Downpatrick, grandson of Kent (1988–   )
Lady Marina Charlotte Windsor, granddaughter of Kent (1992–   )
Lord Nicholas Windsor, son of Kent (1970–   )
Lady Helen Taylor, daughter of Kent (1964–   )
Lord Frederick Windsor, son of Michael (1979–   )
Lady Gabriella Windsor, daughter of Michael (1981–   )
Alexandra, sister of Kent (1936–   )
James, son of Alexandra (1964–   )
Marina, Mrs Paul Mowatt, daughter of Alexandra (1966–   )
George Lascelles, 7th Earl of Harewood, son of sister of George VI (1923–   )
David, Viscount Lascelles, eldest son of Harewood (1950–   )
Hon Alexander Lascelles, son of Viscount Lascelles (1980–   )
Hon Edward Lascelles, youngest son of Viscount Lascelles (1982–   )
Hon James Lascelles, second son of Harewood (1953–   )
Rowan Lascelles, son of Hon James Lascelles (1977–   )
Tewa Lascelles, youngest son of Hon James Lascelles (1985–   )
Sophie Lascelles, daughter of Hon James Lascelles (1973–   )
Hon Jeremy Lascelles, youngest son of Harewood (1955–   )
Thomas Lascelles, son of Hon Jeremy Lascelles (1982–   )
Ellen Lascelles, daughter of Hon Jeremy Lascelles (1984–   )
Amy Lascelles, youngest daughter of Hon Jeremy Lascelles (1986–   )
Hon Gerald Lascelles, younger brother of Harewood (1924–   )
Henry Lascelles, son of Hon Gerald Lascelles (1953–   )

Emmet Robert 1778–1803. Irish nationalist leader. In 1803 he led an unsuccessful revolt in Dublin against British rule and was captured, tried, and hanged. His youth and courage made him an Irish hero.

Employers and Workmen Act UK Act of Parliament 1875 which limited to civil damages the penalty for a breach of contract of employment by a worker. Previously, employees who broke their contracts faced penalties imposed under criminal law.

Employer's Liability Act UK Act of Parliament 1880, which obtained for workers or their families a right to compensation from employers whose negligence resulted in industrial injury or death at work.

enclosure appropriation of common land as private property, or the changing of open-field systems to enclosed fields (often used for sheep). This process began in Britain in the 14th century and became widespread in the 15th and 16th centuries. It caused poverty, homelessness, and rural depopulation, and resulted in revolts 1536, 1569, and 1607.

England largest division of the ◊United Kingdom
area 50,318 sq mi/130,357 sq km
capital London
cities Birmingham, Coventry, Leeds, Leicester, Manchester, Newcastle-upon-Tyne, Nottingham, Sheffield; ports Bristol, Dover, Liverpool, Portsmouth, Southampton
features variability of climate and diversity of scenery; among European countries, only the Netherlands is more densely populated
exports agricultural (cereals, rape, sugar beet, potatoes); meat and meat products; electronic (software), and telecommunications equipment; scientific instruments; textiles and fashion goods; North Sea oil and gas, petrochemicals, and pharmaceuticals; film and television programs; sound recordings. Tourism is important. There are worldwide banking and insurance interests
currency pound sterling
population (1986) 47,255,000
language English, with more than 100 minority languages
religion Christian, with the Church of England as the established church; Jewish; Muslim

England: history for earlier history, see ◊Britain, ancient.

AD 43	Roman invasion.
5th–7th centuries	Anglo-Saxons overran all England except Cornwall and Cumberland, forming independent kingdoms including Northumbria, Mercia, Kent, and Wessex.
c. 597	England converted to Christianity by St Augustine.
829	Egbert of Wessex accepted as overlord of all England.
878	Alfred ceded N and E England to the Danish invaders but kept them out of Wessex.
1066	Norman Conquest; England passed into French hands under William the Conqueror.
1172	Henry II became king of Ireland and established a colony there.
1215	King John forced to sign Magna Carta.
1284	Conquest of Wales, begun by the Normans, completed by Edward I.
1295	Model Parliament set up.
1338–1453	Hundred Years' War with France enabled parliament to secure control of taxation and, by impeachment, of the king's choice of ministers.
1348–49	Black Death killed about 30% of the population.
1381	Social upheaval led to the ◊Peasants' Revolt, which was brutally repressed.
1399	Richard II deposed by Parliament for absolutism.
1414	Lollard revolt repressed.
1455–85	Wars of the Roses.
1497	Henry VII ended the power of the feudal nobility with the suppression of the Yorkist revolts.
1529	Henry VIII became head of the Church of England after breaking with Rome.
1536–43	Acts of Union united England and Wales after conquest.
1547	Edward VI adopted Protestant doctrines.
1553	Reversion to Roman Catholicism under Mary I.
1558	Elizabeth I adopted a religious compromise.
1588	Attempted invasion of England by the Spanish Armada.
1603	James I united the English and Scottish crowns; parliamentary dissidence increased.
1642–52	Civil War between royalists and parliamentarians, resulting in victory for Parliament.
1649	Charles I executed and the Commonwealth set up.
1653	Oliver Cromwell appointed Lord Protector.
1660	Restoration of Charles II.
1685	Monmouth's rebellion.
1688	William of Orange invited to take the throne; flight of James II.
1707	Act of Union between England and Scotland under Queen Anne, after which the countries became known as Great Britain.
	For further history, see ◊United Kingdom.

For *government* and *history*, see ◊Britain, ancient; ◊England: history; ◊United Kingdom.

English Pale territory in Ireland where English rule operated after the English settlement of Ireland 1171. The area of the Pale varied, but in the mid-14th century it comprised the counties of Dublin, Louth, Meath, Trim, Kilkenny and Kildare. It then gradually shrank until the ◊Plantation of Ireland 1556–1660.

Eric Bloodaxe King of Norway, succeeded 942 on the abdication of his father, Harald I Fairhair, and killed seven of his eight half-brothers who had rebelled against him, hence his nickname. He was deposed by his youngest half-brother Haakon 947 and fled to England, where he became ruler of the Norse kingdom of Northumbria 948. He was expelled 954 and killed in battle at Stainmore, Yorkshire (now in Cumbria).

Erskine Thomas, 1st Baron Erskine 1750–1823. British barrister and lord chancellor. He was called to the Bar in 1778 and defended a number of parliamentary reformers on charges of sedition. When the Whig Party returned to power 1806 he became lord chancellor and a baron. Among his speeches were those in defence of Lord George Gordon, Thomas Paine, and Queen Caroline.

Essex Robert Devereux, 2nd Earl of Essex 1566–1601. English soldier and politician. He became a favourite with Queen Elizabeth I from 1587, but was executed because of his policies in Ireland.

Essex Robert Devereux, 3rd Earl of Essex 1591–1646. English soldier. Eldest son of the 2nd earl, he commanded the Parliamentary army at the inconclusive English Civil War battle of Edgehill 1642. Following a disastrous campaign in Cornwall, he resigned his command 1645.

Ethelbert c. 552–616. King of Kent 560-616. He was defeated by the West Saxons 568 but later became ruler of England S of the river Humber. Ethelbert received the Christian missionary Augustine 597 and later converted to become the first Christian ruler of Anglo-Saxon England. He issued the first written code of laws known in England.

Ethelred (II) the Unready *c.* 968–1016. King of England from 978. He tried to buy off the Danish raiders by paying Danegeld. In 1002, he ordered the massacre of the Danish settlers, provoking an invasion by Sweyn I of Denmark. War with Sweyn and Sweyn's son, Canute, occupied the rest of Ethelred's reign. He was nicknamed the 'Unready', meaning 'ill-advised', as a pun on the meaning of his real name, 'noble counsel'.

European Community (EC) political and economic alliance consisting of the European Coal and Steel Community (1952), European Economic Community (EEC, popularly called the Common Market, 1957), and the European Atomic Energy Commission (Euratom, 1957). The original six members – Belgium, France, West Germany, Italy, Luxembourg, and the Netherlands – were joined by the UK, Denmark, and the Republic of Ireland 1973, Greece 1981, and Spain and Portugal 1986. Association agreements – providing for free trade within ten years and the possibility of full EC membership – were signed with Czechoslovakia, Hungary, and Poland 1991, subject to ratification, and with Romania 1992. The aims of the EC include the expansion of trade, reduction of competition, the abolition of restrictive trading practices, the encouragement of free movement of capital and labour within the community, and the establishment of a closer union among European people. The ◊Maastricht Treaty 1991 provides the framework for closer economic and political union. After an original rejection by Denmark in a referendum, it was ratified by all member states in 1993. Common Agricultural Policy (CAP) *established* 1962 *purpose* to ensure reasonable standards of living for farmers in member states by controlling outputs, giving financial grants, and supporting prices to even out fluctuations. *European Atomic Energy Commission* (EURATOM) *established* 1957 *purpose* the cooperation of member states in nuclear research and the development of large-scale nonmilitary nuclear energy. *European Coal and Steel Community* (ECSC) *established* 1952 *purpose* the creation of a single European market for coal, iron ore, and steel by the abolition of customs duties and quantitative restrictions. *European Court of Justice established* 1957 *purpose* to ensure the treaties that established the Community are observed and to adjudicate on disputes between members on the interpretation and application of the laws of the Community *base* Luxembourg. *European Economic Community* (EEC), popularly called the Common Market *established* 1957 *purpose* the creation of a single European market for the products of member states by the abolition of tariffs and other restrictions on trade. *European Investment Bank* (EIB) *established* 1958 *purpose* to finance capital investment that will assist the steady development of the Community. *European Monetary System* (EMS) *established* 1979 *purpose* to bring financial cooperation and monetary stability to the Community.

Central to the EMS is the Exchange Rate Mechanism (ERM), which is a voluntary arrangement whereby members agreed to their currencies being fixed within certain limits. The value of each currency is related to the European Currency Unit (ECU), which, it is anticipated, will eventually become the single currency for all member states. If the currency of any one member state moves outside the agreed limits, its government must buy or sell to avert the trend. *central organs and methods of working of the Community* *European Commission membership* 16: two each from France, Germany, Italy and the UK, and one each from Belgium, Denmark, Greece, Ireland, Luxembourg, the Netherlands, Portugal, and Spain. The members are nominated by each state for a four-year, renewable term of office. One member is chosen as president for a two- year, renewable term. The post of president is a mixture of head of government and head of the European civil service *operational methods* the commissioners are drawn proportionately from member states, and each takes an oath on appointment not to promote national interests. They head a comparatively large bureaucracy, with 20 directorates- general, each responsible for a particular department *base* Brussels. *Council of Ministers membership* one minister from each of the 12 member countries *operational methods* it is the supreme decision-making body of the Community. The representatives vary according to the subject matter under discussion. If it is economic policy it will be the finance ministers, if it is agricultural policy, the agriculture ministers. It is the foreign ministers, however, who tend to be the most active. The presidency of the Council changes hands at six-monthly intervals, each member state taking its turn *base* Brussels. *Committee of Permanent Representatives* (COREPER) *membership* *a* subsidiary body of officials, often called 'ambassadors', who act on behalf of the Council. The members of COREPER are senior civil servants who have been emporarily released by member states to work for the Community *operational methods* COREPER receives proposals from he Council of Ministers for consideration in detail before the Council decides on action *base* Brussels. *Economic and Social Committee membership* representatives from member countries covering a wide range of interests, including employers, trade unionists, professional people, and farmers *operational methods* a consultative body advising the Council of Ministers and the Commission *base* Brussels. *European Parliament membership* determined by the populations of member states. The total number of seats is 518, of which France, Germany, Italy, and the UK have 81 each, Spain has 60, the Netherlands 25, Belgium, Greece, and Portugal 24 each, Denmark 16, Ireland 15, and Luxembourg 6. Members are elected for five-year terms in large Euro- constituencies. Voting is by a system of proportional representation in all countries except he UK. *role and powers* mainly consultative, but it does have power to reject the Community budget and to dismiss the Commission if it has good grounds for doing so. It debates Community present and future policies and its powers will undoubtedly grow as the political nature of the Community becomes clearer *base* Luxembourg and Strasbourg.

European Parliament the parliament of the European Community, which meets in Strasbourg to comment on the legislative proposals of the Commission of the European Communities. Members are elected for a five-year term. The European Parliament has 518 seats, apportioned on the basis of population, of which the UK, France, Germany, and Italy have 81 each; Spain 60; the Netherlands 25; Belgium, Greece, and Portugal 24 each; Denmark 16; the Republic of Ireland 15; and Luxembourg 6.

Evesham town in Hereford and Worcester, England, on the river Avon SE of Worcester; population (1990 est) 18,000. Fruit and vegetables are grown in the fertile *Vale of Evesham*. In the Battle of Evesham, 4 Aug 1265, during the ◊Barons' Wars, Edward, Prince of Wales, defeated Simon de Montfort, who was killed.

eyre in English history, one of the travelling courts set up by Henry II 1176 to enforce conformity to the king's will; they continued into the 13th century. *Justices in eyre* were the judges who heard pleas at these courts.

F

Fabian Society UK socialist organization for research, discussion, and publication, founded in London 1884. Its name is derived from the Roman commander Fabius Maximus, and refers to the evolutionary methods by which it hopes to attain socialism by a succession of gradual reforms. Early members included the playwright George Bernard Shaw and Beatrice and Sidney Webb. The society helped to found the Labour Representation Committee in 1900, which became the Labour Party in 1906.

factory act in Britain, an act of Parliament such as the Health and Safety at Work, etc. Act 1974, which governs conditions of work, hours of labour, safety, and sanitary provision in factories and workshops.

Fairfax Thomas, 3rd Baron Fairfax of Cameron 1612–1671. English general, commander in chief of the Parliamentary army in the English Civil War. With Oliver Cromwell he formed the ◊New Model Army and defeated Charles I at Naseby. He opposed the king's execution, resigned in protest 1650 against the invasion of Scotland, and participated in the restoration of Charles II after Cromwell's death.

Falkirk, Battle of battle 22 July 1298 at Falkirk, 37 km/23 mi west of Edinburgh at which ◊Edward I of England defeated the Scots. Sir William ◊Wallace faced the English in open battle, but his cavalry fled and his spearmen were outmatched by the English archers. The battle led to Wallace's fall from power.

Falkland Lucius Cary, 2nd Viscount c. 1610–1643. English soldier and politician. He was elected to the ◊Long Parliament 1640 and tried hard to secure a compromise peace between Royalists and Parliamentarians. He was killed at the Battle of Newbury in the Civil War.

Falkland Islands, Battle of the British naval victory (under Admiral Sturdee) 8 Dec 1914 over the German admiral von Spee.

Falklands War war between Argentina and Britain over disputed sovereignty of the Falkland Islands initiated when Argentina invaded and occupied the islands 2 April 1982. On the following day, the United Nations Security Council passed a resolution calling for Argentina to withdraw. A British task force was immediately dispatched and, after a fierce conflict in which more than 1,000 Argentine and British lives were lost, 12,000 Argentine troops surrendered and the islands were returned to British rule 14–15 June 1982.

Faulkner Brian 1921–1977. Northern Ireland Unionist politician. He was the last prime minister of Northern Ireland 1971–72 before the Stormont Parliament was suspended.

Fawkes Guy 1570–1606. English conspirator in the ◊Gunpowder Plot to blow up King James I and the members of both Houses of Parliament. Fawkes, a Roman Catholic convert, was arrested in the cellar underneath the House 4 Nov 1605, tortured, and executed. The event is still commemorated in Britain and elsewhere every 5 Nov with bonfires, fireworks, and the burning of the 'guy', an effigy.

Fianna Fáil ('warriors of destiny') Republic of Ireland political party, founded by the Irish nationalist de Valera 1926. It has been the governing party in the Republic of Ireland 1932–48, 1951–54, 1957–73, 1977–81, 1982, and 1987–   .

It aims at the establishment of a united and completely independent all-Ireland republic.

Fidei Defensor Latin for the title of 'Defender of the Faith' (still retained by British sovereigns) conferred by Pope Leo X on Henry VIII of England 1521 to reward his writing of a treatise against the Protestant Martin Luther.

fief estate of lands granted to a vassal by his lord after the former had sworn homage, or fealty, promising to serve the lord. As a noble tenure, it carried with it rights of jurisdiction.

Field of the Cloth of Gold site between Guînes and Ardres near Calais, France, where a meeting took place between Henry VIII of

England and Francis I of France in June 1520, remarkable for the lavish clothes worn and tent pavilions erected. Francis hoped to gain England's support in opposing the Holy Roman emperor, Charles V, but failed.

Fifteen, the ◊Jacobite rebellion of 1715, led by the 'Old Pretender' ◊James Edward Stuart and the Earl of Mar, in order to place the former on the English throne. Mar was checked at Sheriffmuir, Scotland, and the revolt collapsed.

Finn Mac Cumhaill legendary Irish hero, identified with a general who organized an Irish regular army in the 3rd century. James Macpherson (1736–96) featured him (as Fingal) and his followers in the verse of his popular epics 1762–63, which were supposedly written by a 3rd-century bard, Ossian. Although challenged by the critic Dr Johnson, the poems were influential in the Romantic movement.

Fire of London fire 2–5 Sept 1666 that destroyed four fifths of the City of London. It broke out in a bakery in Pudding Lane and spread as far west as the Temple. It destroyed 87 churches, including St Paul's Cathedral, and 13,200 houses, although fewer than 20 people lost their lives.

Fisher John Arbuthnot, 1st Baron Fisher 1841–1920. British admiral, First Sea Lord 1904–10, when he carried out many radical reforms and innovations, including the introduction of the dreadnought battleship.

FitzGerald Garret 1926– . Irish politician. As *Taoiseach* (prime minister) 1981-82 and again 1982–86, he was noted for his attempts to solve the Northern Ireland dispute, ultimately by participating in the Anglo-Irish agreement 1985. He tried to remove some of the overtly Catholic features of the constitution to make the Republic more attractive to Northern Protestants. He retired as leader of the Fine Gael Party 1987.

Fitzherbert Maria Anne 1756–1837. Wife of the Prince of Wales, later George IV. She became Mrs Fitzherbert by her second marriage 1778 and, after her husband's death 1781, entered London society. She secretly married the Prince of Wales 1785 and finally parted from him 1803.

Five Boroughs five East Midlands towns of Leicester, Lincoln, Derby, Stamford, and Nottingham. They were settled by Danish soldiers 9th and 10th centuries and formed an independent confederation within the ◊Danelaw. Their laws contained the first provision in England for a jury to find someone guilty by a majority verdict.

Fletcher Andrew of Salteoun 1653–1716. Scottish patriot, the most outspoken critic of the Union of Scotland with England of 1707. He advocated an independent Scotland, and a republic or limited monarchy, and proposed 'limitations' to the treaty, such as annual Parliaments. After the Treaty of Union he retired to private life.

Flodden, Battle of the defeat of the Scots by the English under the Earl of Surrey 9 Sept 1513 on a site in Northumberland, England, 5 km/3 mi SE of Coldstream; many Scots, including King James IV, were killed.

Foot Dingle 1905–1978. British lawyer and Labour politician, solicitor-general 1964–67. He was the brother of Michael Foot.

Foot Hugh, Baron Caradon 1907–1990. British Labour politician. As governor of Cyprus 1957–60, he guided the independence negotiations, and he represented the UK at the United Nations 1964–70. He was the son of Isaac Foot and brother of Michael Foot.

Foot Isaac 1880–1960. British Liberal politician. A staunch Nonconformist, he was minister of mines 1931–32. He was the father of Dingle, Hugh, and Michael Foot.

Foot Michael 1913– . British Labour politician and writer. A leader of the left-wing Tribune Group, he was secretary of state for employment 1974–76, Lord President of the Council and leader of the House 1976–79, and succeeded James Callaghan as Labour Party leader 1980–83.

footpad thief or mugger, operating on foot, who robbed travellers on the highway in the 18th and 19th centuries in Britain. Thieves on horseback were termed highwaymen.

Forster William Edward 1818–1886. British Liberal reformer. In Gladstone's government 1868–74 he was vice president of the council, and secured the passing of the Education Act 1870 and the Ballot Act 1872. He was chief secretary for Ireland 1880–82.

Forty-Five, the ◊Jacobite rebellion 1745, led by Prince ◊Charles Edward Stuart. With his army of Highlanders 'Bonnie Prince Charlie' occupied Edinburgh and advanced into England as far as Derby, but then turned back. The rising was crushed by the Duke of Cumberland at Culloden 1746.

Fox Charles James 1749–1806. English Whig politician, son of the 1st Baron Holland. He entered Parliament 1769 as a supporter of the court, but went over to the opposition 1774. As secretary of state 1782, leader of the opposition to Pitt, and foreign secretary 1806, he welcomed the French Revolution and brought about the abolition of the slave trade.

franchise in politics, the eligibility, right, or privilege to vote at public elections, especially for the members of a legislative body, or parliament. In the UK adult citizens are eligible to vote from the age of 18, with the exclusion of peers, the insane, and criminals.

freemasonry the beliefs and practices of a group of linked national organizations open to men over the age of 21, united by a common code of morals and certain traditional 'secrets'. Modern freemasonry began in 18th-century Europe. Freemasons do much charitable work, but have been criticized in recent years for their secrecy, their male exclusivity, and their alleged use of influence within and between organizations (for example, the police or local government) to further each other's interests. There are approximately 6 million members.

French John Denton Pinkstone, 1st Earl of Ypres 1852–1925. British field marshal. In the second South African War 1899–1902, he relieved Kimberley and took Bloemfontein; in World War I he was commander in chief of the British Expeditionary Force in France 1914–15; he resigned after being criticized as indecisive.

Friends, Society of or *Quakers* Christian Protestant sect founded by George Fox in England in the 17th century. They were persecuted for their nonviolent activism, and many emigrated to form communities elsewhere, for example in Pennsylvania and New England, USA. They now form a worldwide movement of about 200,000. Their worship stresses meditation and the freedom of all to take an active part in the service (called a meeting, held in a meeting house). They have no priests or ministers.

Frobisher Martin 1535–1594. English navigator. He made his first voyage to Guinea, West Africa, 1554. In 1576 he set out in search of the Northwest Passage, and visited Labrador, and Frobisher Bay, Baffin Island. Second and third expeditions sailed 1577 and 1578.

Froude James Anthony 1818–1894. English historian whose History of England from the Fall of Wolsey to the Defeat of the Spanish Armada in 12 volumes 1856–70 was a classic Victorian work.

Fry Elizabeth (born Gurney) 1780–1845. English Quaker philanthropist. She formed an association for the improvement of conditions for female prisoners 1817, and worked with her brother, *Joseph Gurney* (1788–1847), on an 1819 report on prison reform.

Fyfe David Maxwell, 1st Earl of Kilmuir. Scottish lawyer and Conservative politician; see ◊Kilmuir.

G

Gaitskell Hugh (Todd Naylor) 1906–1963. British Labour politician. In 1950 he became minister of economic affairs, and then chancellor of the Exchequer until Oct 1951. In 1955 he defeated Aneurin Bevan for the succession to Attlee as party leader, and tried to reconcile internal differences on nationalization and disarmament. He was re-elected leader in 1960.

Gardiner Stephen c. 1493–1555. English priest and politician. After being secretary to Cardinal Wolsey, he became bishop of Winchester in 1531. An opponent of Protestantism, he was imprisoned under Edward VI, and as Lord Chancellor 1553–55 under Queen Mary he tried to restore Roman Catholicism.

gavelkind system of land tenure found only in Kent. The tenant paid rent to the lord instead of carrying out services for him, as elsewhere. It came into force in Anglo-Saxon times and was only formally abolished 1926. The term comes from Old English *gafol*, 'tribute' and *gecynd*, 'kind'.

General Belgrano Argentine battle cruiser torpedoed and sunk on 2 May 1982 by the British nuclear-powered submarine Conqueror during the ◊Falklands War.

general strike refusal to work by employees in several key industries, with the intention of paralysing the economic life of a country. In British history, the General Strike was a nationwide strike called by the Trade Union Congress on 3 May 1926 in support of the miners' union. Elsewhere, the general strike was used as a political weapon by anarchists and others, especially in Spain and Italy.

The immediate cause of the 1926 General Strike was the report of a royal commission on the coal mining industry (Samuel Report 1926) which, among other things, recommended a cut in wages. The mine-owners wanted longer hours as well as lower wages. The miners' union under the leadership of A J Cook resisted with the slogan 'not a penny off the pay, not a minute on the day'. A coal strike started in early May 1926 and the miners asked the TUC to bring all major industries out on strike in support of the action; eventually it included more than 2 million workers. The Conservative government under Stanley Baldwin used troops, volunteers, and special constables to maintain food supplies and essential services, and had a monopoly on the information services, including BBC radio. After nine days the TUC ended the general strike, leaving the miners - who felt betrayed by the TUC - to remain on strike, unsuccessfully, until Nov 1926. The Trades Disputes Act of 1927 made general strikes illegal.

George six kings of Great Britain:

George I 1660–1727. King of Great Britain and Ireland from 1714. He was the son of the first elector of Hanover, Ernest Augustus (1629–1698), and his wife Sophia, and a great-grandson of James I. He succeeded to the electorate 1698, and became king on the death of Queen Anne. He attached himself to the Whigs, and spent most of his reign in Hanover, never having learned English.

George II 1683–1760. King of Great Britain and Ireland from 1727, when he succeeded his father, George I. His victory at Dettingen 1743, in the War of the Austrian Succession, was the last battle commanded by a British king. He married Caroline of Anspach 1705. He was succeeded by his grandson George III.

George II 1683–1760. King of Great Britain from 1727, when he succeeded his father, George I, whom he detested. He married Caroline of Anspach 1705. She supported Robert ◊Walpole's position as adviser, and Walpole rallied support for George during the ◊Jacobite rebellions against him.

George III 1738–1820. King of Great Britain and Ireland from 1760, when he succeeded his grandfather George II. His rule was marked by intransigence resulting in the loss of the American colonies, for which he shared the blame with his chief minister Lord North, and the emancipation of Catholics in England. Possibly suffering from porphyria, he had repeated attacks of insanity, permanent from 1811. He was succeeded by his son George IV.

George IV 1762–1830. King of Great Britain and Ireland from 1820, when he succeeded his father George III, for whom he had been regent during the king's period of insanity 1811–20. In 1785 he secretly married a Catholic widow, Maria ◊Fitzherbert, but in 1795 also married Princess ◊Caroline of Brunswick, in return for payment of his debts. He was a patron of the arts. His prestige was undermined by his treatment of Caroline (they separated 1796), his dissipation, and his extravagance. He was succeeded by his brother, the duke of Clarence, who became William IV.

George V 1865–1936. King of Great Britain from 1910, when he succeeded his father Edward VII. He was the second son, and became heir 1892 on the death of his elder brother Albert, Duke of Clarence. In 1893, he married Princess Victoria Mary of Teck (Queen Mary), formerly engaged to his brother. During World War I he made several visits to the front. In 1917, he abandoned all German titles for himself and his family. The name of the royal house was changed from Saxe-Coburg-Gotha (popularly known as Brunswick or Hanover) to Windsor.

George VI 1895–1952. King of Great Britain from 1936, when he succeeded after the abdication of his brother Edward VIII, who had succeeded their father George V. Created Duke of York 1920, he married in 1923 Lady Elizabeth Bowes-Lyon (1900–   ), and their children are Elizabeth II and Princess Margaret. During World War II, he visited the Normandy and Italian battlefields.

Gerald of Wales English name of ◊Giraldus Cambrensis, medieval Welsh bishop and historian.

Gibbon Edward 1737–1794. English historian. He wrote one major work, arranged in three parts, *The History of the Decline and Fall of the Roman Empire* 1776–88, a continuous narrative from the 2nd century AD to the fall of Constantinople 1453.

He began work on it while in Rome 1764. Although immediately successful, he was compelled to reply to attacks on his account of the early development of Christianity by a *Vindication* 1779. His *Autobiography*, pieced together from fragments, appeared 1796.

Giraldus Cambrensis (Welsh *Geralt Gymro*) c. 1146–1220. Welsh historian, born in Pembrokeshire. He was elected bishop of St David's in 1198. He wrote a history of the conquest of Ireland by Henry II, and Itinerarium Cambriae/Journey through Wales 1191.

Gladstone William Ewart 1809–1898. British Liberal politician, repeatedly prime minister. He entered Parliament as a Tory in 1833 and held ministerial office, but left the party 1846 and after 1859 identified himself with the Liberals. He was chancellor of the Exchequer 1852–55 and 1859–66, and prime minister 1868–74, 1880–85, 1886, and 1892–94. He introduced elementary education 1870 and vote by secret ballot 1872 and many reforms in Ireland, although he failed in his efforts to get a ◊Home Rule Bill passed.

Gladstone was born in Liverpool, the son of a rich merchant. In Peel's government he was president of the Board of Trade 1843–45, and colonial secretary 1845–46. He left the Tory Party with the Peelite group in 1846. He was chancellor of the Exchequer in Aberdeen's government 1852–55 and in the Liberal governments of Palmerston and Russell 1859–66. In his first term as prime minister he carried through a series of reforms, including the disestablishment of the Church of Ireland, the Irish Land Act, and the abolition of the purchase of army commissions and of religious tests in the universities.

Gladstone strongly resisted Disraeli's imperialist and pro-Turkish policy during the latter's government of 1874–80, not least because of Turkish pogroms against subject Christians, and by his Midlothian campaign of 1879 helped to overthrow Disraeli. Gladstone's second government carried the second Irish Land Act and the Reform Act 1884 but was confronted with problems in Ireland, Egypt, and South Africa, and lost prestige through its failure to relieve General ◊Gordon. Returning to office in 1886, Gladstone introduced his first Home Rule Bill, which was defeated by the secession of the Liberal Unionists, and he thereupon resigned. After six years' opposition he formed his last government; his second Home Rule Bill was rejected by the Lords, and in 1894 he resigned. He led a final crusade against the massacre of Armenian Christians in 1896.

Glencoe glen in Strathclyde region, Scotland, where members of the Macdonald clan were massacred 1692. John Campbell, Earl of Breadalbane, was the chief instigator. It is now a winter sports area.

Glendower Owen c. 1359–c. 1416. (Welsh *Owain Glyndŵr*) Welsh nationalist leader of a successful revolt against the English in N Wales, who defeated Henry IV in three campaigns 1400–02, although Wales was reconquered 1405–13. Glendower disappeared 1416 after some years of guerrilla warfare.

Glorious Revolution in British history, the events surrounding the removal of James II from the throne and his replacement by Mary (daughter of Charles I) and William of Orange as joint sovereigns in 1689. James had become increasingly unpopular on account of his unconstitutional behaviour and Catholicism. Various elements in England, including seven prominent politicians, plotted to invite the Protestant William to invade. Arriving at Torbay on 5 Nov 1688, William rapidly gained support and James was allowed to flee to France after the army deserted him. William and Mary then accepted a new constitutional settlement, the Bill of Rights 1689, which assured the ascendency of parliamentary power over sovereign rule.

Godiva Lady c. 1040–1080. Wife of Leofric, earl of Mercia (died 1057). Legend has it that her husband promised to reduce the heavy taxes on the people of Coventry if she rode naked through the streets at noon. The grateful citizens remained indoors as she did so, but 'Peeping Tom' bored a hole in his shutters and was struck blind.

Godwin died 1053. Earl of Wessex from 1020. He secured the succession to the throne in 1042 of ◊Edward the Confessor, to whom he married his daughter Edith, and whose chief minister he became. King Harold II was his son.

Gordon Charles (George) 1833–1885. British general sent to Khartoum in the Sudan 1884 to rescue English garrisons that were under attack by the *Mahdi*, Muhammad Ahmed; he was himself besieged for ten months by the Mahdi's army. A relief expedition arrived 28 Jan 1885 to find that Khartoum had been captured and Gordon killed two days before.

Gordon George 1751–1793. British organizer of the so-called *Gordon Riots* of 1778, a protest against removal of penalties imposed on Roman Catholics in the Catholic Relief Act of 1778; he was acquitted on a treason charge. Gordon and the 'No Popery' riots figure in Charles Dickens's novel Barnaby Rudge.

Gorst J(ohn) E(ldon) 1835–1916. English Conservative Party administrator. A supporter of Disraeli, Gorst was largely responsible for extending the Victorian Conservative Party electoral base to include middle- and working-class support. Appointed Conservative Party agent in 1870, he established Conservative Central Office, and became secretary of the National Union in 1871. He was solicitor-general 1885–86.

Goschen George Joachim, 1st Viscount Goschen 1831–1907. British Liberal politician. He held several cabinet posts under Gladstone 1868–74, but broke with him in 1886 over Irish Home Rule. In Salisbury's Unionist government of 1886–92 he was chancellor of the Exchequer, and 1895–1900 was First Lord of the Admiralty.

Grafton Augustus Henry, 3rd Duke of Grafton 1735–1811. British politician. Grandson of the first duke, who was the son of Charles II and Barbara Villiers (1641–1709), Duchess of Cleveland. He became First Lord of the Treasury in 1766 and an unsuccessful acting prime minister 1767–70.

Granby John Manners, Marquess of Granby 1721–1770. British soldier. His head appears on many inn-signs in England as a result of his popularity as a commander of the British forces fighting in Europe in the Seven Years' War.

Grand Remonstrance petition passed by the English Parliament in Nov 1641 that listed all the alleged misdeeds of Charles I and demanded Parliamentary approval for the king's ministers and the reform of the church. Charles refused to accept the Grand Remonstrance and countered by trying to arrest five leading members of the House of Commons (Pym, Hampden, Holles, Hesilrige, and Strode). The worsening of relations between king and Parliament led to the outbreak of the English Civil War in 1642.

Grattan Henry 1746–1820. Irish politician. He entered the Irish parliament in 1775, led the patriot opposition, and obtained free trade and legislative independence for Ireland 1782. He failed to prevent the Act of Union of Ireland and England in 1805, sat in the British Parliament from that year, and pressed for Catholic emancipation.

Great Britain official name for ◊England, ◊Scotland, and ◊Wales, and the adjacent islands (except the Channel Islands and the Isle of Man) from 1603, when the English and Scottish crowns were united under

James I of England (James VI of Scotland). With Northern ◊Ireland it forms the ◊United Kingdom.

Greater London Council (GLC) in the UK, local authority that governed London 1965–86. When the GLC was abolished (see ◊local government), its powers either devolved back to the borough councils or were transferred to certain nonelected bodies.

Great Exhibition world fair held in Hyde Park, London, UK, in 1851, proclaimed by its originator Prince Albert as 'the Great Exhibition of the Industries of All Nations'. In practice, it glorified British manufacture: over half the 100,000 exhibits were from Britain or the British Empire. Over 6 million people attended the exhibition. The exhibition hall, popularly known as the *◊Crystal Palace*, was constructed of glass with a cast-iron frame, and designed by Joseph Paxton.

Green Paper publication issued by a British government department setting out various aspects of a matter on which legislation is contemplated, and inviting public discussion and suggestions. In due course it may be followed by a ◊White Paper, giving details of proposed legislation. The first Green Paper was published 1967.

Green Party political party aiming to 'preserve the planet and its people', based on the premise that incessant economic growth is unsustainable. The leaderless party structure reflects a general commitment to decentralization. Green parties sprang up in W Europe in the 1970s and in E Europe from 1988. Parties in different countries are linked to one another but unaffiliated with any pressure group. The party had a number of parliamentary seats in 1992: Austria 9, Belgium 13, Finland 8, Italy 20, Luxembourg 2, Republic of Ireland 1, Greece 1, and Germany 2; and 29 members in the European Parliament (Belgium 3, France 8, Italy 7, the Netherlands 2, Spain 1, and Germany 8).

Grenville George 1712–1770. British Whig politician, prime minister, and chancellor of the Exchequer, whose introduction of the ◊Stamp Act 1765 to raise revenue from the colonies was one of the causes of the American Revolution. His government was also responsible for prosecuting the radical John ◊Wilkes.

Grenville Richard 1542–1591. English naval commander and adventurer who died heroically aboard his ship The Revenge when attacked by Spanish warships. Grenville fought in Hungary and Ireland 1566–69, and was knighted about 1577. In 1585 he commanded the expedition that founded Virginia, USA, for his cousin Walter ◊Raleigh. From 1586 to 1588 he organized the defence of England against the Spanish Armada.

Grenville William Wyndham, Baron 1759–1834. British Whig politician, foreign secretary from 1791; he resigned along with Prime Minister Pitt the Younger 1801 over George III's refusal to assent to Catholic emancipation. He headed the 'All the Talents' coalition of 1806–07 that abolished the slave trade.

Gretna Green village in Dumfries and Galloway region, Scotland, where runaway marriages were legal after they were banned in England 1754; all that was necessary was the couple's declaration, before witnesses, of their willingness to marry. From 1856 Scottish law required at least one of the parties to be resident in Scotland for a minimum of 21 days before the marriage, and marriage by declaration was abolished 1940.

Grey Charles, 2nd Earl Grey 1764–1845. British Whig politician. He entered Parliament 1786, and in 1806 became First Lord of the Admiralty, and foreign secretary soon afterwards. As prime minister 1830–34, he carried the Great Reform Bill that reshaped the parliamentary representative system 1832 and the act abolishing slavery throughout the British Empire 1833.

Grey Edward, 1st Viscount Grey of Fallodon 1862–1933. British Liberal politician, nephew of Charles Grey. As foreign secretary 1905–16 he negotiated an entente with Russia 1907, and backed France against Germany in the Agadir Incident of 1911. In 1914 he said: 'The lamps are going out all over Europe; we shall not see them lit again in our lifetime.'

Grey Henry, 3rd Earl Grey 1802–1894. British politician, son of Charles Grey. He served under his father as undersecretary for the colonies 1830–33, resigning because the cabinet would not back the immediate emancipation of slaves; he was secretary of war 1835–39 and colonial secretary 1846–52.

Grey Lady Jane 1537–1554. Queen of England for nine days, 10–19

July 1553, the great- granddaughter of Henry VII. She was married 1553 to Lord Guildford Dudley (died 1554), son of the Duke of ◊Northumberland. Edward VI was persuaded by Northumberland to set aside the claims to the throne of his sisters Mary and Elizabeth. When Edward died on 6 July 1553, Jane reluctantly accepted the crown and was proclaimed queen four days later. Mary, although a Roman Catholic, had the support of the populace, and the Lord Mayor of London announced that she was queen 19 July. Grey was executed on Tower Green.

guillotine in politics, a device used by UK governments in which the time allowed for debating a bill in the House of Commons is restricted so as to ensure its speedy passage to receiving the royal assent (that is, to becoming law). The tactic of guillotining was introduced during the 1880s to overcome attempts by Irish members of Parliament to obstruct the passing of legislation. The guillotine is also used as a parliamentary process in France.

Gummer John Selwyn 1939–   . British Conservative politician, secretary of state for the environment from 1993. He was minister of state for employment 1983–84, paymaster general 1984–85, minister for agriculture 1985–88, secretary of state for agriculture 1989–93, and chair of the party 1983–85.

Gunpowder Plot in British history, the Catholic conspiracy to blow up James I and his parliament on 5 Nov 1605. It was discovered through an anonymous letter. Guy ◊Fawkes was found in the cellar beneath the Palace of Westminster, ready to fire a store of explosives. Several of the conspirators were killed, and Fawkes and seven others were executed.

Guthrum Danish king of East Anglia. He led a large Danish invasion of Anglo-Saxon England 878 but was defeated by King ◊Alfred at the Battle of ◊Edington 878. His reign 880–890 was mostly peaceful.

Gwyn (or *Gwynn*) Nell (Eleanor) 1651–1687. English comedy actress from 1665. She was formerly an orange- seller at Drury Lane Theatre, London. The poet Dryden wrote parts for her, and from 1669 she was the mistress of Charles II.

H

habeas corpus in law, a writ directed to someone who has custody of a person, ordering him or her to bring the person before the court issuing the writ and to justify why the person is detained in custody.

Traditional rights to habeas corpus were embodied in the English Habeas Corpus Act 1679, mainly owing to Lord ◊Shaftesbury. The Scottish equivalent is the Wrongous Imprisonment Act 1701.

Hadrian's Wall Roman fortification built AD 122–126 to mark England's northern boundary and abandoned about 383; its ruins run 185 km/115 mi from Wallsend on the river Tyne to Maryport, W Cumbria. In some parts, the wall was covered with a glistening, white coat of mortar. The fort at South Shields, Arbeia, built to defend the eastern end, is being reconstructed.

Haig Douglas, 1st Earl Haig 1861–1928. British army officer, commander in chief in World War I. His Somme offensive in France in the summer of 1916 made considerable advances only at enormous cost to human life, and his Passchendaele offensive in Belgium from July to Nov 1917 achieved little at a similar loss. He was created field marshal 1917 and, after retiring, became first president of the British Legion 1921.

Hailsham Quintin Hogg, Baron Hailsham of St Marylebone 1907– . British lawyer and Conservative politician. The 2nd Viscount Hailsham, he renounced the title in 1963 to re-enter the House of Commons, and was then able to contest the Conservative Party leadership elections, but took a life peerage 1970 on his appointment as Lord Chancellor 1970–74. He was Lord Chancellor again 1979–87.

Haldane Richard Burdon, Viscount Haldane 1856–1928. British Liberal politician. As secretary for war 1905–12, he sponsored the army reforms that established an expeditionary force, backed by a territorial army and under the unified control of an imperial general staff. He was Lord Chancellor 1912–15 and in the Labour government of 1924. His writings on German philosophy led to accusations of his having pro-German sympathies.

Halifax Charles Montagu, Earl of Halifax 1661–1715. British financier. Appointed commissioner of the Treasury 1692, he raised money for the French war by instituting the national debt and in 1694 carried out William Paterson's plan for a national bank (the Bank of England) and became chancellor of the Exchequer.

Halifax Edward Frederick Lindley Wood, Earl of Halifax 1881–1959. British Conservative politician, viceroy of India 1926–31. As foreign secretary 1938–40 he was associated with Chamberlain's 'appeasement' policy. He received an earldom 1944 for services to the Allied cause while ambassador to the USA 1941–46.

Halifax George Savile, 1st Marquess of Halifax 1633–1695. English politician. He entered Parliament 1660, and was raised to the peerage by Charles II, by whom he was also later dismissed. He strove to steer a middle course between extremists, and became known as 'the Trimmer'. He played a prominent part in the revolution of 1688.

Hallam Henry 1777–1859. British historian. He was called to the Bar, but a private fortune enabled him to devote himself to historical study from 1812 and his Constitutional History of England 1827 established his reputation.

Hamilton Emma (born Amy Lyon), Lady Hamilton 1765–1815. Wife of Sir William ◊Hamilton from 1791, envoy to the court of Naples, and mistress of Admiral Horatio ◊Nelson, whom she met in Naples in 1793. After his return from the Nile battle 1798, during the Napoleonic Wars, she became his mistress and their daughter, Horatia, was born 1801. After Nelson's death in battle 1805, Lady Hamilton spent her inheritance and died in poverty in Calais. She had been a great beauty and had posed for the great artists of her youth, especially George Romney (1734–1802).

Hamilton James, 1st Duke of Hamilton 1606–1649. Scottish adviser to Charles I. He led an army against the ◊Covenanters (supporters of the National Covenant 1638 to establish Presbyterianism) 1639 and subsequently took part in the negotiations between Charles and the Scots. In the second Civil War he led the Scottish invasion of England, but was captured at Preston and executed.

Hamilton William 1730–1803. British diplomat, envoy to the court of Naples 1764–1800, whose collection of Greek vases was bought by the British Museum.

Hampden John 1594–1643. English politician. His refusal in 1636 to pay ◊ship money, a compulsory tax levied to support the navy, made him a national figure. In the Short and Long Parliaments he proved himself a skilful debater and parliamentary strategist. King Charles's attempt to arrest him and four other leading MPs made the Civil War inevitable. He raised his own regiment on the outbreak of hostilities, and on 18 June 1643 was mortally wounded at the skirmish of Chalgrove Field in Oxfordshire.

Hampton Court Palace former royal residence near Richmond, London, built 1515 by Cardinal ◊Wolsey and presented by him to Henry VIII 1525. Henry subsequently enlarged and improved it. In the 17th century William and Mary made it their main residence outside London, and the palace was further enlarged by Christopher Wren, although only part of his intended scheme was completed. Part of the building was extensively damaged by fire 1986.

Hanover German royal dynasty that ruled Great Britain and Ireland 1714–1901. Under the Act of ◊Settlement 1701, the succession passed to the ruling family of Hanover, Germany, on the death of Queen Anne. On the death of Queen Victoria, the crown passed to Edward VII of the house of Saxe-Coburg.

Hansard official report of the proceedings of the British Houses of Parliament, named after Luke Hansard (1752–1828), printer of the House of Commons Journal from 1774. It is published by Her Majesty's Stationery Office. The name Hansard was officially adopted 1943.

Harcourt William Vernon 1827–1904. British Liberal politician. Under Gladstone he was home secretary 1880–85 and chancellor of the Exchequer 1886 and 1892–95. He is remembered for his remark 1892: 'We are all Socialists now.'

Hardicanute c. 1019–1042. King of Denmark from 1028, and of England from 1040; son of Canute. In England he was considered a harsh ruler.

Hardie (James) Keir 1856–1915. Scottish socialist, member of Parliament 1892–95 and 1900–15. He worked in the mines as a boy and in 1886 became secretary of the Scottish Miners' Federation. In 1888 he was the first Labour candidate to stand for Parliament; he entered Parliament independently as a Labour member 1892 and was a chief founder of the ◊Independent Labour Party 1893.

Harding (Allan Francis) John, 1st Baron Harding of Petherton 1896–1989. British field marshal. He was Chief of Staff in Italy during World War II. As governor of Cyprus 1955–57, during the period of political agitation prior to independence 1960, he was responsible for the deportation of Makarios III from Cyprus 1955.

Hardy Thomas Masterman 1769–1839. British sailor. At Trafalgar he was Nelson's flag captain in the Victory, attending him during his dying moments. He became First Sea Lord 1830.

Harley Robert, 1st Earl of Oxford 1661–1724. British Tory politician, chief minister to Queen Anne 1711–14, when he negotiated the Treaty of Utrecht 1713. Accused of treason as a ◊Jacobite after the accession of George I, he was imprisoned 1714–17.

Harold two kings of England:

Harold I died 1040. King of England from 1035. The illegitimate son of Canute, known as *Harefoot*, he claimed the throne 1035 when the legitimate heir Hardicanute was in Denmark. He was elected king 1037.

Harold II c. 1020–1066. King of England from Jan 1066. He succeeded his father Earl Godwin 1053 as earl of Wessex. In 1063 William of Normandy (◊William (I) the Conqueror) tricked him into swearing to support his claim to the English throne, and when the ◊Witan elected Harold to succeed Edward the Confessor, William prepared to invade. Meanwhile, Harold's treacherous brother Tostig (died 1066) joined the king of Norway, Harald Hardrada (1015–1066), in invading Northumbria. Harold routed and killed them at Stamford Bridge 25

Sept. Three days later William landed at Pevensey, Sussex, and Harold was killed at the Battle of Hastings 14 Oct 1066.

Hartington Spencer Compton Cavendish 1833–1908. 8th Duke of Devonshire, Marquess of Hartington. British politician, first leader of the Liberal Unionists 1886–1903. As war minister he opposed devolution for Ireland in cabinet and later led the revolt of the Liberal Unionists that defeated Gladstone's Irish Home Rule bill 1886. Hartington refused the premiership three times, 1880, 1886, and 1887, and led the opposition to the Irish Home Rule bill in the House of Lords 1893.

Hastings, Battle of battle 14 Oct 1066 at which William the Conqueror, Duke of Normandy, defeated Harold, King of England. The site is 10 km/6 mi inland from Hastings, at Senlac, Sussex; it is marked by Battle Abbey.

Haughey Charles 1925– . Irish Fianna Fáil politician of Ulster descent. Dismissed 1970 from Jack Lynch's cabinet for alleged complicity in IRA gun-running, he was afterward acquitted. He was prime minister 1979–81, March–Nov 1982, and 1986–92, when he was replaced by Albert Reynolds.

Hawkins John 1532–1595. English navigator, born in Plymouth. Treasurer to the navy 1573–89, he was knighted for his services as a commander against the Spanish Armada 1588.

Hawkins Richard c. 1562–1622. English navigator, son of John Hawkins. He held a command against the Spanish Armada 1588, was captured in an expedition against Spanish possessions 1593–94 and released 1602.

Heath Edward (Richard George) 1916– . British Conservative politician, party leader 1965–75. As prime minister 1970–74 he took the UK into the European Community but was brought down by economic and industrial relations crises at home. He was replaced as party leader by Margaret Thatcher 1975, and became increasingly critical of her policies and her opposition to the UK's full participation in the EC. In 1990 he undertook a mission to Iraq in an attempt to secure the release of British hostages.

Hebrides group of more than 500 islands (fewer than 100 inhabited) off W Scotland; total area 2,900 sq km/1,120 sq mi. The Hebrides were settled by Scandinavians during the 6th to 9th centuries and passed under Norwegian rule from about 890 to 1266.

Henderson Arthur 1863–1935. British Labour politician, foreign secretary 1929–31, when he accorded the Soviet government full recognition. He was awarded the Nobel Peace Prize 1934.

Hengist 5th century AD. Legendary leader, with his brother *Horsa*, of the Jutes, who originated in Jutland and settled in Kent about 450, the first Anglo-Saxon settlers in Britain.

Henrietta Maria 1609–1669. Queen of England 1625–49. The daughter of Henry IV of France, she married Charles I of England 1625. By encouraging him to aid Roman Catholics and make himself an absolute ruler, she became highly unpopular and was exiled 1644–60. She returned to England at the Restoration but retired to France 1665.

Henry eight kings of England:

Henry I 1068–1135. King of England from 1100. Youngest son of William the Conqueror, he succeeded his brother William II. He won the support of the Saxons by granting them a charter and marrying a Saxon princess. An able administrator, he established a professional bureaucracy and a system of travelling judges. He was succeeded by Stephen.

Henry II 1133–1189. King of England from 1154, when he succeeded ◊Stephen. He was the son of ◊Matilda and Geoffrey of Anjou (1113–1151). He curbed the power of the barons, but his attempt to bring the church courts under control had to be abandoned after the murder of Thomas à ◊Becket. During his reign the English conquest of Ireland began. He was succeeded by his son Richard I.

Henry III 1207–1272. King of England from 1216, when he succeeded John, but he did not rule until 1227. His financial commitments to the papacy and his foreign favourites led to de ◊Montfort's revolt 1264. Henry was defeated at Lewes, Sussex, and imprisoned. He was restored to the throne after the royalist victory at Evesham 1265. He was succeeded by his son Edward I.

Henry IV (Bolingbroke) 1367–1413. King of England from 1399, the son of ◊John of Gaunt. In 1398 he was banished by ◊Richard II for political activity but returned 1399 to head a revolt and be accepted as king by Parliament. He was succeeded by his son Henry V.

Henry V 1387–1422. King of England from 1413, son of Henry IV. Invading Normandy 1415 (during the Hundred Years' War), he captured Harfleur and defeated the French at ◊Agincourt. He invaded again 1417–19, capturing Rouen. His military victory forced the French into the Treaty of Troyes 1420, which gave Henry control of the French government. He married ◊Catherine of Valois 1420 and gained recognition as heir to the French throne by his father-in-law Charles VI, but died before him. He was succeeded by his son Henry VI.

Henry VI 1421–1471. King of England from 1422, son of Henry V. He assumed royal power 1442 and sided with the party opposed to the continuation of the Hundred Years' War with France. After his marriage 1445, he was dominated by his wife, ◊Margaret of Anjou. The unpopularity of the government, especially after the loss of the English conquests in France, encouraged Richard, Duke of ◊York, to claim the throne, and though York was killed 1460, his son Edward IV proclaimed himself king 1461 (see Wars of the ◊Roses). Henry was captured 1465, temporarily restored 1470, but again imprisoned 1471 and then murdered.

Henry VII 1457–1509. King of England from 1485, son of Edmund Tudor, Earl of Richmond (c. 1430–1456), and a descendant of ◊John of Gaunt. He spent his early life in Brittany until 1485, when he landed in Britain to lead the rebellion against Richard III which ended with Richard's defeat and death at ◊Bosworth. By his marriage to Elizabeth of York 1486, he united the houses of York and Lancaster. Yorkist revolts continued until 1497, but Henry restored order after the Wars of the ◊Roses by the ◊Star Chamber and achieved independence from Parliament by amassing a private fortune through confiscations. He was succeeded by his son Henry VIII.

Henry VIII 1491–1547. King of England from 1509, when he succeeded his father Henry VII and married Catherine of Aragon, the widow of his brother. During the period 1513–29 Henry pursued an active foreign policy, largely under the guidance of his Lord Chancellor, Cardinal Wolsey who shared Henry's desire to make England stronger. Wolsey was replaced by Thomas More 1529 for failing to persuade the pope to grant Henry a divorce. After 1532 Henry broke with papal authority, proclaimed himself head of the church in England, dissolved the monasteries, and divorced Catherine. His subsequent wives were Anne Boleyn, Jane Seymour, Anne of Cleves, Catherine Howard, and Catherine Parr. He was succeeded by his son Edward VI.

He divorced Catherine 1533 because she was too old to give him an heir, and married Anne Boleyn, who was beheaded 1536, ostensibly for adultery. Henry's third wife, Jane Seymour, died 1537. He married Anne of Cleves 1540 in pursuance of Thomas Cromwell's policy of allying with the German Protestants, but rapidly abandoned this policy, divorced Anne, and beheaded Cromwell. His fifth wife, Catherine Howard, was beheaded 1542, and the following year he married Catherine Parr, who survived him. Henry never completely lost his popularity, but wars with France and Scotland towards the end of his reign sapped the economy, and in religion he not only executed Roman Catholics, including Thomas More, for refusing to acknowledge his supremacy in the church, but also Protestants who maintained his changes had not gone far enough.

Henry Frederick Prince of Wales 1594–1612. Eldest son of James I of England and Anne of Denmark; a keen patron of Italian art.

heptarchy the seven Saxon kingdoms thought to have existed in England before AD 800: Northumbria, Mercia, East Anglia, Essex, Kent, Sussex, and Wessex. The term was coined by 16th-century historians.

Herbert of Lea Sidney Herbert, 1st Baron Herbert of Lea 1810–1861. British politician. He was secretary for war in Aberdeen's Liberal-Peelite coalition of 1852–55, and during the Crimean War was responsible for sending Florence Nightingale to the front.

Hereward the Wake 11th century. English leader of a revolt against the Normans 1070. His stronghold in the Isle of Ely was captured by William the Conqueror 1071. Hereward escaped, but his fate is unknown.

Heseltine Michael (Ray Dibdin) 1933– . English Conservative politician, member of Parliament from 1966 (for Henley from 1974), secretary of state for the environment 1990-92 and for trade and industry from 1992.

hide Anglo-Saxon unit of land regarded as sufficient to support a peasant and his household. It varied from about 296 ha/120 acres in the east of England to as little as 99 ha/40 acres in ◊Wessex. It was the basic unit of assessment for taxation and military service.

Highland Clearances forced removal of tenants from large estates in Scotland during the early 19th century, as landowners 'improved' their estates by switching from arable to sheep farming. It led ultimately to widespread emigration to North America.

highwayman in English history, a thief on horseback who robbed travellers on the highway (those who did so on foot were known as *footpads*). Highwaymen continued to flourish well into the 19th century.

With the development of regular coach services in the 17th and 18th centuries, the highwaymen's activities became notorious, and the Bow Street runners were organized to suppress them; (see ◊police).

hill figure in Britain, any of a number of ancient figures, usually of animals, cut from downland turf to show the underlying chalk. Examples include the various White Horses, the Long Man of Wilmington, East Sussex, and the Cerne Abbas Giant, Dorset. Their origins are variously attributed to Celts, Romans, Saxons, Druids, or Benedictine monks.

hillfort European Iron Age site with massive banks and ditches for defence, used as both a military camp and a permanent settlement. An example is Maiden Castle, Dorset, England.

Hillsborough Agreement another name for the ◊Anglo-Irish Agreement 1985.

Hobbes Thomas 1588–1679. English political philosopher and the first thinker since Aristotle to attempt to develop a comprehensive theory of nature, including human behaviour. In The Leviathan 1651, he advocates absolutist government as the only means of ensuring order and security; he saw this as deriving from the social contract.

Holinshed Ralph c. 1520–c. 1580. English historian who published two volumes of the Chronicles of England, Scotland and Ireland 1578, on which Shakespeare based his history plays.

Holland Henry Richard Vassall Fox, 3rd Baron 1773–1840. British Whig politician. He was Lord Privy Seal 1806–07. His home, at Holland House, London, was for many years the centre of Whig political and literary society.

Hollis Roger 1905–1973. British civil servant, head of the secret intelligence service MI5 1956–65. He was alleged to have been a double agent together with Kim Philby, but this was denied by the KGB 1991.

home front the organized sectors of domestic activity in wartime, mainly associated with World Wars I and II. Features of the UK home front in World War II included the organization of the black-out, evacuation, air-raid shelters, the Home Guard, rationing, and distribution of gas masks. With many men on active military service, women were called upon to carry out jobs previously undertaken only by men.

Home Guard unpaid force formed in Britain May 1940 to repel the expected German invasion, and known until July 1940 as the Local Defence Volunteers.

It consisted of men aged 17–65 who had not been called up, formed part of the armed forces of the crown, and was subject to military law. Over 2 million strong in 1944, it was disbanded 31 Dec 1945, but revived 1951, then placed on a reserve basis 1955, and ceased activities 1957.

Home Rule, Irish movement to repeal the Act of ◊Union 1801 that joined Ireland to Britain and to establish an Irish parliament responsible for internal affairs. In 1870 Isaac Butt (1813–1879) formed the Home Rule Association and the movement was led in Parliament from 1880 by Charles ◊Parnell. After 1918 the demand for an independent Irish republic replaced that for home rule.

Gladstone's Home Rule bills 1886 and 1893 were both defeated. A third bill was introduced by the Liberals in 1912, which aroused opposition in Ireland where the Protestant minority in Ulster feared domination by the Catholic majority. Ireland appeared on the brink of civil war but the outbreak of World War I rendered further consideration of Home

Rule inopportune. In 1920 the Government of Ireland Act introduced separate parliaments in the North and South and led to the treaty 1921 that established the Irish Free State.

Hon. abbreviation for *Honourable*.

Hood Samuel, 1st Viscount Hood 1724–1816. British admiral. A masterly tactician, he defeated the French at Dominica in the West Indies 1783, and in the Revolutionary Wars captured Toulon and Corsica.

Hore-Belisha Leslie, Baron Hore-Belisha 1895–1957. British politician. A National Liberal, he was minister of transport 1934–37, introducing *Belisha beacons* to mark pedestrian crossings. As war minister from 1937, until removed by Chamberlain 1940 on grounds of temperament, he introduced peacetime conscription 1939.

Hornby v. Close UK court case in 1867, in which it was decided that trade unions were illegal associations. The decision, overturned two years later by a special act of Parliament, indirectly led to the full legalization of trade unions under the Trade Union Acts 1871–76.

Horse, Master of the head of the department of the British royal household, responsible for the royal stables. The Earl of Westmorland became Master of the Horse 1978.

House of Commons lower chamber of the UK ◊Parliament.

House of Lords upper chamber of the UK ◊Parliament.

Household, Royal see ◊royal household.

Howard Catherine c. 1520–1542. Queen consort of ◊Henry VIII of England from 1540. In 1541 the archbishop of Canterbury, Thomas Cranmer, accused her of being unchaste before marriage to Henry and she was beheaded 1542 after Cranmer made further charges of adultery.

Howard Charles, 2nd Baron Howard of Effingham and 1st Earl of Nottingham 1536–1624. English admiral, a cousin of Queen Elizabeth I. He commanded the fleet against the Spanish Armada while Lord High Admiral 1585-1618.

Howard Michael 1941–   . British Conservative politician. He began his career as a barrister, then took up politics, becoming MP for Folkstone and Hythe 1983. Under Margaret ◊Thatcher, he was appointed minister for local government 1987 and Secretary of State for Employment 1990. John ◊Major appointed him Secretary of State for the Environment 1992, a post he held until succeeding Kenneth ◊Clarke as Home Secretary 1993.

Howe Geoffrey 1926– . British Conservative politician, member of Parliament for Surrey East. Under Edward ◊Heath he was solicitor general 1970-72 and minister for trade 1972-74; as chancellor of the Exchequer 1979-83 under Margaret Thatcher, he put into practice the monetarist policy which reduced inflation at the cost of a rise in unemployment. In 1983 he became foreign secretary, and in 1989 deputy prime minister and leader of the House of Commons. On 1 Nov 1990 he resigned in protest at Thatcher's continued opposition to Britain's greater integration in Europe.

Howe Richard Earl 1726–1799. British admiral. He cooperated with his brother William against the colonists during the American Revolution and in the French Revolutionary Wars commanded the Channel fleets 1792–96.

Howe William, 5th Viscount Howe 1729–1814. British general. During the War of American Independence he won the Battle of Bunker Hill 1775, and as commander in chief in America 1776–78 captured New York and defeated Washington at Brandywine and Germantown. He resigned in protest at lack of home government support.

HRH abbreviation for *His/Her Royal Highness*.

Hudson's Bay Company chartered company founded by Prince ◊Rupert 1670 to trade in furs with North American Indians. In 1783 the rival North West Company was formed, but in 1851 this became amalgamated with the Hudson's Bay Company. It is still Canada's biggest fur company, but today also sells general merchandise through department stores and has oil and natural gas interests.

Huguenot French Protestant in the 16th century; the term referred mainly to Calvinists. Severely persecuted under Francis I and Henry II, the Huguenots survived both an attempt to exterminate them (the *Massacre of* St Bartholomew 24 Aug 1572) and the religious wars of the next 30 years. In 1598 Henry IV (himself formerly a Huguenot) granted them toleration under the *Edict of Nantes*. Louis XIV revoked the edict 1685, attempting their forcible conversion, and 400,000 emigrated.

Hume John 1937–   . Northern Ireland Catholic politician, leader of the ◊Social Democratic and Labour Party (SDLP) from 1979. Hume is widely respected for his moderate nationalist views but has recently caused controversy by participating in talks with Gerry ◊Adams as part of a broad attempt to include Sinn Féin in the Nothern Ireland peace process.

Hume Joseph 1777–1855. British Radical politician. Born in Montrose, Scotland, he went to India as an army surgeon 1797, made a fortune, and on his return bought a seat in Parliament. In 1818 he secured election as a Philosophic Radical and supported many progressive measures.

hundred subdivision of a shire in England, Ireland, and parts of the USA. The term was originally used by Germanic peoples to denote a group of 100 warriors, also the area occupied by 100 families or equalling 100 hides (one hide being the amount of land necessary to support a peasant family). When the Germanic peoples settled in England, the hundred remained the basic military and administrative division of England until its abolition 1867.

Hundred Years' War series of conflicts between England and France 1337–1453. Its origins lay with the English kings' possession of Gascony (SW France), which the French kings claimed as their ◊fief, and with trade rivalries over Flanders.

The two kingdoms had a long history of strife before 1337, and the Hundred Years' War has sometimes been interpreted as merely an intensification of these struggles. It was caused by fears of French intervention in Scotland, which the English were trying to subdue, and by the claim of England's ◊Edward III (through his mother Isabel, daughter of Charles IV) to the crown of France.

hunger march procession of the unemployed, a feature of social protest in interwar Britain.

Hurd Douglas (Richard) 1930–   . English Conservative politician, home secretary 1985–89, appointed foreign secretary 1989 in the reshuffle that followed Nigel Lawson's resignation as chancellor of the Exchequer. In Nov 1990 he was an unsuccessful candidate in the Tory leadership contest following Margaret Thatcher's unexpected

chronology: Hundred Years' War

1340	The English were victorious at the naval battle of Sluys.
1346	Battle of Crécy, a victory for the English.
1347	The English took Calais.
1356	Battle of Poitiers, where Edward the Black Prince defeated the French. King John of France was captured.
late 1350s– early 1360s	France had civil wars, brigandage, and the popular uprising of the ◊Jacquerie.
1360	Treaty of Brétigny-Calais. France accepted English possession of Calais and of a greatly enlarged duchy of Gascony. John was ransomed for £500,000.
1369–1414	The tide turned in favour of the French, and when there was another truce in 1388, only Calais, Bordeaux, and Bayonne were in English hands. A state of half-war continued for many years.
1415	Henry V invaded France and won a victory at Agincourt, followed by conquest of Normandy.
1419	In the Treaty of Troyes, Charles VI of France was forced to disinherit his son, the Dauphin, in favour of Henry V, who was to marry Catherine, Charles's daughter. Most of N France was in English hands.
1422–28	After the death of Henry V his brother Bedford was generally successful.
1429	Joan of Arc raised the siege of Orléans, and the Dauphin was crowned Charles VII at Rheims.
1430–53	Even after Joan's capture and death the French continued their successful counter-offensive, and in 1453 only Calais was left in English hands.

resignation. He retained his post as foreign secretary in Prime Minister John Major's new cabinet formed after the 1992 general election.

Huskisson William 1770–1830. British Conservative politician, financier, and advocate of free trade. He served as secretary to the Treasury 1807–09 and colonial agent for Ceylon (now Sri Lanka). He was active in the ◊Corn Law debates and supported their relaxation in 1821.

Hyde Douglas 1860–1949. Irish scholar and politician. Founder president of the Gaelic League 1893– 1915 (aiming to promote a cultural, rather than political, nationalism), he was president of Eire 1938–45. He was the first person to write a book in modern Irish and to collect Irish folklore, as well as being the author of the first literary history of Ireland. His works include Love Songs of Connacht 1894.

Hywel Dda (Hywel the Good) Welsh king. He succeeded his father Cadell as ruler of Seisyllwg (roughly former Cardiganshire and present Towy Valley), at first jointly with his brother Clydog c. 910–920 then alone 920–950. He extended his realm to Dyfed, Gwynedd, and Powys 942, creating a larger Welsh kingdom than any before. His reign was peaceful, mainly because he was subservient to English kings. He is said to have codified Welsh laws, but there is no contemporary record of this.

Iceni ancient people of E England, who revolted against occupying Romans under ◊Boudicca.

Independent Labour Party (ILP) British socialist party, founded in Bradford 1893 by the Scottish member of Parliament Keir Hardie. In 1900 it joined with trades unions and Fabians in founding the Labour Representation Committee, the nucleus of the ◊Labour Party. Many members left the ILP to join the Communist Party 1921, and in 1932 all connections with the Labour Party were severed. After World War II the ILP dwindled, eventually becoming extinct. James Maxton (1885–1946) was its chair 1926–46.

Indian Mutiny or *Sepoy Rebellion* or *Mutiny* revolt 1857–58 of Indian soldiers (Sepoys) against the British in India. The uprising was confined to the north, from Bengal to the Punjab, and central India. It led to the end of rule by the British ◊East India Company and its replacement by direct British crown administration.

Industrial Revolution the sudden acceleration of technical and economic development that began in Britain in the second half of the 18th century. The traditional agrarian economy was replaced by one dominated by machinery and manufacturing, made possible through technical advances such as the steam engine. This transferred the balance of political power from the landowner to the industrial capitalist and created an urban working class. From 1830 to the early 20th century, the Industrial Revolution spread throughout Europe and the USA and to Japan and the various colonial empires.

INLA abbreviation for ◊Irish National Liberation Army.

intelligence services the British secret intelligence service (founded 1909) is M(ilitary) I(ntelligence) 6 and its agents operate abroad, whereas MI5 is responsible for domestic counter-intelligence. MI5 has as its executive arm Scotland Yard's ◊Special Branch. Britain also has the electronic surveillance centre GCHQ.

MI5 has an estimated annual budget of £175 million and 2,000 full-time staff. It was found in breach of the European Convention on Human Rights 1990 in having carried out secret surveillance of civil-liberties campaigners and covert vetting of applicants for jobs with military contractors. Until 1992 MI6 did not officially exist in peace-time, and Parliament still has no control over the expenditure of the security and intelligence agencies.

Invergordon Mutiny incident in the British Atlantic Fleet, Cromarty Firth, Scotland, 15 Sept 1931. Ratings refused to prepare the ships for sea following the government's cuts in their pay; the cuts were conse-quently modified.

IRA abbreviation for ◊Irish Republican Army.

Ireland: history in prehistoric times Ireland underwent a number of invasions from Europe, the most important of which was that of the Gaels in the 3rd century BC. Gaelic Ireland was divided into kingdoms, nominally subject to an *Ardri* or High King; the chiefs were elected under the tribal or Brehon law, and were usually at war with one another. Christianity was introduced by St ◊Patrick about 432, and dur-ing the 5th and 6th centuries Ireland became the home of a civilization which sent out missionaries to Britain and Europe. From about 800 the Danes began to raid Ireland, and later founded Dublin and other coastal towns, until they were defeated by Brian Boru (king from 976) at Clontarf 1014. Anglo-Norman adventurers invaded Ireland 1167, but by the end of the medieval period English rule was still confined to the Pale, the territory around Dublin. The Tudors adopted a policy of con-quest, confiscation of Irish land, and plantation by English settlers, and further imposed the ◊Reformation and English law on Ireland. The most important of the plantations was that of Ulster, carried out under James I 1610. In 1641 the Irish took advantage of the developing strug-gle in England between king and Parliament to begin a revolt which was crushed by Oliver ◊Cromwell 1649, the estates of all 'rebels' being confiscated. Another revolt 1689–91 was also defeated, and the Roman

Ireland: chronology to 1800

432	St Patrick's mission to Ireland.
563	St Columba founds the monastery at Iona.
590	St Columbanus sails to France.
795	First Viking raids on Ireland.
841	Vikings found Dublin.
1002	Brian Boru acknowledged High King of Ireland.
1014	Brian Boru killed as he defeats Norsemen at Battle of Clontarf.
1169	Norman invasion of Ireland begins.
1171	Henry II lands at Waterford.
1175	Treaty of Windsor.
1315	Edward Bruce invades Ireland.
1318	Edward Bruce killed at Battle of Faughart.
1366	Statutes of Kilkenny.
1394	First visit of Richard II to Ireland.
1399	Second visit of Richard II to Ireland.
1494	Poynings' parliament.
1513	Rule of Garret More, Earl of Kildare.
1534	Rebellion of 'Silken Thomas'.
1541	Irish parliament confirms Henry VIII as king of Ireland.
1569	First Desmond rebellion.
1579	Second Desmond rebellion.
1586	Plantation of Munster.
1594	Rebellion of Hugh O'Neill, Earl of Tyrone.
1598	Battle of the Yellow Ford.
1601	Battle of Kinsale; O'Neill defeated.
1603	Treaty of Mellifont.
1607	Flight of the Earls.
1609	Plantation of Ulster.
1633	Sir Thomas Wentworth becomes Lord Deputy of Ireland.
1641	Ulster rising begins.
1642	Confederation of Kilkenny formed.
1646	Owen Roe O'Neill defeats Robert Monro at Battle of Benburb.
1649	Oliver Cromwell captures Drogheda and Wexford.
1652	Land confiscation begins.
1681	Oliver Plunkett executed in London.
1689	Siege of Londonderry.
1690	William III wins Battle of the Boyne.
1691	Treaty of Limerick, followed by land confiscation.
1695	Penal laws introduced against Catholics.
1720	Act declaring British parliament's right to legislate for Ireland passed.
1779	Volunteers parade in Dublin; trade restrictions repealed.

1782	Convention of Volunteers at Dungannon; Irish parliamentary independence conceded.
1791	Society of United Irishmen formed.
1792	Catholic Relief Acts ease penal laws against Catholics.
1795	Orange Order founded in Co Armagh.
1798	United Irishmen's rising fails; Wolfe Tone commits suicide.
1800	Acts of Union passed; end of Grattan's parliament.

Ireland 1801–1921

1800	Act of Union established United Kingdom of Great Britain and Ireland. Effective 1801.
1823	Catholic Association founded by Daniel O'Connell to campaign for Catholic political rights.
1828	O'Connell elected for County Clare; forces granting of rights for Catholics to sit in Parliament.
1829	Catholic Emancipation Act.
1838	Tithe Act (abolishing payment) removed a major source of discontent.
1840	Franchise in Ireland reformed. 'Young Ireland' formed.
1846–51	Potato famine resulted in widespread death and emigration. Population reduced by 20%.
1850	Irish Franchise Act extended voters from 61,000 to 165,000.
1858	Fenian Brotherhood formed.
1867	Fenian insurrection failed.
1869	Church of Ireland disestablished.
1870	Land Act provided greater security for tenants but failed to halt agrarian disorders. Protestant Isaac Butt formed Home Government Association (Home Rule League).
1874	Home Rule League won 59 Parliamentary seats and adopted a policy of obstruction.
1880	Charles Stuart Parnell became leader of Home Rulers, dominated by Catholic groups. 'Boycotts' against landlords unwilling to agree to fair rents.
1881	Land Act greeted with hostility. Parnell imprisoned. 'No Rent' movement began.
1882	'Kilmainham Treaty' between government and Parnell agreed conciliation. Chief Secretary Cavendish and Under Secretary Burke murdered in Phoenix Park, Dublin.
1885	Franchise Reform gave Home Rulers 85 seats in new parliament and ba ance between Liberals and Tories. Home Rule Bill rejected.
1886	Home Rule Bill rejected again.

1890	Parnell cited in divorce case, which split Home Rule movement.
1893	Second Home Rule Bill defeated in House of Lords; Gaelic League founded.
1900	Irish Nationalists reunited under Redmond. 82 MPs elected.
1902	Sinn Féin founded by Arthur Griffith.
1906	Bill for devolution of power to Ireland rejected by Nationalists.
1910	Sir Edward Carson led Unionist opposition to Home Rule.
1912	Home Rule Bill for whole of Ireland introduced. (Protestant) Ulster Volunteers formed to resist.
1913	Home Rule Bill defeated in House of Lords but overridden. (Catholic) Irish Volunteers founded in the South.
1914	Nationalists persuaded to exclude Ulster from Bill for six years but Carson rejected it. Curragh 'mutiny' cast doubt on reliability of British troops against Protestants. Extensive gun-running by both sides. World War I deferred implementation.
1916	Easter Rising by members of Irish Republican Brotherhood. Suppressed by troops and leaders executed.
1919	Irish Republican Army (IRA) formed.
1921	Partition of Ireland; creation of Irish Free State. For subsequent history, see ◊Ireland, Republic of and ◊Ireland, Northern.

Catholic majority held down by penal laws. In 1739–41 a famine killed one-third of the population of 1.5 million.

The subordination of the Irish parliament to that of England, and of Irish economic interests to English, led to the rise of a Protestant patriot party, which in 1782 forced the British government to remove many commercial restrictions and grant the Irish parliament its independence. This did not satisfy the population, who in 1798, influenced by French revolutionary ideas, rose in rebellion, but were again defeated; and in 1800 William ◊Pitt induced the Irish parliament to vote itself out of existence by the Act of ◊Union, effective 1 Jan 1801, which brought Ireland under the aegis of the British crown. During another famine 1846–51, 1.5 million people emigrated, mostly to the USA.

By the 1880s there was a strong movement for home rule for Ireland; Gladstone supported it but was defeated by the British Parliament. By 1914, home rule was conceded but World War I delayed implementation.

The *Easter Rising* took place April 1916, when nationalists seized the Dublin general post office and proclaimed a republic. After a week of fighting, the revolt was suppressed by the British army and most of its leaders executed. From 1918 to 1921 there was guerrilla warfare against the British army, especially by the ◊Irish Republican Army(IRA), formed by Michael Collins 1919. This led to a split in the rebel forces, but in 1921 the Anglo-Irish Treaty resulted in partition and the creation of the Irish Free State in S Ireland. For history since that date, see ◊Ireland, Republic of; ◊Ireland, Northern.

Ireland, Northern constituent part of the United Kingdom
area 13,460 sq km/5,196 sq mi
capital Belfast
towns Londonderry, Enniskillen, Omagh, Newry, Armagh, Coleraine
features Mourne Mountains, Belfast Lough and Lough Neagh; Giant's Causeway; comprises the six counties (Antrim, Armagh, Down, Fermanagh, Londonderry, and Tyrone) that form part of Ireland's northernmost province of Ulster
exports engineering, especially shipbuilding, textile machinery, air-craft components; linen and synthetic textiles; processed foods, especially dairy and poultry products
currency pound sterling
population (1988 est) 1,578,100
language English
religion Protestant 54%, Roman Catholic 31%
famous people Viscount Montgomery, Lord Alanbrooke
government direct rule from the UK since 1972. Northern Ireland is entitled to send 12 members to the Westminster Parliament. The province costs the UK government £3 billion annually
history for history pre-1921, see ◊Ireland, history. The creation of Northern Ireland dates from 1921 when the mainly Protestant counties of Ulster withdrew from the newly established Irish Free State. Spasmodic outbreaks of violence by the ◊Irish Republican Army continued, but only in 1968–69 were there serious disturbances arising from Protestant polit-ical dominance and discrimination against the Roman Catholic minority in employment and housing. British troops were sent to restore peace and protect Catholics, but disturbances continued and in 1972 the parliament at Stormont was prorogued and superseded by direct rule from Westminster. Under the ◊Anglo-Irish Agreement 1985, the Republic of Ireland was given a consultative role (via an Anglo-Irish conference) in

Ireland, Northern: counties

county	administrative headquarters	area sq km
Ulster province		
Antrim	Belfast	2,830
Armagh	Armagh	1,250
Down	Downpatrick	2,470
Fermanagh	Enniskillen	1,680
Londonderry	Derry	2,070
Tyrone	Omagh	3,160
		13,460

Northern Ireland 1967–   : chronology

1967	Northern Ireland Civil Rights Association set up to press for equal treatment for Catholics in the provinces.
1968	Series of civil rights marches sparked off rioting and violence, especially in Londonderry.
1969	Election results weakened Terence O'Neil's Unionist government. Further rioting led to call-up of (Protestant-based) B-Specials to Royal Ulster Constabulary. Chichester-Clark replaced O'Neil. IRA split into 'official' and 'provisional' wings. RUC disarmed and B-Specials replaced by nonsectarian Ulster Defence Regiment (UDR). British Army deployed in Belfast and Londonderry.
1971	First British soldier killed. Brian Faulkner replaced Chichester-Clark. IRA stepped up bombing campaign.
1972	'Bloody Sunday' in Londonderry when British Army killed 13 demonstrators. Direct rule from Westminster introduced.
1974	'Power sharing' between Protestant and Catholic groups tried but failed. IRA extended bombing campaign to UK mainland. Bombs in Guildford and Birmingham caused a substantial number of fatalities.
1976	British Ambassador in Dublin, Christopher Ewart Biggs, assassinated. Peace Movement founded by Betty Williams and Mairead Corrigan.
1979	British MP Airey Neave assassinated by INLA at the House of Commons.
1980	Meeting of Margaret Thatcher and Irish premier Charles Haughey on a peaceful settlement to the Irish question. Hunger strikes and 'dirty protests' started by Republican prisoners in pursuit of political status.
1981	Hunger strikes led to deaths of Bobby Sands and Francis Hughes; Anglo-Irish Intergovernmental Council formed.

1982	Northern Ireland Assembly created to devolve legislative and executive powers back to the province. SDLP (19%) and Sinn Féin (10%) boycotted the assembly.
1984	Series of reports from various groups on the future of the province. IRA bomb at Conservative Party conference in Brighton killed five people. Second Anglo-Irish Intergovernmental Council summit meeting agreed to oppose violence and cooperate on security; Britain rejected ideas of confederation or joint sovereignty.
1985	Meeting of Margaret Thatcher and Irish premier Garret FitzGerald at Hillsborough produced Anglo-Irish agreement on the future of Ulster; regarded as a sell- out by Unionists.
1986	Unionist opposition to Anglo-Irish agreement included protests and strikes. Loyalist violence against police and Unionist MPs boycotted Westminster.
1987	IRA bombed British Army base in West Germany. Unionist boycott of Westminster ended. Extradition clauses of Anglo-Irish Agreement approved in Eire. IRA bombed Remembrance Day service at Enniskillen – later admitted it to be a 'mistake'.
1988	Three IRA bombers killed by security forces on Gibraltar.
1989	After serving fourteen years in prison, the 'Guildford Four' were released when their convictions were ruled unsound by the Court of Appeal.
1990	Anglo-Irish Agreement threatened when Eire refused extraditions. Convictions of 'Birmingham Six' also called into question and sent to the Court of Appeal.
1991	IRA renewed bombing campaign on British mainland, targetting a meeting of the cabinet in Downing Street and mainline railway stations.
1992	Jan: government sent 100 extra troops following futher acts of terrorism. June: leaders of four main political parties as well as British and Irish government ministers hold round-table talks for first time in 70 years; an agenda for further talks on the future of the province agreed. Aug: UDA officially proscribed as an illegal organization. Nov: round-table talks on furture of province ended without agreement.
1993	May: Northern Ireland Secretary, Sir Patrick Mayhew, denied secret talks with IRA, but it emerged that there had been clandestine contact between the government and Sinn Féin/IRA representatives on possible end to conflict. June: Irish president Mary Robinson met Sinn Féin leader Gerry Adams during visit to Belfast. Dec: Major and Reynolds issue joint Anglo-Irish peace proposal for Northern Ireland, the Downing Street Declaration. Gerry Adams calls for 'direct and unconditional talks' between Britain and Ireland and Sinn Féin/IRA.

the government of Northern Ireland, but agreed that there should be no change in its status except by majority consent. The agreement was approved by Parliament, but all 12 Ulster members gave up their seats, so that by-elections could be fought as a form of 'referendum' on the views of the province itself. A similar boycotting of the Northern Ireland Assembly led to its dissolution 1986 by the UK government. Job discrimination was outlawed under the Fair Employment Act 1975, but in 1987 Catholics were two and a half times more likely to be unemployed than their Protestant counterparts – a differential that had not improved since 1971. In 1993, unemployment was running at 14.2%, and 75% of the unemployed were Catholic. Residential integration is still sparse: in 1993 650,000 people live in areas that are 90% Catholic or Protestant. Between 1969 and 1991 violence had claimed 2,872 lives in Northern Ireland; another 94 people were killed 1991. At the end of 1991 there were 11,000 regular soldiers and 6,000 Ulster Defence Regiment members in Northern Ireland.

The question of Northern Ireland's political future was debated in talks held in Belfast April–Sept 1991 — the first direct negotiations between the political parties for 16 years. These preliminary discussions laid the foundations for a dialogue between the British government and the main Northern Ireland parties, which was set in motion 1992.

Ireland, Republic of country occupying the main part of the island of Ireland, NW Europe. It is bounded E by the Irish Sea, S and W by the Atlantic Ocean, and NE by Northern Ireland.

government The 1937 constitution provides for a president, elected by universal suffrage for a seven-year term, and a two-chamber national parliament, consisting of a senate, Seanad éireann, and a house of representatives, Dáil éireann, serving a five-year term. The senate has 60 members, 11 nominated by the prime minister (Taoiseach) and 49 elected by panels representative of most aspects of Irish life. The Dáil consists of 166 members elected by universal suffrage through a system of proportional representation. The president appoints a prime minister who is nominated by the Dáil, which is subject to dissolution by the president when the government has ceased to retain the support of a majority in the Dáil.

Ireland, Republic of: counties

county	administrative headquarters	area sq km
Ulster province		
Cavan	Cavan	1,890
Donegal	Lifford	4,830
Monaghan	Monaghan	1,290
Munster province		
Clare	Ennis	3,190
Cork	Cork	7,460
Kerry	Tralee	4,700
Limerick	Limerick	2,690
Tipperary (N)	Nenagh	2,000
Tipperary (S)	Clonmel	2,260
Waterford	Waterford	1,840
Leinster province		
Carlow	Carlow	900
Dublin	Dublin	920
Kildare	Naas	1,690
Kilkenny	Kilkenny	2,060
Laois	Port Laoise	1,720
Longford	Longford	1,040
Louth	Dundalk	820
Meath	Trim	2,340
Offaly	Tullamore	2,000
Westmeath	Mullingar	1,760
Wexford	Wexford	2,350
Wicklow	Wicklow	2,030
Connacht province		
Galway	Galway	5,940
Leitrim	Carrick-on-Shannon	1,530
Mayo	Castlebar	5,400
Roscommon	Roscommon	2,460
Sligo	Sligo	1,800
		68,910

Ireland, Republic of: chronology

1916	Easter Rising: nationalists against British rule seized the Dublin general post office and proclaimed a republic; the revolt was suppressed by the British army and most of the leaders were executed.
1918–21	Guerrilla warfare against British army led to split in rebel forces.
1921	Anglo-Irish Treaty resulted in creation of the Irish Free State (Southern Ireland).
1937	Independence achieved from Britain.
1949	Eire left the Commonwealth and became the Republic of Ireland.
1973	Fianna Fáil defeated after 40 years in office; Liam Cosgrave formed a coalition government.
1977	Fianna Fáil returned to power, with Jack Lynch as prime minister.
1979	Lynch resigned, succeeded by Charles Haughey.
1981	Garret FitzGerald formed a coalition.
1983	New Ireland Forum formed, but rejected by the British government.
1985	Anglo-Irish Agreement signed.
1986	Protests by Ulster Unionists against the agreement.
1987	General election won by Charles Haughey.
1988	Relations with UK at low ebb because of disagreement over extradition decisions.
1989	Haughey failed to win majority in general election. Progressive Democrats given cabinet positions in coalition government.
1990	Mary Robinson elected president; John Bruton became Fine Gael leader.
1992	Jan: Haughey resigned after losing parliamentary majority. Feb: Albert Reynolds became Fianna Fáil leader and prime minister. June: National referendum approved ratification of Maastricht Treaty. Nov: Reynolds lost confidence vote; election result inconclusive.
1993	Jan: Fianna Fáil–Labour coalition formed; Reynolds re-elected prime minister. May: Irish President, Mary Robinson, meets Queen Elizabeth in London. Dec: Major and Reynolds issue joint Anglo-Irish peace proposal for Northern Ireland, the Downing Street Declaration. Gerry Adams calls for 'direct and unconditional talks' between Britain and Ireland and Sinn Fein/IRA.

history For history pre-1921, see ◊Ireland, history. In 1921 a treaty gave Southern Ireland dominion status within the ◊Commonwealth, while six out of the nine counties of Ulster remained part of the UK, with limited self-government. The Irish Free State, as Southern Ireland was formally called 1921, was accepted by IRA leader Michael Collins but not by many of his colleagues, who shifted their allegiance to the Fianna Fáil party leader éamon ◊de Valera. A civil war ensued, in which Collins was killed.

The partition was eventually acknowledged 1937 when a new constitution established the country as a sovereign state under the name of Eire.

after independence The IRA continued its fight for an independent, unified Ireland through a campaign of violence, mainly in Northern Ireland but also on the British mainland and, to a lesser extent, in the Irish republic. Eire remained part of the Commonwealth until 1949, when it left, declaring itself the Republic of Ireland, while Northern Ireland remained a constituent part of the UK. In 1973 Fianna Fáil, having held office for over 40 years, was defeated, and Liam Cosgrave formed a coalition of the Fine Gael and Labour parties.

In 1977 Fianna Fáil returned to power, with Jack Lynch as prime minister. In 1979 IRA violence intensified with the killing of Earl Mountbatten in Ireland and 18 British soldiers in Northern Ireland. Lynch resigned later the same year, and was succeeded by Charles Haughey. His aim was a united Ireland, with considerable independence for the six northern counties. After the 1981 election Garret FitzGerald, leader of Fine Gael, formed another coalition with Labour but was defeated the following year on budget proposals and resigned. Haughey returned to office with a minority government, but he, too, had to resign later that year, resulting in the return of FitzGerald.

Anglo-Irish Agreement In 1983 all the main Irish and Northern Irish political parties initiated the New Ireland Forum as a vehicle for discussion. Its report was rejected by Margaret Thatcher's Conservative government in the UK, but discussions between London and Dublin resulted in the signing of the Anglo-Irish Agreement 1985, providing for regular consultation and exchange of information on political, legal, security, and cross-border matters. The agreement also said that the status of Northern Ireland would not be changed without the consent of a majority of the people. The agreement was criticized by the Unionist parties of Northern Ireland, who asked that it be rescinded. FitzGerald's coalition ended 1986, and the Feb 1987 election again returned Fianna Fáil and Charles Haughey.

relations with UK In 1988 relations between the Republic of Ireland and the UK were at a low ebb because of disagreements over extradition decisions. In 1989 Haughey failed to win a majority in the election and entered into a coalition with the Progressive Democrats (a breakaway party from Fianna Fáil), putting two of their members into the cabinet. In Nov 1990, after being dismissed as deputy prime minister, Brian Lenihan was defeated in the presidential election by the left-wing-backed Mary Robinson. In the same month Alan Dukes resigned the leadership of Fine Gael, to be replaced by the right-winger John Bruton.

Haughey resigns The Progressive Democrat leader Desmond O'Malley withdrew from the coalition after allegations Jan 1992 against Haughey of illegal telephone-tapping. As a result, Haughey lost his parliamentary majority and resigned as Fianna Fáil leader and prime minister. He was succeeded Feb 1992 by Albert Reynolds. Reynolds immediately reconstructed the cabinet, with David Andrews as foreign minister and Bertie Ahern as finance minister.

In a national referendum June 1992, Ireland showed its approval of the Maastricht Treaty on European union when 69% voted in favour in a turnout of 57%. Campaigning hard for the treaty, Reynolds said that it was essential for Ireland's economy to maintain close links with the European Community.

Fianna Fáil–Labour coalition Having failed to win a confidence vote in the Dáil, Reynolds called a general election Nov 1992. The result gave no party a working majority, although Labour made substantial gains under Dick Spring. In Jan 1993, after prolonged negotiations, Reynolds succeeded in forming a Fianna Fáil–Labour coalition, with Spring as deputy to Reynolds in the post of minister for foreign affairs.

Ireton Henry 1611–1651. English Civil War general. He joined the parliamentary forces and fought at ◊Edgehill 1642, Gainsborough 1643, and ◊Naseby 1645. After the Battle of Naseby, Ireton, who was opposed to both the extreme republicans and ◊Levellers, strove for a compromise with Charles I, but then played a leading role in his trial and execution. He married his leader Cromwell's daughter in 1646. Lord Deputy in Ireland from 1650, he died after the capture of Limerick.

Irish nationalism political movement objecting to British rule of Ireland (which had no elected government of its own but sent members to the British Parliament in Westminster) and campaigned for ◊Home Rule.

In the ◊Easter Rising 1916 an armed rebellion that aimed to secure Irish independence from British rule was crushed by the British army. In 1919 fighting broke out in Ireland between the British army and the Irish Republican Army (IRA), a guerrilla unit formed by the political group Sinn Féin. In the 1921 treaty partitioning Ireland, southern Ireland became independent (Irish Free State 1922) with the province of Northern Ireland voting to remain part of Britain.

Irish nationalism see ◊Ireland, history and ◊Ireland, Northern.

Irish National Liberation Army (INLA) guerrilla organization committed to the end of British rule in Northern Ireland and the incorporation of Ulster into the Irish Republic. The INLA was a 1974 offshoot of the Irish Republican Army (IRA). Among the INLA's activities was the killing of British politician Airey Neave in 1979. From the late 1980s, the INLA was riven with internal disputes and often bloody factionalism, although it still claimed responsibility for attacks periodically.

Irish Republican Army (IRA) militant Irish nationalist organization whose aim is to create a united Irish socialist republic including Ulster. The paramilitary wing of ◊Sinn Féin, it was founded 1919 by Michael ◊Collins and fought a successful war against Britain 1919-21. It came to the fore again 1939 with a bombing campaign in Britain, having been declared illegal in 1936. Its activities intensified from 1968 onwards, as the civil-rights disorders ('the Troubles') in Northern Ireland developed. In 1970 a group in the north broke away to become the *Provisional IRA*; its objective is the expulsion of the British from Northern Ireland.

In 1974 a further breakaway occurred, of the left-wing Irish

Republican Socialist Party with its paramilitary wing, the Irish National Liberation Army (INLA).

The IRA is committed to the use of force in trying to achieve its objectives, and it regularly carries out bombings and shootings. In 1979 it murdered Louis ◊Mountbatten, and its bomb attacks in Britain have included: Birmingham, Guildford, and Woolwich pub bombs 1974; Chelsea Barracks, London, 1981; Harrods department store, London, 1983; Brighton 1984 (an attempt to kill members of the UK cabinet during the Conservative Party conference); 10 Downing Street, London, 1991 (an assassination attempt on John Major and senior cabinet ministers); Victoria Station, London, 1991; City of London, 1992; Oxford Street, London, 1992; Harrods department store, London, 1993; Camden High Street, London, 1993; Warrington, 1993; City of London, 1993.

In 1993 there was controversy when it emerged the British government had been conducting secret discussions with the IRA on ways to end the conflict, with both sides disputing the nature and content of the dialogue.

Ironsides nickname of regiment raised by ◊Cromwell 1643 during the ◊Civil War. It was noted for its discipline and religious fanaticism, and first won fame at the Battle of ◊Marston Moor 1644. The nickname came from that of 'Ironside' given Cromwell by Prince ◊Rupert.

Isaacs Rufus Daniel, 1st Marquess of Reading 1860–1935. British Liberal lawyer and politician. As Lord Chief Justice he tried the Irish nationalist Roger Casement in 1916. Viceroy of India 1921–26; foreign secretary 1931.

Isle of Man see ◊Man, Isle of.

Isle of Wight see ◊Wight, Isle of.

J

Jack the Ripper popular name for the unidentified murderer and mutilator of at least five women prostitutes in the Whitechapel area of London in 1888.

Jacobite in Britain, a supporter of the royal house of Stuart after the deposition of James II in 1688. They include the Scottish Highlanders, who rose unsuccessfully under ◊Claverhouse in 1689; and those who rose in Scotland and N England under the leadership of ◊James Edward Stuart, the Old Pretender, in 1715, and followed his son ◊Charles Edward Stuart in an invasion of England that reached Derby in 1745–46. After the defeat at ◊Culloden, Jacobitism disappeared as a political force.

James two kings of Britain:

James I 1566–1625. King of England from 1603 and Scotland (as *James VI*) from 1567. The son of Mary Queen of Scots and Lord Darnley, he succeeded on his mother's abdication from the Scottish throne, assumed power 1583, established a strong centralized authority, and in 1589 married Anne of Denmark (1574–1619). As successor to Elizabeth I in England, he alienated the Puritans by his High Church views and Parliament by his assertion of ◊divine right, and was generally unpopular because of his favourites, such as ◊Buckingham, and his schemes for an alliance with Spain. He was succeeded by his son Charles I.

James II 1633–1701. King of England and Scotland (as *James VII*) from 1685, second son of Charles I. He succeeded Charles II. James married Anne Hyde 1659 (1637–1671, mother of Mary II and Anne) and ◊Mary of Modena 1673 (mother of James Edward Stuart). He became a Catholic 1671, which led first to attempts to exclude him from the succession, then to the rebellions of ◊Monmouth and ◊Argyll, and finally to the Whig and Tory leaders' invitation to William of Orange to take the throne in 1688. James fled to France, then led an uprising in Ireland 1689, but after defeat at the Battle of the ◊Boyne 1690 remained in exile in France.

James seven kings of Scotland:

James I 1394–1437. King of Scotland 1406–37, who assumed power 1424. He was a cultured and strong monarch whose improvements in the administration of justice brought him popularity among the common people. He was assassinated by a group of conspirators led by the Earl of Atholl.

James II 1430–1460. King of Scotland from 1437, who assumed power 1449. The only surviving son of James I, he was supported by most of the nobles and parliament. He sympathized with the Lancastrians during the Wars of the ◊Roses, and attacked English possessions in S Scotland. He was killed while besieging Roxburgh Castle.

James III 1451–1488. King of Scotland from 1460, who assumed power 1469. His reign was marked by rebellions by the nobles, including his brother Alexander, Duke of Albany. He was murdered during a rebellion supported by his son, who then ascended the throne as James IV.

James IV 1473–1513. King of Scotland from 1488, who married Margaret (1489–1541, daughter of Henry VII) in 1503. He came to the throne after his followers murdered his father, James III, at Sauchieburn. His reign was internally peaceful, but he allied himself with France against England, invaded 1513 and was defeated and killed at the Battle of ◊Flodden. James IV was a patron of poets and architects as well as a military leader.

James V 1512–1542. King of Scotland from 1513, who assumed power 1528. During the long period of his minority, he was caught in a struggle between pro-French and pro-English factions. When he assumed power, he allied himself with France and upheld Catholicism against the Protestants. Following an attack on Scottish territory by Henry VIII's forces, he was defeated near the border at Solway Moss 1542.

James VI of Scotland. See ◊James I of England.

James VII of Scotland. See ◊James II of England.

James Edward Stuart 1688–1766. British prince, known as the *Old Pretender* (for the ◊Jacobites, he was James III). Son of James II, he was born at St James's Palace and after the revolution of 1688 was taken to France. He landed in Scotland in 1715 to head a Jacobite rebellion but withdrew through lack of support. In his later years he settled in Rome.

Jamestown first permanent British settlement in North America, established by Captain John Smith 1607, named after James I. It was capital of Virginia 1624–99.

Jarrow Crusade march in 1936 from Jarrow to London, protesting at the high level of unemployment following the closure of Palmer's shipyard in the town.

Jeffreys George, 1st Baron 1648–1689. Welsh judge, popularly known as the hanging judge. He became Chief Justice of the King's Bench in 1683, and presided over many political trials, notably those of Philip Sidney, Titus Oates, and Richard Baxter, becoming notorious for his brutality.

Jellicoe John Rushworth, 1st Earl 1859–1935. British admiral who commanded the Grand Fleet 1914–16 during World War I; the only action he fought was the inconclusive battle of ◊Jutland. He was First Sea Lord 1916–17, when he failed to push the introduction of the convoy system to combat U-boat attack. Created 1st Earl 1925.

Jenkins Roy (Harris), Lord Jenkins 1920–   . British politician. He became a Labour minister 1964, was home secretary 1965–67 and 1974–76, and chancellor of the Exchequer 1967–70. He was president of the European Commission 1977–81. In 1981 he became one of the founders of the Social Democratic Party and was elected 1982, but lost his seat 1987. In the same year, he was elected chancellor of Oxford University and made a life peer.

Jenkins's Ear, War of war 1739 between Britain and Spain, arising from Britain's illicit trade in Spanish America; it merged into the War of the ◊Austrian Succession 1740–48. The name derives from the claim of Robert Jenkins, a merchant captain, that his ear had been cut off by Spanish coastguards near Jamaica. The incident was seized on by opponents of Robert ◊Walpole who wanted to embarrass his government's antiwar policy and force war with Spain.

Jervis John, Earl of St Vincent 1735–1823. English admiral who secured the blockage of Toulon, France, 1795 in the Revolutionary Wars, and the defeat of the Spanish fleet off Cape St Vincent 1797, in which Admiral ◊Nelson played a key part. Jervis was a rigid disciplinarian.

Joan of Kent 1328–1385. Countess of Kent. She married ◊Edward the Black Prince 1361 and their younger son became ◊Richard II. ◊John of Gaunt took refuge at her home in Kennington when his palace was besieged by Londoners 1376. Her beauty and gentleness earned her the nickname 'Fair Maid of Kent'.

John (I) Lackland 1167–1216. King of England from 1199 and acting king from 1189 during his brother Richard the Lion-Heart's absence on the third Crusade. He lost Normandy and almost all the other English possessions in France to Philip II of France by 1205. His repressive policies and excessive taxation brought him into conflict with his barons, and he was forced to seal the ◊Magna Carta 1215. Later repudiation of it led to the first Barons' War 1215–17, during which he died.

John of Gaunt 1340–1399. English nobleman and politician, born in Ghent, fourth son of Edward III, Duke of Lancaster from 1362. He distinguished himself during the Hundred Years' War. During Edward's last years, and the years before Richard II attained the age of majority, he acted as head of government, and Parliament protested against his corrupt rule.

John of Lancaster Duke of Bedford 1389–1435. English prince, third son of Henry IV. He was regent of France 1422–31 during the minority of Henry VI, his nephew, and protector of England 1422–35. He mostly left English affairs to his brother, Humphrey, duke of Gloucester. He allowed Joan of Arc to be burnt as a witch 1431 and had Henry VI crowned king of France 1431.

Johnson Amy 1903–1941. English aviator. She made a solo flight from England to Australia 1930, in 9 1/2 days, and in 1932 made the fastest ever solo flight from England to Cape Town, South Africa. Her plane ditched in the English Channel in World War II while she was serving with the Air Transport Auxiliary.

Jones Thomas 1870–1955. Welsh politician who gave up an academic career (professor of economics at Queens University, Belfast, 1909) to become a political advisor. He acted first for Lloyd George, as assisstant secretary of the War Cabinet 1916, and then successively for Bonar Law, Baldwin, and MacDonald. He was also highly successful as a fundraiser.

Joyce William 1906–1946. Born in New York, son of a naturalized Irish-born American, he carried on fascist activity in the UK as a 'British subject'. During World War II he made propaganda broadcasts from Germany to the UK, his upper-class accent earning him the nickname *Lord Haw Haw*. He was hanged for treason.

Jute member of a Germanic people who originated in Jutland but later settled in Frankish territory. They occupied Kent, SE England, about 450, according to tradition under Hengist and Horsa, and conquered the Isle of Wight and the opposite coast of Hampshire in the early 6th century.

Jutland, Battle of naval battle of World War I, fought between England and Germany on 31 May 1916, off the W coast of Jutland. Its outcome was indecisive, but the German fleet remained in port for the rest of the war.

K

KBE abbreviation for *Knight* (Commander of the Order) of the British Empire.

Keble John 1792–1866. Anglican priest and religious poet. His sermon on the decline of religious faith in Britain, preached 1833, heralded the start of the ◊Oxford Movement, a Catholic revival in the Church of England. Keble College, Oxford, was founded 1870 in his memory.

Keeler Christine 1942– . British prostitute of the 1960s. She became notorious in 1963 after revelations of affairs with both a Soviet attaché and the war minister John ◊Profumo, who resigned after admitting lying to the House of Commons about their relationship. Her patron, the osteopath Stephen Ward, convicted of living on immoral earnings, committed suicide and Keeler was subsequently imprisoned for related offences.

Keeper of the Great Seal in the Middle Ages, an officer who had charge of the Great Seal of England (the official seal authenticating state documents).

Kells, Book of 8th-century illuminated manuscript of the Gospels produced at the monastery of Kells in County Meath, Ireland. It is now in Trinity College library, Dublin.

Kenneth two kings of Scotland:

Kenneth I (called *MacAlpin*) died 858. King of Scotland from about 844. Traditionally, he is regarded as the founder of the Scottish kingdom (Alba) by virtue of his final defeat of the Picts about 844. He invaded Northumbria six times, and drove the Angles and the Britons over the river Tweed.

Kenneth II died 995. King of Scotland from 971, son of Malcolm I. He invaded Northumbria several times, and his chiefs were in constant conflict with Sigurd the Norwegian over the area of Scotland north of the river Spey. He is believed to have been murdered by his subjects.

Kent Bruce 1929– . British peace campaigner who was general secretary of the Campaign for Nuclear Disarmament 1980–85. He has published numerous articles on disarmament, Christianity, and peace. He was a Catholic priest until 1987.

Kent Edward George Nicholas Paul Patrick, 2nd Duke of Kent 1935– . British prince, grandson of George V. His father, *George* (1902–1942), was created Duke of Kent just before his marriage in 1934 to Princess Marina of Greece and Denmark (1906–1968). The second duke succeeded when his father (George Edward Alexander Edmund) was killed in an air crash on active service with the RAF.

Kent and Strathearn Edward, Duke of Kent and Strathearn 1767–1820. British general. The fourth son of George III, he married Victoria Mary Louisa (1786–1861), widow of the Prince of Leiningen, in 1818, and had one child, the future Queen Victoria.

Ketch Jack died 1686. English executioner who included ◊Monmouth in 1685 among his victims; his name was once a common nickname for an executioner.

Kett's Rebellion rebellion 1549 in Norfolk against enclosures of common land. Its leader, Robert Kett, was defeated and executed 1549.

KG abbreviation for *Knight of the Order of the Garter*.

Kidd 'Captain' (William) c. 1645–1701. Scottish pirate. He spent his youth privateering for the British against the French off the North American coast, and in 1695 was given a royal commission to suppress piracy in the Indian Ocean. Instead, he joined a group of pirates in Madagascar. On his way to Boston, Massachusetts, he was arrested 1699, taken to England, and hanged.

Killiecrankie, Battle of in British history, during the first ◊Jacobite uprising, defeat on 7 May 1689 of General Mackay (for William of Orange) by John Graham of ◊Claverhouse, a supporter of James II, at Killiecrankie, Scotland. Despite the victory, Claverhouse was killed and the revolt soon petered out; the remaining forces were routed on 21 Aug.

Kilmainham Treaty in Irish history, an informal secret agreement in April 1882 that secured the release of the nationalist Charles ◊Parnell from Kilmainham jail, Dublin, where he had been imprisoned for six months for supporting Irish tenant farmers who had joined the Land League's campaign for agricultural reform.

Kilmuir David Patrick Maxwell Fyfe, 1st Earl of Kilmuir 1900–1967. British lawyer and Conservative politician. He was solicitor- general 1942–45 and attorney-general in 1945 during the Churchill governments. He was home secretary 1951–54 and lord chancellor 1954–62.

King/Queen's Champion in English history, ceremonial office held by virtue of possessing the lordship of Scrivelsby, Lincolnshire. Sir John Dymoke established his right to champion the monarch on coronation day 1377 and it is still held by his descendant.

Kinglake Alexander William 1809–1891. British historian of the Crimean War who also wrote a Middle East travel narrative Eothen 1844.

King's Council in medieval England, a court that carried out much of the monarch's daily administration. It was first established in the reign of Edward I, and became the Privy Council 1534–36.

Kinnock Neil 1942– . British Labour politician, party leader 1983–92. Born and educated in Wales, he was elected to represent a Welsh constituency in Parliament 1970 (Islwyn from 1983). He was further left than prime ministers Wilson and Callaghan, but as party leader (in succession to Michael Foot) adopted a moderate position, initiating a major policy review 1988–89. He resigned as party leader after Labour's defeat in the 1992 general election.

Kitchener Horatio Herbert, Earl Kitchener of Khartoum 1850–1916. British soldier and administrator. He defeated the Sudanese dervishes at Omdurman 1898 and reoccupied Khartoum. In South Africa, he was Chief of Staff 1900–02 during the Boer War, and commanded the forces in India 1902–09. He was appointed war minister on the outbreak of World War I, and drowned when his ship was sunk on the way to Russia.

Kitchener was born in County Kerry, Ireland. He was commissioned 1871, and transferred to the Egyptian army 1882. Promoted to commander in chief 1892, he forced a French expedition to withdraw in the Fashoda Incident. During the South African War he acted as Lord Roberts's Chief of Staff. He conducted war by scorched-earth policy and created the earliest concentration camps for civilians. Subsequently he commanded the forces in India and acted as British agent in Egypt, and in 1914 received an earldom. As British secretary of state for war from 1914, he modernized the British forces.

knighthood, order of fraternity carrying with it the rank of knight, admission to which is granted as a mark of royal favour or as a reward for public services. During the Middle Ages in Europe such fraternities fell into two classes, religious and secular. The first class, including the *Templars* and the Knights of *St John*, consisted of knights who had taken religious vows and devoted themselves to military service against the Saracens (Arabs) or other non-Christians. The secular orders probably arose from bands of knights engaged in the service of a prince or great noble.

These knights wore the badge of their patrons or the emblems of their patron saints. A knight *bachelor* belongs to the lowest stage of knighthood, not being a member of any specially named order.

The *Order of the Garter*, founded about 1347, is the oldest now in existence; there are eight other British orders: the *Thistle* founded 1687, the Bath *1725, the* St Patrick *1788, the* St Michael and St George *1818, the* Star of India *1861, the* Indian Empire *1878, the* Royal Victorian Order *1896, and the* Order of the British Empire *(OBE) 1917. The* Order of Merit *(OM), founded 1902, comprises the sovereign and no more than 24 prominent individuals.*

Knox John c. 1505–1572. Scottish Protestant reformer, founder of the Church of Scotland. He spent several years in exile for his beliefs, including a period in Geneva where he met John Calvin. He returned to Scotland 1559 to promote Presbyterianism. His books include First Blast of the Trumpet Against the Monstrous Regiment of Women 1558.

L

Labour Party UK political party based on socialist principles, originally formed to represent workers. It was founded in 1900 and first held office in 1924. The first majority Labour government 1945–51 introduced ◊nationalization and the National Health Service, and expanded ◊social security. Labour was again in power 1964–70 and 1974–79. The party leader is elected by Labour members of Parliament.

Labour Representation Committee in British politics, a forerunner 1900–1906 of the Labour Party. The committee was founded in Feb 1900 after a resolution drafted by Ramsay ◊MacDonald and moved by the Amalgamated Society of Railway Workers (now the National Union of Railwaymen) was carried at the 1899 Trades Union Congress (TUC). The resolution called for a special congress of the TUC parliamentary committee to campaign for more Labour members of Parliament. Ramsay MacDonald became its secretary.

Following his efforts, 29 Labour members of Parliament were elected in the 1906 general election, and the Labour Representation Committee was renamed the Labour Party.

Lady in the UK, the formal title of the daughter of an earl, marquis, or duke; and of any woman whose husband is above the rank of baronet or knight, as well as (by courtesy only) the wives of these latter ranks.

laissez faire theory that the state should not intervene in economic affairs, except to break up a monopoly. The phrase originated with the Physiocrats, 18th-century French economists whose maxim was *laissez faire et laissez passer* (literally, 'let go and let pass' – that is, leave the individual alone and let commodities circulate freely). The degree to which intervention should take place is still one of the chief problems of economics. The Scottish economist Adam Smith justified the theory in The Wealth of Nations.

lake dwelling prehistoric village built on piles driven into the bottom of a lake. Such villages are found throughout Europe, in W Africa, South America, Borneo, and New Guinea. British examples include a lake village of the 1st centuries BC and AD excavated near Glastonbury, Somerset.

Lambert John 1619–1683. English general, a cavalry commander in the Civil War under Cromwell (at the battles of Marston Moor, Preston, Dunbar, and Worcester). Lambert broke with Cromwell over the proposal to award him the royal title. After the Restoration he was imprisoned for life.

Lancaster House Agreement accord reached at a conference held in Sept 1979 at Lancaster House, London, between Britain and representative groups of Rhodesia, including the Rhodesian government under Ian Smith and black nationalist groups. The agreement enabled a smooth transition to the independent state of Zimbabwe in 1980.

Lancaster, House of English royal house, a branch of the Plantagenets.

Land League Irish peasant-rights organization, formed 1879 by Michael ◊Davitt and Charles ◊Parnell to fight against tenant evictions. Through its skilful use of the boycott against anyone who took a farm from which another had been evicted, it forced Gladstone's government to introduce a law in 1881 restricting rents and granting tenants security of tenure.

Langton Stephen c. 1150–1228. English priest who was mainly responsible for drafting the charter of rights, the ◊Magna Carta.

Lansbury George 1859–1940. British Labour politician, leader in the Commons 1931–35. He was a member of Parliament for Bow 1910–12 – when he resigned to force a by-election on the issue of votes for women, which he lost – and again 1922–40. In 1921, while mayor of the London borough of Poplar, he went to prison with most of the council rather than modify their policy of more generous unemployment relief.

Lansdowne Henry Charles, 5th Marquis of Lansdowne 1845–1927. British Liberal Unionist politician, governor-general of Canada 1883–88, viceroy of India 1888–93, war minister 1895–1900, and foreign secretary 1900–06. While at the Foreign Office he abandoned Britain's isolationist policy by forming an alliance with Japan and an entente cordiale with France. His letter of 1917 suggesting an offer of peace to Germany created a controversy.

Latimer Hugh 1490–1555. English Christian church reformer and bishop. After his conversion to Protestantism in 1524 he was imprisoned several times but was protected by Cardinal Wolsey and Henry VIII. After the accession of the Catholic Mary, he was burned for heresy.

Laud William 1573–1645. English priest; archbishop of Canterbury from 1633. Laud's High Church policy, support for Charles I's unparliamentary rule, censorship of the press, and persecution of the Puritans all aroused bitter opposition, while his strict enforcement of the statutes against enclosures and of laws regulating wages and prices alienated the propertied classes. His attempt to impose the use of the Prayer Book on the Scots precipitated the English ◊Civil War. Impeached by Parliament 1640, he was imprisoned in the Tower of London, summarily condemned to death, and beheaded.

Lauderdale John Maitland, Duke of Lauderdale 1616–1682. Scottish politician. Formerly a zealous ◊Covenanter, he joined the Royalists 1647, and as high commissioner for Scotland 1667–79 persecuted the Covenanters. He was created duke of Lauderdale 1672, and was a member of the ◊Cabal ministry 1667–73.

Law Andrew Bonar 1858–1923. British Conservative politician. Elected leader of the opposition 1911, he became colonial secretary in Asquith's coalition government 1915–16, chancellor of the Exchequer 1916–19, and Lord Privy Seal 1919–21 in Lloyd George's coalition. He formed a Conservative Cabinet 1922, but resigned on health grounds.

Lawrence T(homas) E(dward), known as *Lawrence of Arabia* 1888–1935. English soldier, scholar, and translator. Appointed to the military intelligence department in Cairo, Egypt, during World War I, he took part in negotiations for an Arab revolt against the Ottoman Turks, and in 1916 attached himself to the emir Faisal. He became a guerrilla leader of genius, combining raids on Turkish communications with the organization of a joint Arab revolt, described in The Seven Pillars of Wisdom 1926.

Lee Jennie, Baroness Lee 1904–1988. British socialist politician. She became a member of Parliament for the Independent Labour Party at the age of 24, and in 1934 married Aneurin ◊Bevan. On the left wing of the Labour Party, she was on its National Executive Committee 1958–70 and was minister of education 1967–70, during which time she was responsible for founding the Open University in 1969. She was made a baroness in 1970.

Leicester Robert Dudley, Earl of Leicester *c.* 1532–1588. English courtier. Son of the Duke of Northumberland, he was created Earl of Leicester 1564. Queen Elizabeth I gave him command of the army sent to the Netherlands 1585–87 and of the forces prepared to resist the threat of Spanish invasion 1588. His lack of military success led to his recall, but he retained Elizabeth's favour until his death.

Leland John 1506–1552. English antiquary whose manuscripts have proved a valuable source for scholars. He became chaplain and librarian to Henry VIII, and during 1534–43 toured England collecting material for a history of English antiquities. The Itinerary was published in 1710.

Lenthall William 1591–1662. English lawyer. Speaker of the House of Commons in the ◊Long Parliament of 1640–60, he played an active part in the Restoration of Charles II.

Leofric Earl of Mercia. English nobleman. He was created earl c. 1034 by King ◊Canute, and was a rival of ◊Godwin, Earl of Essex, supporting ◊Edward the Confessor against him 1051. His wife was Lady ◊Godiva.

Levellers (or Levelers) democratic party in the English Civil War. The Levellers found wide support among Cromwell's New Model Army and the yeoman farmers, artisans, and small traders, and proved a powerful political force 1647–49. Their programme included the establishment of a republic, government by a parliament of one house elected by male suffrage, religious toleration, and sweeping social reforms.

Leven Alexander Leslie, 1st Earl of Leven c. 1580–1661. Scottish general in the English Civil War. He led the ◊Covenanters' army which invaded England in 1640, commanded the Scottish army sent to aid the English Puritans in 1643–46, and shared in the Parliamentarians' victory over the Royalists in the Battle of Marston Moor.

Leveson-Gower Granville George, 2nd Earl Granville 1815–1891. English politician. He held several cabinet posts 1851–86, including that of foreign secretary 1870–74 and 1880–85 under ♦Gladstone. He supported Gladstone's ♦Home Rule policy and played a leading part in the decision to send General ♦Gordon to Khartoum 1884.

Liberal Democrats in UK politics, common name for the ♦Social and Liberal Democrats.

liberalism political and social theory that favours representative government, freedom of the press, speech, and worship, the abolition of class privileges, the use of state resources to protect the welfare of the individual, and international free trade. It is historically associated with the Liberal Party in the UK and the Democratic Party in the USA.

Liberal Party British political party, the successor to the ♦Whig Party, with an ideology of liberalism. In the 19th century, it represented the interests of commerce and industry. Its outstanding leaders were Palmerston, Gladstone, and Lloyd George. From 1914 it declined, and the rise of the Labour Party pushed the Liberals into the middle ground. The Liberals joined forces with the Social Democratic Party (SDP) as the Alliance for the 1983 and 1987 elections. In 1988, a majority of the SDP voted to merge with the Liberals to form the ♦Social and Liberal Democrats.

The term 'Liberal', used officially from about 1840 and unofficially from about 1815, marked a shift of support for the party from aristocrats to include also progressive industrialists, backed by supporters of the utilitarian reformer ♦Bentham, Nonconformists (especially in Welsh and Scottish constituencies), and the middle classes. During the Liberals' first period of power 1830–41, they promoted parliamentary and municipal government reform and the abolition of slavery, but their laissez-faire theories led to the harsh Poor Law of 1834. Except for two short periods the Liberals were in power 1846–66, but the only major change was the general adoption of free trade. Liberal pressure forced Peel to repeal the Corn Laws 1846, thereby splitting the Tory party. Extended franchise in 1867 and Gladstone's emergence as leader began a new phase, dominated by the Manchester school with a programme of 'peace, retrenchment, and reform'. Gladstone's 1868–74 government introduced many important reforms, including elementary education and vote by ballot. The party's left, mainly composed of working-class Radicals and led by Charles ◊Bradlaugh (a lawyer's clerk) and Joseph ◊Chamberlain (a wealthy manufacturer), repudiated laissez-faire and inclined towards republicanism, but in 1886 the Liberals were split over the policy of Home Rule for Ireland, and many became Liberal Unionists or joined the Conservatives. Except for 1892–95, the Liberals remained out of power until 1906, when, reinforced by Labour and Irish support, they returned with a huge majority. Old-age pensions, National Insurance, limitation of the powers of the Lords, and the Irish Home Rule Bill followed. Lloyd George's alliance with the Conservatives 1916–22 divided the Liberal Party between him and his predecessor Asquith, and although reunited in 1923 the Liberals continued to lose votes. They briefly joined the National Government 1931–32. After World War II they were reduced to a handful of members of Parliament. A revival began under the leadership 1956–67 of Jo Grimond and continued under Jeremy Thorpe, who resigned after a period of controversy within the party in 1976. After a caretaker return by Grimond, David Steel became the first party leader in British politics to be elected by party members who were not MPs. In 1977–78 Steel entered into an agreement to support Labour in any vote of confidence in return for consultation on measures undertaken. He resigned in 1988 and was replaced by Paddy Ashdown.

Liberator, the title given to Daniel ◊O'Connell, Irish political leader.

Lilburne John 1614–1657. English republican agitator. He was imprisoned 1638–40 for circulating Puritan pamphlets, fought in the Parliamentary army in the Civil War, and by his advocacy of a democratic republic won the leadership of the Levellers, the democratic party in the English Revolution.

Lindsey, Parts of former administrative division within Lincolnshire, England. It was the largest of the three administrative divisions (or 'parts') of the county, with its headquarters at Lincoln.

In 1974 Lindsey was divided between the new county of Humberside and a reduced Lincolnshire.

Liverpool Robert Banks Jenkinson, 2nd Earl Liverpool 1770–1825. British Tory politician. He entered Parliament 1790 and was foreign secretary 1801–03, home secretary 1804–06 and 1807–09, war minister 1809–12, and prime minister 1812–27. His government conducted the Napoleonic Wars to a successful conclusion, but its ruthless suppression of freedom of speech and of the press aroused such opposition that during 1815–20 revolution frequently seemed imminent.

Llewelyn two princes of Wales:

Llewelyn I 1173–1240. Prince of Wales from 1194 who extended his rule to all Wales not in Norman hands, driving the English from N Wales 1212, and taking Shrewsbury 1215. During the early part of Henry III's reign, he was several times attacked by English armies. He was married to Joanna, illegitimate daughter of King John.

Llewelyn II ap Gruffydd c. 1225–1282. Prince of Wales from 1246, grandson of Llewelyn I. In 1277 Edward I of England compelled Llewelyn to acknowledge him as overlord and to surrender S Wales. His death while leading a national uprising ended Welsh independence.

Lewes, Battle of battle in 1264 caused by the baronial opposition to the English King Henry III, led by Simon de Montfort, Earl of Leicester (1208–65). The king was defeated and captured at the battle.

Lloyd John, known as *John Scolvus*, 'the skilful', lived 15th century. Welsh sailor who carried on an illegal trade with Greenland and is claimed to have reached North America, sailing as far south as Maryland, in 1477 (15 years before the voyage of Columbus).

Lloyd Selwyn. See ◊Selwyn Lloyd, British Conservative politician.

Lloyd George David 1863–1945. Welsh Liberal politician, prime minister of Britain 1916–22. A pioneer of social reform, as chancellor of the Exchequer 1908–15 he introduced old-age pensions 1908 and health and unemployment insurance 1911. High unemployment, intervention in the Russian Civil War, and use of the military police force, the ◊Black and Tans, in Ireland eroded his support as prime minister, and the creation of the Irish Free State in 1921 and his pro-Greek policy against the Turks caused the collapse of his coalition government.

Lloyd George was born in Manchester, became a solicitor, and was member of Parliament for Caernarvon Boroughs from 1890. During the Boer War, he was prominent as a pro-Boer. His 1909 budget (with graduated direct taxes and taxing land values) provoked the Lords to reject it, and resulted in the Act of 1911 limiting their powers. He held ministerial posts during World War I until 1916 when there was an open breach between him and Prime Minister ◊Asquith, and he became prime minister of a coalition government. Securing a unified Allied command, he enabled the Allies to withstand the last German offensive and achieve victory. After World War I he had a major role in the Versailles peace treaty.

In the 1918 elections, he achieved a huge majority over Labour and Asquith's followers. He had become largely distrusted within his own party by 1922, and never regained power.

lobby individual or pressure group that sets out to influence government action. The lobby is prevalent in the USA, where the term originated in the 1830s from the practice of those wishing to influence state policy waiting for elected representatives in the lobby of the Capitol.

local government that part of government dealing mainly with matters concerning the inhabitants of a particular area or town, usually financed at least in part by local taxes. In the USA and UK, local government has comparatively large powers and responsibilities.

Lollard follower of the English religious reformer John ◊Wycliffe in the 14th century. The Lollards condemned the doctrine of the transubstantiation of the bread and wine of the Eucharist, advocated the diversion of ecclesiastical property to charitable uses, and denounced war and capital punishment. They were active from about 1377; after the passing of the statute *De heretico comburendo* ('The Necessity of Burning Heretics') 1401 many Lollards were burned, and in 1414 they raised an unsuccessful revolt in London, known as Oldcastle's rebellion.

London capital of England and the United Kingdom, on the river Thames; area 1,580 sq km/610 sq mi; population (1991) 6,378,600, larger metropolitan area about 9 million. The *City of London*, known as the 'square mile', area 274 hectares/677 acres, is the financial and

Population of Greater London 1801 to present day (millions)

1801	1.09
1811	1.30
1821	1.57
1831	1.87
1841	2.20
1851	2.65
1861	3.18
1871	3.84
1881	4.71
1891	5.57
1901	6.50
1911	7.16
1921	7.38
1931	8.11
1939	8.61 (est.)
1951	8.19
1961	7.99
1971	7.45
1981	6.71
1991	6.67

commercial centre of the UK. *Greater London* from 1965 comprises the City of London and 32 boroughs. Popular tourist attractions include the Tower of London, St Paul's Cathedral, Buckingham Palace, and Westminster Abbey.

Roman *Londinium* was established soon after the Roman invasion AD 43; in the 2nd century London became a walled city; by the 11th century, it was the main city of England and gradually extended beyond the walls to link with the originally separate Westminster. Throughout the 19th century London was the largest city in the world (in population).

features The Tower of London, built by William the Conqueror on a Roman site, houses the crown jewels and the royal armouries; 15th-century Guildhall; the Monument (a column designed by Christopher Wren) marks the site in Pudding Lane where the Great Fire of 1666 began; Mansion House (residence of the lord mayor); Barbican arts and conference centre; Central Criminal Court (Old Bailey) and the Inner and Middle Temples; Covent Garden, once a vegetable market, is now a tourist shopping and entertainment area.

architecture London contains buildings in all styles of English architecture since the 11th century. *Norman*: the White Tower, Tower of London; St Bartholomew's, Smithfield; the Temple Church. *Gothic*: Westminster Abbey; Westminster Hall; Lambeth Palace; Southwark Cathedral. *Tudor*: St James's Palace; Staple Inn. *17th century*: Banqueting Hall, Whitehall (Inigo Jones); St Paul's, Kensington Palace; many City churches (Wren). *18th century*: Somerset House (Chambers); St Martin-in-the- Fields; Buckingham Palace. *19th century*: British Museum (Neo-Classical); Houses of Parliament; Law Courts (Neo- Gothic); Westminster Cathedral (Byzantine style). *20th century*: Lloyd's of London.

government There has since 1986 been no central authority for Greater London; responsibility is divided between individual boroughs and central government.

The City of London has been governed by a corporation from the 12th century. Its structure and the electoral procedures for its common councillors and aldermen are medievally complex, and it is headed by the lord mayor (who is, broadly speaking, nominated by the former and elected annually by the latter). After being sworn in at the Guildhall, he or she is presented the next day to the lord chief justice at the Royal Courts of Justice in Westminster, and the *Lord Mayor's Show* is a ceremonial procession there in November.

London County Council (LCC) former administrative authority for London created in 1888 by the Local Government Act; it incorporated parts of Kent, Surrey, and Middlesex in the metropolis. It was replaced by the Greater London Council 1964-86.

London, Museum of museum of London's history. It was formed by the amalgamation of the former Guildhall (Roman and medieval) and London (Tudor and later) Museums, housed from 1976 in a building at the junction of London Wall and Aldersgate, near the Barbican.

London Working Men's Association (LWMA) campaigning organization for political reform, founded June 1836 by William Lovett and others, who in 1837 drew up the first version of the People's Charter (see ◊Chartism). It was founded in the belief that popular education, achieved through discussion and access to a cheap and honest press, was a means of obtaining political reform. By 1837 the LWMA had 100 members.

Longford Frank (Francis Aungier) Pakenham, 7th Earl of Longford 1905– . Anglo-Irish Labour politician. He was brought up a Protestant but is now a leading Catholic. He is an advocate of penal reform.

Long Parliament English Parliament 1640–53 and 1659–60, which continued through the Civil War. After the Royalists withdrew in 1642 and the Presbyterian right was excluded in 1648, the remaining ◊Rump ruled England until expelled by Oliver Cromwell in 1653. Reassembled 1659–60, the Long Parliament initiated the negotiations for the restoration of the monarchy.

Lord in the UK, prefix used informally as alternative to the full title of a marquess, earl, or viscount; normally also in speaking of a baron, and as a courtesy title before the forename and surname of younger sons of dukes and marquesses.

Lord Chancellor UK state official; see ◊Chancellor, Lord.

Lords, House of upper house of the UK ◊Parliament.

Louis, Prince of Battenberg 1854–1921. German-born British admiral who took British nationality in 1917 and translated his name to Mountbatten.

Lovat Simon Fraser, 12th Baron Lovat c. 1667–1747. Scottish ◊Jacobite. Throughout a political career lasting 50 years he constantly intrigued with both Jacobites and Whigs, and was beheaded for supporting the 1745 rebellion.

Loyalist member of approximately 30% of the US population remaining loyal to Britain in the American Revolution. Many went to E Ontario, Canada, after 1783. Known as Tories, most Loyalists were crown officials, Anglican clergy, and economically advantaged, although they were represented in every segment of colonial society.

The term also refers to people in Northern Ireland who wish to remain part of the United Kingdom rather than unifying with the Republic of Ireland.

Luddite one of a group of people involved in machine-wrecking riots in N England 1811–16. The organizer of the Luddites was referred to as

General Ludd, but may not have existed. Many Luddites were hanged or transported to penal colonies, such as Australia.

Lugard Frederick John Dealtry, 1st Baron Lugard 1858–1945. British colonial administrator. He served in the army 1878–89 and then worked for the British East Africa Company, for whom he took possession of Uganda in 1890. He was high commissioner for N Nigeria 1900–07, governor of Hong Kong 1907–12, and governor general of Nigeria 1914–19.

Lutine British bullion ship that sank in the North Sea in 1799. Its bell, salvaged in 1859, is at the headquarters in London of Lloyd's, the insurance organization. It is sounded once when a ship is missing and twice for good news.

Lynch 'Jack' (John) 1917– . Irish politician, prime minister 1966–73 and 1977–79. A Gaelic footballer and a barrister, in 1948 he entered the parliament of the republic as a Fianna Fáil member.

Lytton Edward Robert Bulwer-Lytton, 1st Earl of Lytton 1831–1891. British diplomat, viceroy of India 1876–80, where he pursued a controversial 'forward' policy. Only son of the novelist, he was himself a poet under the pseudonym *Owen Meredith*, writing 'King Poppy' 1892 and other poems.

M

Maastricht Treaty treaty on European union, signed 10 Dec 1991 by leaders of European Community (EC) nations at Maastricht in the Netherlands, at a meeting convened to agree on terms for political union. The treaty was formally endorsed by the European Parliament April 1992 but its subsequent rejection by the Danish in a June referendum placed its future in jeopardy. Survival of the treaty appeared more certain after an Edinburgh summit Dec 1992, at which EC leaders agreed to a set of compromises, including limited Danish participation.

Macaulay Thomas Babington, Baron Macaulay 1800–1859. English historian, essayist, poet, and politician, secretary of war 1839–41. His History of England in five volumes 1849–61 celebrates the Glorious Revolution of 1688 as the crowning achievement of the Whig party.

Macbeth died 1057. King of Scotland from 1040. The son of Findlaech, hereditary ruler of Moray, he was commander of the forces of Duncan I, King of Scotia, whom he killed in battle 1040. His reign was prosperous until Duncan's son Malcolm III led an invasion and killed him at Lumphanan.

Macdonald Flora 1722–1790. Scottish heroine who rescued Prince Charles Edward Stuart, the Young Pretender, after his defeat at Culloden 1746. Disguising him as her maid, she escorted him from her home in the Hebrides as far as Skye, whence he fled to France. She was arrested, but released 1747.

MacDonald (James) Ramsay 1866–1937. British politician, first Labour prime minister Jan–Oct 1924 and 1929–31. Failing to deal with worsening economic conditions, he left the party to form a coalition government 1931, which was increasingly dominated by Conservatives, until he was replaced by Stanley Baldwin 1935.

Macleod Iain Norman 1913–1970. British Conservative politician. As colonial secretary 1959–61, he forwarded the independence of former British territories in Africa; he died in office as chancellor of the Exchequer.

Macmillan (Maurice) Harold, 1st Earl of Stockton 1894–1986. British Conservative politician, prime minister 1957–63; foreign secretary 1955 and chancellor of the Exchequer 1955–57. In 1963 he attempted to negotiate British entry into the European Economic Community, but was blocked by French president de Gaulle. Much of his career as prime minister was spent defending the retention of a UK nuclear weapon, and he was responsible for the purchase of US Polaris missiles 1962.

Macmillan was MP for Stockton 1924–29 and 1931–45, and for Bromley 1945–64. As minister of housing 1951–54 he achieved the construction of 300,000 new houses a year. He became prime minister on the resignation of Anthony ◊Eden after the Suez crisis, and led the Conservative Party to victory in the 1959 elections on the slogan 'You've never had it so good' (the phrase was borrowed from a US election campaign). Internationally, his realization of the 'wind of change' in Africa advanced the independence of former colonies. Macmillan's nickname Supermac was coined by the cartoonist Vicky.

Magna Carta in English history, the charter granted by King John 1215, traditionally seen as guaranteeing human rights against the excessive use of royal power. As a reply to the king's demands for excessive feudal dues and attacks on the privileges of the church, Archbishop Langton proposed to the barons the drawing-up of a binding document 1213. John was forced to accept this at Runnymede (now in Surrey) 15 June 1215.

Magna Carta begins by reaffirming the rights of the church. Certain clauses guard against infringements of feudal custom: for example, the king was prevented from making excessive demands for money from his barons without their consent. Others are designed to check extortions by officials or maladministration of justice: for example, no freeman to be arrested, imprisoned, or punished except by the judgement of his peers or the law of the land. The privileges of London and the cities were also guaranteed.

As feudalism declined Magna Carta lost its significance, and under the Tudors was almost forgotten. During the 17th century it was rediscovered and reinterpreted by the Parliamentary party as a democratic document. Four original copies exist, one each in Salisbury and Lincoln cathedrals and two in the British Library.

maid of honour in Britain, the closest attendant on a queen. They are chosen generally from the daughters and granddaughters of peers, but in the absence of another title bear that of Honourable.

Maiden Castle prehistoric hillfort and later earthworks near Dorchester, Dorset, England. The site was inhabited from Neolithic times (about 2000 BC) and was stormed by the Romans AD 43.

Major John 1943– . British Conservative politician, prime minister from Nov 1990.

He was foreign secretary 1989 and chancellor of the Exchequer 1989–90. His earlier positive approach to European Community (EC) matters was hindered during 1991 by divisions within the Conservative Party. Despite continuing public dissatisfaction with the poll tax, the National Health Service, and the recession, Major was returned to power in the April 1992 general election. His subsequent handling of a series of political crises called into question his ability to govern the country effectively.

major-general after the English Civil War, one of the officers appointed by Oliver Cromwell 1655 to oversee the 12 military districts into which England had been divided. Their powers included organizing the militia, local government, and the collection of some taxes.

Malcolm four kings of Scotland, including:

Malcolm III called *Canmore* c. 1031–1093. King of Scotland from 1058, the son of Duncan I (murdered by ◊Macbeth 1040). He fled to England when the throne was usurped by Macbeth, but recovered S Scotland and killed Macbeth in battle 1057. He was killed at Alnwick while invading Northumberland, England.

malt tax in Britain, a tax first imposed 1697 on the use of malt in brewing. It supplemented the existing beer duty when a hop duty was imposed between 1711 and 1862. The malt tax was abolished 1880 when replaced by a tax on drinking beer.

Man, Isle of island in the Irish Sea, a dependency of the British crown, but not part of the UK
area 570 sq km/220 sq mi
capital Douglas
towns Ramsey, Peel, Castletown
features Snaefell 620 m/2,035 ft; annual TT (Tourist Trophy) motorcycle races, gambling casinos, Britain's first free port, tax haven; tailless Manx cat
products light engineering products; tourism, banking, and insurance are important
currency the island produces its own coins and notes in UK currency denominations
population (1986) 64,300
language English (Manx, nearer to Scottish than Irish Gaelic, has been almost extinct since the 1970s)
government crown-appointed lieutenant-governor, a legislative council, and the representative House of Keys, which together make up the Court of Tynwald, passing laws subject to the royal assent. Laws passed at Westminster only affect the island if specifically so provided
history Norwegian until 1266, when the island was ceded to Scotland; it came under UK administration 1765.

manumission in medieval England, the act of freeing a villein or serf from his or her bondage. The process took place in a county court and freedom could either be bought or granted as a reward for services rendered.

Mappa Mundi 13th-century symbolic map of the world. It is circular and shows Asia at the top, with Europe and Africa below and Jerusalem at the centre (reflecting Christian religious rather than geographical belief). It was drawn by David de Bello, a canon at Hereford Cathedral, England, who left the map to the cathedral, where it was used as an altarpiece.

Marconi Scandal scandal 1912 in which UK chancellor Lloyd George and two other government ministers were found by a French newspaper to have dealt in shares of the US Marconi company shortly before it was announced that the Post Office had accepted the British

Marconi company's bid to construct an imperial wireless chain. A parliamentary select committee, biased towards the Liberal government's interests, found that the other four wireless systems were technically inadequate and therefore the decision to adopt Marconi's tender was not the result of ministerial corruption. The scandal did irreparable harm to Lloyd George's reputation.

Margaret (called *the Maid of Norway*) 1282–1290. Queen of Scotland from 1285, the daughter of Eric II, King of Norway, and Princess Margaret of Scotland. When only two years old she became queen of Scotland on the death of her grandfather, Alexander III, but died in the Orkneys on the voyage from Norway to her kingdom.

Margaret of Anjou 1430–1482. Queen of England from 1445, wife of ◊Henry VI of England. After the outbreak of the Wars of the ◊Roses 1455, she acted as the leader of the Lancastrians, but was defeated and captured at the battle of Tewkesbury 1471 by Edward IV.

Margaret, St 1045–1093. Queen of Scotland, the granddaughter of King Edmund Ironside of England. She went to Scotland after the Norman Conquest, and soon after married Malcolm III. The marriage of her daughter Matilda to Henry I united the Norman and English royal houses.

Markievicz Constance Georgina, Countess Markievicz (born Gore Booth) 1868–1927. Irish nationalist who married the Polish count Markievicz 1900. Her death sentence for taking part in the Easter Rising of 1916 was commuted, and after her release from prison 1917 she was elected to the Westminster Parliament as a Sinn Féin candidate 1918 (technically the first British woman member of Parliament), but did not take her seat.

Marlborough John Churchill, 1st Duke of Marlborough 1650–1722. English soldier, created a duke 1702 by Queen Anne. He was granted the Blenheim mansion in Oxfordshire in recognition of his services, which included defeating the French army outside Vienna in the Battle of ◊Blenheim 1704, during the War of the ◊Spanish Succession.

marquess or *marquis* title and rank of a nobleman who in the British peerage ranks below a duke and above an earl. The wife of a marquess is a marchioness.

marshal title given in some countries to a high officer of state. Originally it meant one who tends horses, in particular one who shoes them.

Marston Moor, Battle of battle fought in the English Civil War 2 July 1644 on Marston Moor, 11 km/7 mi W of York. The Royalists were conclusively defeated by the Parliamentarians and Scots.

Martello tower circular tower for coastal defence. Formerly much used in Europe, many were built along the English coast, especially in Sussex and Kent, in 1804, as a defence against the threatened French invasion. The name is derived from a tower on Cape Mortella, Corsica, which was captured by the British with great difficulty 1794, and was taken as a model. They are round towers of solid masonry, sometimes moated, with a flat roof for mounted guns.

Mary Queen of Scots 1542–1587. Queen of Scotland 1542–67. Also known as *Mary Stuart*, she was the daughter of James V. Mary's connection with the English royal line from Henry VII made her a threat to Elizabeth I's hold on the English throne, especially as she represented a champion of the Catholic cause. She was married three times. After her forced abdication she was imprisoned but escaped 1568 to England. Elizabeth I held her prisoner, while the Roman Catholics, who regarded Mary as rightful queen of England, formed many conspiracies to place her on the throne, and for complicity in one of these she was executed.

Mary's mother was the French Mary of Guise. Born in Linlithgow (now in Lothian region, Scotland), Mary was sent to France, where she married the dauphin, later Francis II. After his death she returned to Scotland 1561, which, during her absence, had become Protestant. She married her cousin, the Earl of ◊Darnley, 1565, but they soon quarrelled, and Darnley took part in the murder of Mary's secretary, ◊Rizzio. In 1567 Darnley was assassinated as the result of a conspiracy formed by the Earl of ◊Bothwell, possibly with Mary's connivance, and shortly after Bothwell married her. A rebellion followed; defeated at Carberry Hill, Mary abdicated and was imprisoned. She escaped 1568, raised an army, and after its defeat at Langside fled to England, only to be imprisoned again. A plot against Elizabeth I devised by Anthony Babington led to her trial and execution at Fotheringay Castle 1587.

Mary of Guise, or Mary of Lorraine 1515–1560. French wife of James V of Scotland from 1538, and from 1554 regent of Scotland for her daughter ◊Mary Queen of Scots. A Catholic, she moved from reconciliation with Scottish Protestants to repression, and died during a Protestant rebellion in Edinburgh.

Mary Queen 1867–1953. Consort of George V of the UK. The daughter of the Duke and Duchess of Teck, the latter a grand-daughter of George II, in 1891 she became engaged to the Duke of Clarence, eldest son of the Prince of Wales (later Edward VII). After his death 1892, she married 1893 his brother George, Duke of York, who succeeded to the throne 1910.

Mary two queens of England:

Mary I (called *Bloody Mary*) 1516–1558. Queen of England from 1553. She was the eldest daughter of Henry VIII by Catherine of Aragon. When Edward VI died, Mary secured the crown without difficulty in spite of the conspiracy to substitute Lady Jane ◊Grey. In 1554 Mary married Philip II of Spain, and as a devout Roman Catholic obtained the restoration of papal supremacy and sanctioned the persecution of Protestants. She was succeeded by her half-sister Elizabeth I.

Mary II 1662–1694. Queen of England, Scotland, and Ireland from 1688. She was the Protestant elder daughter of the Catholic ◊James II, and in 1677 was married to her cousin ◊William of Orange. After the 1688 revolution she accepted the crown jointly with William.

Mary of Modena 1658–1718. Queen consort of England and Scotland. She was the daughter of the Duke of Modena, Italy, and married James, Duke of York, later James II, 1673. The birth of their son James Francis Edward Stuart was the signal for the revolution of 1688 that overthrew James II. Mary fled to France.

Mary Rose greatest warship of Henry VIII of England, which sank off Southsea, Hampshire, 19 July 1545. The wreck was located 1971, and raised for preservation in dry dock in Portsmouth harbour 1982.

Matilda *the Empress Maud* 1102–1167. Claimant to the throne of England. On the death of her father, Henry I, 1135, the barons elected her cousin Stephen to be king. Matilda invaded England 1139, and was crowned by her supporters 1141. Civil war ensued until Stephen was finally recognized as king 1153, with Henry II (Matilda's son) as his successor.

Maudling Reginald 1917–1979. British Conservative politician, chancellor of the Exchequer 1962–64, contender for the party leadership 1965, and home secretary 1970–72. He resigned when referred to during the bankruptcy proceedings of the architect John Poulson, since (as home secretary) he would have been in charge of the Metropolitan Police investigating the case.

MBE abbreviation for *Member (of the Order) of the British Empire*, an honour first awarded 1917.

megalith prehistoric stone monument of the late Neolithic or early Bronze Age. Most common in Europe, megaliths include single, large uprights (*menhirs*, for example, the Five Kings, Northumberland, England); *rows* (for example, Carnac, Brittany, France); *circles*, generally with a central 'altar stone'; and the remains of burial chambers with the covering earth removed, looking like a hut (*dolmens*, for example Kits Coty, Kent, England).

Melbourne William Lamb, 2nd Viscount 1779–1848. British Whig politician. Home secretary 1830–34, he was briefly prime minister in 1834 and again 1835–41. Accused in 1836 of seducing Caroline Norton, he lost the favour of William IV.

Melville Henry Dundas, Viscount Melville 1742–1811. British Tory politician, born in Edinburgh. He entered Parliament 1774, and as home secretary 1791–94 persecuted the parliamentary reformers. His impeachment for malversation (misconduct) 1806 was the last in English history.

Mercia Anglo-Saxon kingdom that emerged in the 6th century. By the late 8th century it dominated all England south of the Humber, but from about 825 came under the power of ◊Wessex. Mercia eventually came to denote an area bounded by the Welsh border, the river Humber, East Anglia, and the river Thames.

Merit, Order of British order of chivalry, founded on the lines of an order of ◊knighthood.

Methodism evangelical Protestant Christian movement that was founded by John ◊Wesley 1739 within the Church of England, but became a separate body 1795. The Methodist Episcopal Church was founded in the USA 1784. There are over 50 million Methodists worldwide.

metropolitan county in England, a group of six county councils (1974–86) established under the Local Government Act 1972 in the largest urban areas outside London: Tyne and Wear, South Yorkshire, Merseyside, West Midlands, Greater Manchester, and West Yorkshire. Their elected assemblies were abolished 1986 when their areas of responsibility reverted to district councils, although the counties themselves remain.

Militant Tendency in British politics, left-wing faction originally within the Labour Party, aligned with the publication Militant. It became active in the 1970s, with radical socialist policies based on Trotskyism, and gained some success in local government, for example in the inner-city area of Liverpool. In the mid-1980s the Labour Party considered it to be a separate organization within the party and banned it.

Milner Alfred, Viscount Milner 1854–1925. British colonial administrator. As governor of Cape Colony 1897–1901, he negotiated with Kruger but did little to prevent the second South African War; and as governor of the Transvaal and Orange River colonies 1902–05 after their annexation, he reorganized their administration. In 1916 he became a member of Lloyd George's war cabinet.

Model Parliament English parliament set up 1295 by Edward I; it was the first to include representatives from outside the clergy and aristocracy, and was established because Edward needed the support of the whole country against his opponents: Wales, France, and Scotland. His sole aim was to raise money for military purposes, and the parliament did not pass any legislation.

monarchy, succession to the in the UK, the people who are in line to ascend the throne in the event of the death of the person preceding them. In order they are:

Monck or *Monk* George, 1st Duke of Albemarle 1608–1669. English soldier. During the Civil War he fought for King Charles I, but after being captured changed sides and took command of the Parliamentary forces in Ireland. Under the Commonwealth he became commander in chief in Scotland, and in 1660 he led his army into England and brought about the restoration of Charles II.

Monmouth James Scott, Duke of Monmouth 1649–1685. Claimant to the English crown, the illegitimate son of Charles II and Lucy Walter. After James II's accession 1685, Monmouth landed in England at Lyme Regis, Dorset, claimed the crown, and raised a rebellion, which was crushed at ◊Sedgemoor in Somerset. He was executed with 320 of his accomplices.

Montfort Simon de Montfort, Earl of Leicester c. 1208–1265. English politician and soldier. From 1258 he led the baronial opposition to Henry III's misrule during the second ◊Barons' War and in 1264 defeated and captured the king at Lewes, Sussex. In 1265, as head of government, he summoned the first parliament in which the towns were represented; he was killed at the Battle of Evesham during the last of the Barons' Wars.

Montgomery Bernard Law, 1st Viscount Montgomery of Alamein 1887–1976. British field marshal. In World War II he commanded the 8th Army in N Africa in the Second Battle of El Alamein 1942. As commander of British troops in N Europe from 1944, he received the German surrender 1945.

Montrose James Graham, 1st Marquess of Montrose 1612–1650. Scottish soldier, son of the 4th earl of Montrose. He supported the ◊Covenanters against Charles I, but after 1640 changed sides. Defeated in 1645 at Philiphaugh, he escaped to Norway. Returning in 1650 to raise a revolt, he survived shipwreck only to have his weakened forces defeated, and (having been betrayed to the Covenanters) was hanged in Edinburgh.

Moore (John) Jeremy 1928– . British major general of the Commando Forces, Royal Marines, 1979–82. He commanded the land forces in the UK's conflict with Argentina over the Falklands 1982.

Moore John 1761–1809. British general, born in Glasgow. In 1808 he commanded the British army sent to Portugal in the Peninsular War.

After advancing into Spain he had to retreat to Corunna in the NW, and was killed in the battle fought to cover the embarkation.

moot legal and administrative assembly found in nearly every community in medieval England.

Moray another spelling of ◊Murray, regent of Scotland 1567–70.

More (St) Thomas 1478–1535. English politician and author. From 1509 he was favoured by ◊Henry VIII and employed on foreign embassies. He was a member of the privy council from 1518 and Lord Chancellor from 1529 but resigned over Henry's break with the pope. For refusing to accept the king as head of the church, he was executed. The title of his political book Utopia 1516 has come to mean any supposedly perfect society.

Morgan Henry c. 1635–1688. Welsh buccaneer in the Caribbean. He made war against Spain, capturing and sacking Panama 1671. In 1674 he was knighted and appointed lieutenant governor of Jamaica.

Morley John, 1st Viscount Morley of Blackburn 1838–1923. British Liberal politician and writer. He entered Parliament in 1883, and was secretary for Ireland in 1886 and 1892–95. As secretary for India 1905–10, he prepared the way (with Viceroy Gilbert Minto) for more representative government.

Morrison Herbert Stanley, Baron Morrison of Lambeth 1888–1965. British Labour politician. He was a founder member and later secretary of the London Labour Party 1915–45, and a member of the London County Council 1922–45. He entered Parliament in 1923, and organized the Labour Party's general election victory in 1945. He was twice defeated in the contest for leadership of the party, once to Clement Attlee in 1932, and then to Hugh Gaitskell 1955. A skilful organizer, he lacked the ability to unite the party.

Mortimer Roger de, 8th Baron of Wigmore and 1st Earl of March c. 1287–1330. English politician and adventurer. He opposed Edward II and with Edward's queen, Isabella, led a rebellion against him 1326, bringing about his abdication. From 1327 Mortimer ruled England as the queen's lover, until Edward III had him executed.

Mosley Oswald (Ernald) 1896–1980. British politician, founder of the British Union of Fascists (BUF) 1932. He was a member of Parliament

1918–31, then led the BUF until his internment 1940–43 during World War II. In 1946 Mosley was denounced when it became known that Italy had funded his prewar efforts to establish fascism in Britain, but in 1948 he resumed fascist propaganda with his Union Movement, the revived BUF.

Mountbatten Louis, 1st Earl Mountbatten of Burma 1900–1979. British admiral and administrator. In World War II he became chief of combined operations 1942 and commander in chief in SE Asia 1943. As last viceroy of India 1947 and first governor general of India until 1948, he oversaw that country's transition to independence. He was killed by an ◊Irish Republican Army bomb aboard his yacht in the Republic of Ireland.

Munich Agreement pact signed on 29 Sept 1938 by the leaders of the UK (Neville ◊Chamberlain), France (Edouard Daladier), Germany (Hitler), and Italy (Mussolini), under which Czechoslovakia was compelled to surrender its Sudeten-German districts (the *Sudetenland*) to Germany. Chamberlain claimed it would guarantee 'peace in our time', but it did not prevent Hitler from seizing the rest of Czechoslovakia in March 1939.

Municipal Corporations Act English act of Parliament 1835 that laid the foundations of modern local government. The act made local government responsible to a wider electorate of ratepayers through elected councils. Boroughs incorporated in this way were empowered to take on responsibility for policing, public health, and education, and were also subject to regulation and auditing which served to reduce corruption. Similar acts were passed for Scotland (1833) and Ireland (1840).

Murray James Stuart, Earl of Murray, or Moray 1531–1570. Regent of Scotland from 1567, an illegitimate son of James V. He was one of the leaders of the Scottish ◊Reformation, and after the deposition of his half-sister ◊Mary Queen of Scots, he became regent. He was assassinated by one of her supporters.

Mutiny Act in Britain, an act of Parliament, passed 1689 and re-enacted annually since then (since 1882 as part of the Army Acts), for the establishment and payment of a standing army. The act is intended to prevent an army from existing in peacetime without Parliament's consent.

N

Napier Charles James 1782–1853. British general. He conquered Sind in India (now a province of Pakistan) 1841–43 with a very small force and governed it until 1847. He was the first commander to mention men from the ranks in his dispatches.

Napier Robert Cornelis, 1st Baron Napier of Magdala 1810–1890. British field marshal. Knighted for his services in relieving Lucknow during the Indian Mutiny, he took part in capturing Peking (Beijing) 1860 during the war against China in 1860. He was commander in chief in India 1870-76 and governor of Gibraltar 1876-82.

Napoleonic Wars series of European wars (1803–15) conducted by Napoleon I following the Revolutionary Wars, aiming for French conquest of Europe.
1803 Britain renewed the war against France, following an appeal from the Maltese against Napoleon's 1798 seizure of the island.
1805 Napoleon's planned invasion of Britain from Boulogne ended with Nelson's victory at ◊*Trafalgar*. Coalition formed against France by Britain, Austria, Russia, and Sweden. Austria defeated at Ulm; Austria and Russia at *Austerlitz*.
1806 Prussia joined the coalition and was defeated at Jena; Napoleon instituted an attempted blockade, the *Continental System*, to isolate Britain from Europe.
1807 Russia defeated at Eylau and Friedland and, on making peace with Napoleon under the *Treaty of Tilsit*, changed sides, agreeing to attack Sweden, but was forced to retreat.
1808 Napoleon's invasion of Portugal and strategy of installing his relatives as puppet kings led to the ◊*Peninsular War*.
1809 Revived Austrian opposition to Napoleon was ended by defeat at *Wagram*.

1812 The Continental System finally collapsed on its rejection by Russia, and Napoleon made the fatal decision to invade; he reached *Moscow* but was defeated by the Russian resistance and by the bitter winter as he retreated through a countryside laid waste by the retreating Russians (380,000 French soldiers died).

1813 Britain, Prussia, Russia, Austria, and Sweden formed a new coalition, which defeated Napoleon at the *Battle of the Nations*, Leipzig, Germany. He abdicated and was exiled to Elba.

1814 Louis XVIII became king of France, and the Congress of Vienna met to conclude peace.

1815 Napoleon returned to Paris. On 16 June the British commander Wellington defeated the French marshal Ney at Quatre Bras (in Belgium, SE of Brussels), and Napoleon was finally defeated at *Waterloo*, S of Brussels, 18 June.

Naseby, Battle of decisive battle of the English Civil War 14 June 1645, when the Royalists, led by Prince Rupert, were defeated by Oliver Cromwell and General Fairfax. It is named after the nearby village of Naseby, 32 km/20 mi S of Leicester.

Nassau agreement treaty signed 18 Dec 1962 whereby the USA provided Britain with Polaris missiles, marking a strengthening in Anglo-American relations.

National Front in the UK, extreme right-wing political party founded 1967. Despite some elctoral success in the late 1970s, it has now been largely eclipsed by the ◊British National Party. In 1991, the party claimed 3,000 members. Its founding members had links with the National Socialist Movement of the 1960s.

National Government (1931) in British politics, a government of Labour, Liberal and Conservative MPs formed in 1931, and consequent upon a rapidly declining financial situation which had led to a split in the Labour government. The Labour leader, Ramsay ◊Macdonald, was prime minister of the National Government but the majority of his own party refused to support him. Thus the National Government was mainly Conservative, and Macdonald (who resigned in 1935) was succeeded as prime minister by the Conservative leader Stanley ◊Baldwin.

National Insurance Act UK act of Parliament 1911, introduced by Lloyd George, Liberal chancellor, which first provided insurance for workers against ill health and unemployment.

nationalization policy of bringing a country's essential services and industries under public ownership. It was pursued, for example, by the UK Labour government 1945–51. In recent years the trend towards nationalization has slowed and in many countries (the UK, France, and Japan) reversed (◊privatization). Assets in the hands of foreign governments or companies may also be nationalized; for example, Iran's oil industry, the ◊Suez Canal, and US- owned fruit plantations in Guatemala, all in the 1950s.

National Liberal Foundation central organization of the British ◊Liberal Party, established 1877 in Birmingham. The first president was Joseph Chamberlain.

Navigation Acts in British history, a series of acts of Parliament passed from 1381 to protect English shipping from foreign competition and to ensure monopoly trading between Britain and its colonies. The last was repealed 1849 (coastal trade exempt until 1853). The Navigation Acts helped to establish England as a major sea power, although they led to higher prices. They ruined the Dutch merchant fleet in the 17th century, and were one of the causes of the American Revolution.

1650 'Commonwealth Ordinance' forbade foreign ships to trade in English colonies.

1651 Forbade the importation of goods except in English vessels or in vessels of the country of origin of the goods. This act led to the Anglo-Dutch War 1652–54.

1660 All colonial produce was required to be exported in English vessels.

1663 Colonies were prohibited from receiving goods in foreign (rather than English) vessels.

Neave Airey (Middleton Sheffield) 1916–1979. British intelligence officer and Conservative member of Parliament 1953-79, a close adviser to Prime Minister Thatcher. During World War II he escaped from Colditz, a German high-security prison camp. As shadow under-secretary of state for Northern Ireland from 1975, he became a target for extremist groups and was assassinated by an Irish terrorist bomb.

Nelson Horatio, Viscount Nelson 1758–1805. English admiral. He joined the navy in 1770. In the Revolutionary Wars against France he lost the sight in his right eye 1794 and lost his right arm 1797. He became a national hero, and rear admiral, after the victory off Cape St Vincent, Portugal. In 1798 he tracked the French fleet to Aboukir Bay where he almost entirely destroyed it. In 1801 he won a decisive victory over Denmark at the Battle of ◊Copenhagen, and in 1805, after two years of blockading Toulon, another over the Franco-Spanish fleet at the Battle of ◊Trafalgar, near Gibraltar.

Newcastle Thomas Pelham-Holles, Duke of Newcastle 1693–1768. British Whig politician, prime minster 1754–56 and 1757–62. He served as secretary of state for 30 years from 1724, then succeeded his younger brother, Henry ◊Pelham, as prime minister 1754. In 1756 he resigned as a result of setbacks in the Seven Years' War, but returned to office 1757 with ◊Pitt the Elder (1st Earl of Chatham) taking responsibility for the conduct of the war.

Newgate prison in London, which stood on the site of the Old Bailey central criminal court. Originally a gatehouse (hence the name), it was established in the 12th century, rebuilt after the Great Fire of 1666 and again in 1780, and was demolished 1903. Public executions were held outside it 1783–1868.

New Ireland Forum meeting between politicians of the Irish Republic and Northern Ireland May 1983. It offered three potential solutions to the Northern Irish problem, but all were rejected by the UK the following year.

The Forum was the idea of John Hume (1923–   ), leader of the Northern Irish Social Democratic Labour Party, and brought together representatives of the three major political parties of the republic, including Fianna Fáil and Fine Gael. The Forum suggested three possibilities for a solution to the Northern Irish problem: unification under a nonsectarian constitution, a federation of North and South, or joint rule from London and Dublin. It recognized that any solution would have to be agreed by a majority in the North, which seemed unlikely. All three options were rejected by the UK government after talks between the British and Irish leaders, Thatcher and Garret FitzGerald, in Nov 1984 (known as the Anglo-Irish summit), although the talks led to improved communication between the two governments.

Newman John Henry 1801–1890. English Roman Catholic theologian. While still an Anglican, he wrote a series of *Tracts for the Times*, which gave their name to the Tractarian Movement (subsequently called the ◊Oxford Movement) for the revival of Catholicism. He became a Catholic 1845 and was made a cardinal 1879. In 1864 his autobiography, *Apologia pro vita sua*, was published.

New Model Army army created 1645 by Oliver Cromwell to support the cause of Parliament during the English ◊Civil War. It was characterized by organization and discipline. Thomas Fairfax was its first commander.

Newport Riots violent demonstrations by the ◊Chartists in 1839 in Newport, Wales, in support of the Peoples' Charter. They were suppressed with the loss of 20 lives.

Nightingale Florence 1820–1910. English nurse, the founder of nursing as a profession. She took a team of nurses to Scutari (now Üsküdar, Turkey) in 1854 and reduced the ◊Crimean War hospital death rate from 42% to 2%. In 1856 she founded the Nightingale School and Home for Nurses in London.

Nineteen Propositions demands presented by the English Parliament to Charles I 1642. They were designed to limit the powers of the crown, and their rejection represented the beginning of the Civil War.

Nithsdale William Maxwell, 5th Earl of Nithsdale 1676–1744. English ◊Jacobite leader who was captured at Preston, brought to trial in Westminster Hall, London, and condemned to death 1716. With his wife's assistance he escaped from the Tower of London in women's dress, and fled to Rome.

Noel-Baker Philip John 1889–1982. British Labour politician. He was involved in drafting the charters of both the League of Nations and the United Nations. He published The Arms Race 1958, and was awarded the 1959 Nobel Peace Prize.

Nonjuror any of the priests of the Church of England who, after the revolution of 1688, refused to take the oaths of allegiance to William and Mary. They continued to exist as a rival church for over a century, and consecrated their own bishops, the last of whom died 1805.

Nore mutiny British naval mutiny in 1797, caused by low pay and bad conditions. It took place at anchorage by the Nore in the Thames.

Norman any of the descendants of the Norsemen (to whose chief, Rollo, Normandy was granted by Charles III of France 911) who adopted French language and culture. During the 11th and 12th centuries they conquered England 1066 (under William the Conqueror), Scotland 1072, parts of Wales and Ireland, S Italy, Sicily, and Malta, and took a prominent part in the Crusades.

Norman Conquest invasion and settlement of England by the Normans, following the victory of ◊William the Conqueror at the Battle of ◊Hastings 1066.

North Frederick, 8th Lord North 1732–1792. British Tory politician. He entered Parliament in 1754, became chancellor of the Exchequer in 1767, and was prime minister in a government of Tories and 'king's friends' from 1770. His hard line against the American colonies was supported by George III, but in 1782 he was forced to resign by the failure of his policy. In 1783 he returned to office in a coalition with Charles ◊Fox. After its defeat, he retired from politics.

Northumberland John Dudley, Duke of Northumberland c. 1502–1553. English politician, son of the privy councillor Edmund Dudley (beheaded 1510), and chief minister until Edward VI's death 1553. He tried to place his daughter-in-law Lady Jane ◊Grey on the throne, and was executed on Mary I's accession.

Northumbria Anglo-Saxon kingdom that covered NE England and SE Scotland, comprising the 6th-century kingdoms of Bernicia (Forth–Tees) and Deira (Tees–Humber), united in the 7th century. It accepted the supremacy of Wessex 827 and was conquered by the Danes in the late 9th century.

O

Oakeshott Michael 1901–1991. British political philosopher, author of On Civilization 1969. A conservative, he was praised by the right for emphasizing experience over ideals, summed up as 'Tory anarchism'. He was professor of politics at the London School of Economics 1951–69. His other books include A Guide to the Classics 1936 on picking winners in horseracing.

Oastler Richard 1789–1861. English social reformer. He opposed child labour and the ◊poor law 1834, which restricted relief, and was largely responsible for securing the Factory Act 1833 and the Ten Hours Act 1847. He was given the nickname of the 'Factory King' for his achievements on behalf of workers.

Oates Titus 1649–1705. English conspirator. A priest, he entered the Jesuit colleges at Valladolid, Spain, and St Omer, France, as a spy 1677–78, and on his return to England announced he had discovered a 'Popish Plot' to murder Charles II and re-establish Catholicism. Although this story was almost entirely false, many innocent Roman Catholics were executed during 1678–80 on Oates's evidence.

OBE abbreviation for *Officer of the Order of the British Empire*, a British honour.

O'Brien James Bronterre 1805–1864. Irish Chartist. He moved from Ireland to London 1829 where he became leader of the Chartist working class movement (see ◊Chartism). He was editor of the *Poor Man's Guardian* 1831–35 and was imprisoned for his seditious speeches 1840–41. He helped found the socialist National Reform League 1850.

O'Connell Daniel 1775–1847. Irish politician, called 'the Liberator'. Although ineligible, as a Roman Catholic, to take his seat, he was elected member of Parliament for County Clare 1828 and so forced the government to grant Catholic emancipation. In Parliament he cooperated with the Whigs in the hope of obtaining concessions until 1841, when he launched his campaign for repeal of the union.

O'Connor Feargus 1794–1855. Irish parliamentarian, a follower of Daniel ◊O'Connell. He sat in Parliament 1832–35, and as editor of the *Northern Star* became an influential figure of the radical working-class Chartist movement (see ◊Chartism).

Offa died 796. King of Mercia, England, from 757. He conquered Essex, Kent, Sussex, and Surrey; defeated the Welsh and the West Saxons; and established Mercian supremacy over all England south of the river Humber.

Official Secrets Act UK act of Parliament 1989, prohibiting the disclosure of confidential material from government sources by employees; it remains an absolute offence for a member or former member of the security and intelligence services (or those working closely with them) to disclose information about their work. There is no public- interest defence, and disclosure of information already in the public domain is still a crime. Journalists who repeat disclosures may also be prosecuted.

OHMS abbreviation for *On Her (His) Majesty's Service*.

old-age pension regular payment made by the state or a private institution to persons who have reached a specified age and are eligible for such assistance. As part of German chancellor Bismarck's 'state socialism' of the 1880s the Old-Age and Invalidity Insurance Law 1889 provided pensions, with the costs divided between employers, employees, and the state. In 1908 the British Parliament passed the Old Age Pensions Act that provided a weekly pension of five shillings to people over 70 years of age (7s 6d for a married couple) with an income of less than ten shillings a week. Old-age pensions are a form of social security.

Old Bailey popular name for the Central Criminal Court in London, situated in a street of that name in the City of London, off Ludgate Hill.

Old Pretender nickname of ◊James Edward Stuart, the son of James II of England.

OM abbreviation for ◊*Order of Merit*.

ombudsman official who acts on behalf of the private citizen in investigating complaints against the government. The post is of Scandinavian origin; it was introduced in Sweden 1809, Denmark 1954, and Norway 1962, and spread to other countries from the 1960s.

Omdurman, Battle of battle on 2 Sept 1898, in which the Sudanese, led by the Khalifa, were defeated by British and Egyptian troops under General Kitchener.

O'Neill Terence, Baron O'Neill of the Maine 1914–1990. Northern Irish Unionist politician. In the Ulster government he was minister of finance 1956–63, then prime minister 1963–69. He resigned when opposed by his party on measures to extend rights to Roman Catholics, including a universal franchise.

Orange, House of royal family of the Netherlands. The title is derived from the small principality of Orange in S France, held by the family from the 8th century to 1713. They held considerable possessions in the Netherlands, to which, after 1530, was added the German county of Nassau.

Order of Merit British order of chivalry founded 1902 by Edward VII and limited in number to 24 at any one time within the British Isles, plus additional honorary OMs for overseas peoples. It ranks below a knighthood. There are two types of OM, military and civil.

Orford, 1st Earl of title of the British politician Robert ◊Walpole.

Orkney Islands island group off the northeast coast of Scotland *area* 970 sq km/375 sq mi *towns* Kirkwall (administrative headquarters), on Mainland (Pomona) *features* comprises about 90 islands and islets, low- lying and treeless; mild climate owing to the Gulf Stream; Skara Brae, a well-preserved Neolithic village on Mainland. Population, long falling, has in recent years risen as the islands' remoteness from the rest of the world attracts new settlers. Scapa Flow, between Mainland and Hoy, was a naval base in both world wars, and the German fleet scuttled itself here 21 June 1919 *products* fishing and farming, wind power (Burgar Hill has the world's most productive wind-powered generator; a 300 KW wind turbine with blades 60 m/197 ft diameter, capable of producing 20% of the islands' energy needs) *population* (1989) 19,400 *famous people* Edwin Muir, John Rae *history* Harald I (Fairhair) of Norway conquered the islands 876; they were pledged to James III of Scotland 1468 for the dowry of Margaret of Denmark and annexed by Scotland (the dowry unpaid) 1472.

Ormonde James Butler, Duke of Ormonde 1610–1688. Irish general. He commanded the Royalist troops in Ireland 1641–50 during the Irish rebellion and the English Civil War, and was lord lieutenant 1644–47, 1661–69, and 1677–84. He was created a marquess 1642 and a duke 1661.

Osborne Judgement UK legal ruling of 1909 that prevented trade unions from using membership subscriptions to finance the Labour Party. In 1913 the judgement was negated by the Trade Union Act, which permitted them to raise political levies and provide financial support to the Labour Party. Individual trade unionists could 'contract out' of the political levy by signing a form saying they did not wish to pay.

Ossory ancient kingdom, lasting until 1110, in Leinster, Ireland; the name is preserved in some Church of Ireland and Roman Catholic bishoprics.

Oswald, St c. 605–642. King of Northumbria from 634, after killing the Welsh king Cadwallon. He became a Christian convert during exile on the Scottish island of Iona. With the help of St Aidan he furthered the spread of Christianity in N England.

Oswy Anglo-Saxon king. He became king of Bernicia (one of the two divisions of Northumbria) on the death of his brother Oswald 641 and defeated and killed King ◊Penda of Mercia 655. As King of Northumbria 655–70 he gained supremacy over all Mercia, the South Angles, East Angles, and East Saxons, as well as many Britons and Scots, He presided at the Synod of ◊Whitby 664.

Outram James 1803–1863. British general, born in Derbyshire. He entered the Indian Army 1819, served in the Afghan and Sikh wars, and commanded in the Persian campaign of 1857. On the outbreak of the Indian Mutiny, he cooperated with General Henry Havelock (1795–1857) to raise the siege of Lucknow, and held the city until relieved by Sir Colin ◊Campbell (later Baron Clyde).

Owen David 1938–   . British politician, Labour foreign secretary 1977-79. In 1981 he was one of the founders of the ◊Social Democratic Party (SDP), and in 1983 became its leader. Opposed to the decision of the majority of the party to merge with the Liberals 1987, Owen stood down, but emerged 1988 as leader of a rump SDP, which was eventually disbanded 1990.

In 1992 he was chosen to replace Lord Carrington as EC mediator in the peace talks on Bosnia-Herzegovina. Together with UN mediator Cyrus Vance, he was responsible for devising a peace plan dividing the republic into 10 semi-autonomous provinces, although its implementation is proving fraught with problems.

Owen Robert 1771–1858. British socialist, born in Wales. In 1800 he became manager of a mill at New Lanark, Scotland, where by improving working and housing conditions and providing schools he created a model community. His ideas stimulated the ◊cooperative movement (the pooling of resources for joint economic benefit).

Oxford and Asquith, Earl of title of British Liberal politician Herbert Henry ◊Asquith.

Oxford Movement also known as *Tractarian Movement* or *Catholic Revival* movement that attempted to revive Catholic religion in the Church of England. Cardinal Newman dated the movement from ◊Keble's sermon in Oxford 1833. The Oxford Movement by the turn of the century had transformed the Anglican communion, and survives today as Anglo-Catholicism.

Oxford University oldest British university established during the 12th century, the earliest existing college being founded 1249. After suffering from land confiscation during the Reformation, it was reorganized by Elizabeth I 1571. In 1985 there were 9,000 undergraduates and 3,000 post-graduate students..

P

Paine Thomas 1737–1809. English left-wing political writer. He was active in the American and French revolutions. His pamphlet Common Sense 1776 ignited passions in the American Revolution; others include The Rights of Man 1791 and The Age of Reason 1793. He advocated republicanism, deism, the abolition of slavery, and the emancipation of women.

Paisley Ian (Richard Kyle) 1926– . Northern Ireland politician and cleric, leader of the Democratic Unionist Party from 1972. A member of the Northern Ireland parliament from 1969, he has represented North Antrim in the House of Commons since 1974. An almost fanatical loyalist, he resigned his Commons seat 1985 in protest against the ◊Anglo-Irish Agreement, but returned 1986 to continue his opposition to closer co-operation with the South. His blunt and forthright manner, stentorian voice, and pugnaciousness are hallmarks of his political career.

Palmerston Henry John Temple, 3rd Viscount Palmerston 1784–1865. British politician. Initially a Tory, in Parliament from 1807, he was secretary-at-war 1809–28. He broke with the Tories 1830 and sat in the Whig cabinets of 1830–34, 1835–41, and 1846–51 as foreign secretary. He was prime minister 1855–58 (when he rectified Aberdeen's mismanagement of the Crimean War, suppressed the Indian Mutiny, and carried through the Second Opium War) and 1859–65 (when he almost involved Britain in the American Civil War on the side of the South).

Palmerston succeeded to an Irish peerage 1802. He served under five Tory prime ministers before joining the Whigs. His foreign policy was marked by distrust of France and Russia, against whose designs he backed the independence of Belgium and Turkey. He became home secretary in the coalition government of 1852, and prime minister on its fall, and was responsible for the warship Alabama going to the Confederate side in the American Civil War. He was popular with the people and made good use of the press, but his high-handed attitude annoyed Queen Victoria and other ministers.

Paris Matthew c. 1200–1259. English chronicler. He entered St Albans Abbey 1217, and wrote a valuable history of England up to 1259.

Parker Matthew 1504–1575. English cleric. He was converted to Protestantism at Cambridge University. He received high preferment under Henry VIII and Edward VI, and as archbishop of Canterbury from 1559 was largely responsible for the Elizabethan religious settlement (the formal establishment of the Church of England).

Parkinson Cyril Northcote 1909–1993 . English writer and historian, celebrated for his study of public and business administration, Parkinson's Law 1958, which included the dictum: 'Work expands to fill the time available for its completion.'

parliament legislative body of a country. The world's oldest parliament is the Icelandic *Althing* which dates from about 930. The UK Parliament is usually dated from 1265.

   In the UK, Parliament is the supreme legislature, comprising the ◊*House of Commons* and the ◊*House of Lords*. The origins of Parliament are in the 13th century, but its powers were not established until the late 17th century. The powers of the Lords were curtailed 1911, and the duration of parliaments was fixed at five years, but any parliament may extend its own life, as happened during both world wars. The UK Parliament meets in the Palace of Westminster, London.
history Parliament originated under the Norman kings as the Great Council of royal tenants-in-chief, to which in the 13th century representatives of the shires were sometimes summoned. The Parliament summoned by Simon de Montfort 1265 (as head of government in the Barons' War) set a precedent by including representatives of the boroughs as well as the shires. Under Edward III the burgesses and knights of the shires began to meet separately from the barons, thus forming the House of Commons. By the 15th century Parliament had acquired the right to legislate, vote, and appropriate supplies, examine public

accounts, and impeach royal ministers. The powers of Parliament were much diminished under the Yorkists and Tudors but under Elizabeth I a new spirit of independence appeared. The revolutions of 1640 and 1688 established parliamentary control over the executive and judiciary, and finally abolished all royal claim to tax or legislate without parliamentary consent. During these struggles the two great parties (Whig and Tory) emerged, and after 1688 it became customary for the sovereign to choose ministers from the party dominant in the Commons. The English Parliament was united with the Scottish 1707, and with the Irish 1801–1922. The ◊franchise was extended to the middle classes 1832, to the urban working classes 1867, to agricultural labourers 1884, and to women 1918 and 1928. The duration of parliaments was fixed at three years 1694, at seven 1716, and at five 1911. Payment of MPs was introduced 1911. A *public bill* that has been passed is an act of Parliament.

Parliament, European governing body of the European Community; see ◊European Parliament.

Parliament, Houses of building where the UK legislative assembly meets. The present Houses of Parliament in London, designed in Gothic Revival style by the architects Charles Barry and A W N Pugin, were built 1840–60, the previous building having burned down 1834. It incorporates portions of the medieval Palace of Westminster.

parliamentary reform acts UK acts of Parliament 1918, 1928, and 1971. The 19th century witnessed the gradual reform of the voting system in Britain and suffrage was extended in the 20th century. In 1918 the Representation of the People Act gave the vote in the UK to men over 21 years and to women over 30. In 1928 a further act gave women the vote from the age of 21. In 1971 the voting age for men and women was lowered to the age of 18.

Parnell Charles Stewart 1846–1891. Irish nationalist politician. He supported a policy of obstruction and violence to attain ◊Home Rule, and became the president of the Nationalist Party 1877. In 1879 he approved the ◊Land League, and his attitude led to his imprisonment 1881. His career was ruined 1890 when he was cited as co-respondent in a divorce case.

parliamentary reform in the UK:chronology

1822	Lord John Russell proposed a redistribution of seats. Whig Party espoused cause of reform.
1830	Duke of Wellington resigned as prime minister bringing in Whig ministry under Lord Grey, committed to reform. (Electorate 516,000 = 2% of population.)
1832	Reform Act involved redistribution of parliamentary seats from 'rotten boroughs' to urban constituencies. Franchise extended to householders paying £10 per year rent in towns and 40–shilling freeholders in counties. (Electorate 813,000 = 3% of population.)
1867	Reform Act involved further redistribution of seats and extension of franchise to all ratepayers in boroughs. (Electorate 2,500,000 = 8% of population.)
1872	Ballot Act introduced secret ballots for elections.
1883	Corrupt and Illegal Practices Act set limits to election expenses.
1884	Reform Act again involved redistribution of seats and equalization of franchise for boroughs and counties, to include all householders and ratepayers. (Electorate 5,600,000 = 16% of population.)
1885	Further redistribution of parliamentary seats.
1918	Representation of the People Act gave the vote to all men over 21 and all women ratepayers (or wives of ratepayers) over 30.
1928	Representation of the People (Equal Franchise) Act gave the vote to all women over 21.
1948	Plural voting abolished. Permanent Boundary Commission established.
1970	Voting age reduced to 18.
1979	Constituencies established for direct election to European Parliament in Strasbourg.
1983	Number of parliamentary seats raised from 635 to 650.
1985	Representation of the People Act gave the vote to British citizens living abroad for a period of five years after they have left Britain.
1989	Representation of the People Act extended the period during which British citizens abroad may vote to 20 years after leaving Britain.
1992	Number of parliamentary seats raised from 650 to 651.
1994	Number of UK seats in European parliament raised from 81 to 87.

Parr Catherine 1512–1548. Sixth wife of Henry VIII of England. She had already lost two husbands when in 1543 she married Henry VIII. She survived him, and in 1547 married Lord Seymour of Sudeley (1508–1549).

Paston family family of Norfolk, England, whose correspondence and documents (known as the Paston letters) for 1422–1509 throw valuable light on the period.

Patrick, St 389–c. 461. Patron saint of Ireland. Born in Britain, probably in S Wales, he was carried off by pirates to six years' slavery in Antrim, Ireland, before escaping either to Britain or Gaul – his poor Latin suggests the former – to train as a missionary. He is variously said to have landed again in Ireland 432 or 456, and his work was a vital factor in the spread of Christian influence there. His symbols are snakes and shamrocks; feast day 17 March.

Pearse Patrick Henry 1879–1916. Irish poet. He was prominent in the Gaelic revival, a leader of the ◊Easter Rising 1916. Proclaimed president of the provisional government, he was court-martialled and shot after its suppression.

Peasants' Revolt the rising of the English peasantry in June 1381, the culminative result of economic, social, and political disillusionment. It was sparked off by the imposition of a new poll tax, three times the rates of those imposed in 1377 and 1379. Led by Wat ◊Tyler and John ◊Ball, rebels from SE England marched on London and demanded reforms. The revolt was put down by deceit and force by the authorities.

Peel Robert 1788–1850. British Conservative politician. As home secretary 1822–27 and 1828–30, he founded the modern police force and in 1829 introduced Roman Catholic emancipation. He was prime minister 1834–35 and 1841–46, when his repeal of the ◊Corn Laws caused him and his followers to break with the party.

Peel, born in Lancashire, entered Parliament as a Tory 1809. After the passing of the Reform Bill of 1832, which he had resisted, he reformed the Tories under the name of the Conservative Party, on a basis of accepting necessary changes and seeking middle-class support. He fell from prime ministerial office because his repeal of the Corn Laws 1846 was opposed by the majority of his party. He and his followers then formed a third party standing between the Liberals and Conservatives; the majority of the Peelites, including Gladstone, subsequently joined the Liberals.

peerage in the UK, holders, in descending order, of the titles of duke, marquess, earl, viscount, and baron. Some of these titles may be held by a woman in default of a male heir. In the late 19th century the peerage was augmented by the Lords of Appeal in Ordinary (the nonhereditary life peers) and, from 1958, by a number of specially created life peers of either sex (usually long-standing members of the House of Commons). Since 1963 peers have been able to disclaim their titles, usually to enable them to take a seat in the Commons (where peers are disqualified from membership).

Pelham Henry 1696–1754. British Whig politician. He held a succession of offices in Robert Walpole's cabinet 1721–42, and was prime minister 1743–54. His brother Thomas Pelham-Holles, 1st Duke of ◊Newcastle, succeeded him as prime minister.

Penda c. 577–654. King of Mercia, an Anglo-Saxon kingdom in England, from about 632. He raised Mercia to a powerful kingdom, and defeated and killed two Northumbrian kings, Edwin 632 and ◊Oswald 641. He was killed in battle by Oswy, king of Northumbria.

Peninsular War war 1808–14 caused by the French emperor Napoleon's invasion of Portugal and Spain. British expeditionary forces under Sir Arthur Wellesley (Duke of ◊Wellington), combined with Spanish and Portuguese resistance, succeeded in defeating the French at Vimeiro 1808, Talavera 1809, Salamanca 1812, and Vittoria 1813. The results were inconclusive, and the war was ended by Napoleon's abdication.

People's Budget in UK history, the Liberal government's budget of 1909 to finance social reforms and naval rearmament. The chancellor of the Exchequer David Lloyd George proposed graded and increased income tax and a 'supertax' on high incomes. The budget aroused great debate and precipitated a constitutional crisis.

People's Charter the key document of ◊Chartism, a movement for reform of the British political system in the 1830s. It was used to mobilize working-class support following the restricted extension of the franchise specified by the 1832 Reform Act. It was drawn up in Feb 1837.

Perceval Spencer 1762–1812. British Tory politician. He became chancellor of the Exchequer 1807 and prime minister 1809. He was shot in the lobby of the House of Commons 1812 by a merchant who blamed government measures for his bankruptcy.

Percy Henry 'Hotspur' 1364–1403. English soldier, son of the 1st Earl of Northumberland. In repelling a border raid, he defeated the Scots at Homildon Hill in Northumberland 1402. He was killed at the battle of Shrewsbury while in revolt against Henry IV.

Peterloo massacre the events in St Peter's Fields, Manchester, England, 16 Aug 1819, when an open-air meeting in support of parliamentary reform was charged by yeomanry and hussars. Eleven people were killed and 500 wounded. The name was given as an analogy with the Battle of Waterloo.

petition of right in British law, the procedure whereby, before the passing of the Crown Proceedings Act 1947, a subject petitioned for legal relief against the crown, for example for money due under a contract, or for property of which the crown had taken possession.

Philby Kim (Harold) 1912–1988. British intelligence officer from 1940 and Soviet agent from 1933. He was liaison officer in Washington 1949–51, when he was confirmed to be a double agent and asked to resign. Named in 1963 as having warned Guy Burgess and Donald Maclean (similarly double agents) that their activities were known, he fled to the USSR and became a Soviet citizen and general in the KGB. A fourth member of the ring was Anthony Blunt.

Philip Duke of Edinburgh 1921–   . Prince of the UK, husband of Elizabeth II, a grandson of George I of Greece and a great-great-grandson of Queen Victoria. He was born in Corfu, Greece but brought up in England.

Philippa of Hainault 1311–1369. Daughter of William III Count of Holland; wife of King Edward III of England, whom she married in York Minster 1328, and by whom she had 12 children (including Edward the Black Prince, Lionel Duke of Clarence, John Duke of Lancaster, Edmund Duke of York, and Thomas Duke of Gloucester). She was admired for her clemency and successfully pleaded for the lives of the six burghers of Calais who surrendered to to save the town from destruction 1347.

Phoenix Park Murders the murder of several prominent members of the British government in Phoenix Park, Dublin on 6 May 1882. The murders threatened the cooperation between the Liberal government and the Irish nationalist members at Westminster which had been secured by the ◊Kilmainham Treaty.

phoney war the period in World War II between Sept 1939, when the Germans had occupied Poland, and April 1940, when the invasions of Denmark and Norway took place. During this time there were few signs of hostilities in Western Europe; indeed, Hitler made some attempts to arrange a peace settlement with Britain and France.

Pict Roman term for a member of the peoples of N Scotland, possibly meaning 'painted' (tattooed). Of pre-Celtic origin, and speaking a Celtic language which died out in about the 10th century, the Picts are thought to have inhabited much of England before the arrival of the Celtic Britons. They were united with the Celtic Scots under the rule of Kenneth MacAlpin 844. Their greatest monument is a series of carved stones, whose symbols remain undeciphered.

Pilgrimage of Grace rebellion against Henry VIII of England 1536–37, originating in Yorkshire and Lincolnshire. The uprising was directed against the policies of the monarch (such as the dissolution of the monasteries and the effects of the enclosure of common land).

Pinkie, Battle of battle on 10 Sept 1547 near Musselburgh, Lothian, Scotland, in which the Scots were defeated by the English under the Duke of Somerset.

Pitt William, *the Elder*, 1st Earl of Chatham 1708–1778. British Whig politician, 'the Great Commoner'. As paymaster of the forces 1746–55, he broke with tradition by refusing to enrich himself; he was dismissed for attacking the Duke of Newcastle, the prime minister. He served effectively as prime minister in coalition governments 1756–61 (successfully conducting the Seven Years' War) and 1766–68.

Entering Parliament 1735, Pitt led the Patriot faction opposed to the Whig prime minister Robert Walpole and attacked Walpole's successor, Carteret, for his conduct of the War of the Austrian Succession. Recalled by popular demand to form a government on the outbreak of the Seven Years' War 1756, he was forced to form a coalition with Newcastle 1757. A 'year of victories' ensued 1759, and the French were expelled from India and Canada. In 1761 Pitt wished to escalate the war by a declaration of war on Spain, George III disagreed and Pitt resigned, but was again recalled to form an all-party government 1766. He championed the Americans against the king, though rejecting independence, and collapsed during his last speech in the House of Lords - opposing the withdrawal of British troops - and died a month later.

Pitt William, *the Younger* 1759–1806. British Tory prime minister 1783–1801 and 1804–06. He raised the importance of the House of Commons, clamped down on corruption, carried out fiscal reforms, and effected the union with Ireland. He attempted to keep Britain at peace but underestimated the importance of the French Revolution and became embroiled in wars with France from 1793; he died on hearing of Napoleon's victory at Austerlitz.

Son of William Pitt the Elder, he entered Cambridge University at 14 and Parliament at 22. He was the Whig Shelburne's chancellor of the Exchequer 1782–83, and with the support of the Tories and king's friends became Britain's youngest prime minister 1783. He reorganized the country's finances and negotiated reciprocal tariff reduction with France. In 1793, however, the new French republic declared war and England fared badly. Pitt's policy in Ireland led to the 1798 revolt, and he tried to solve the Irish question by the Act of Union 1800, but George III rejected the Catholic emancipation Pitt had promised as a condition, and Pitt resigned 1801.

On his return to office 1804, he organized an alliance with Austria, Russia, and Sweden against Napoleon, which was shattered at Austerlitz. In declining health, he died on hearing the news, saying: 'Oh, my country! How I leave my country!' He was buried in Westminster Abbey.

Place Francis 1771–1854. English Radical. He showed great powers as a political organizer, and made Westminster a centre of pro-labour union Radicalism. He secured the repeal of the anti-union Combination Acts 1824.

Plaid Cymru Welsh nationalist political party established 1925, dedicated to an independent Wales. In 1966 the first Plaid Cymru member of Parliament was elected.

Plantagenet English royal house, reigning 1154–1399, whose name comes from the nickname of Geoffrey, Count of Anjou (1113–1151), father of Henry II, who often wore in his hat a sprig of broom, *planta genista*. In the 1450s, Richard, Duke of York, took 'Plantagenet' as a surname to emphasize his superior claim to the throne over Henry VI's.

Plantation of Ireland colonisation and conquest of Ireland by English and Scottish settlers 1556–1660. There were several rebellions against the plantation by the Irish and the Anglo-Irish aristocracy. The final stages of the conquest took place under ◊Cromwell.

Plassey, Battle of victory in India 23 June 1757, for the British under Robert ◊Clive, which brought Bengal under British rule.

Pole Reginald 1500–1558. English cardinal from 1536 who returned from Rome as papal legate on the accession of Mary I in order to readmit England to the Catholic church. He succeeded Cranmer as archbishop of Canterbury 1556.

police civil law-and-order force. In the UK it is responsible to the Home Office, with 52 autonomous police forces, generally organized on a county basis; mutual aid is given in circumstances such as mass picketing in the 1984–85 miners' strike, but there is no national police force or police riot unit (such as the French CRS riot squad). The predecessors of these forces were the ineffective medieval watch and London's Bow Street runners, introduced 1749 by Henry Fielding which formed a model for the London police force established by Robert ◊Peel's government 1829 (hence 'peelers' or 'bobbies'); the system was introduced throughout the country from 1856.

poll tax tax levied on every individual, without reference to income or property. Being simple to administer, it was among the earliest sorts of tax (introduced in England 1379), but because of its indiscriminate nature (it is a regressive tax, in that it falls proportionately more on poorer people) it has often proved unpopular. The *community charge*, a type of poll tax, was introduced in Scotland by the British government April 1989, and in England and Wales 1990, replacing the property-based local taxation (the rates). Its unpopularity led to its replacement 1993–94 by a ◊council tax, based both on property values and on the size of households.

poor law English system for poor relief, established by the Poor Relief Act 1601. Each parish was responsible for its own poor, paid for by a parish tax. The care of the poor was transferred to the Ministry of Health 1918, but the poor law remained in force until 1930.

Popish Plot supposed plot to murder Charles II; see under Titus ◊Oates.

Portland William Bentinck, 1st Earl of Portland 1649–1709. Dutch politician who accompanied William of Orange to England 1688, and was created an earl 1689. He served in William's campaigns.

Portland William Henry Cavendish Bentinck, 3rd Duke of Portland 1738–1809. British politician, originally a Whig, who in 1783 became nominal prime minister in the Fox–North coalition government. During the French Revolution he joined the Tories, and was prime minister 1807–09.

Pound (Alfred) Dudley Pickman Rogers 1877–1943. British admiral of the fleet. As First Sea Lord and chief of the British naval staff 1939–43, he was responsible for the effective measures taken against the German submarine U-boats in World War II.

Powell (John) Enoch 1912– . British Conservative politician. He was minister of health 1960–63, and contested the party leadership 1965. In 1968 he made a speech against immigration that led to his dismissal from the shadow cabinet. He resigned from the party 1974, and was Official Unionist Party member for South Down, Northern Ireland 1974–87.

praemunire three English acts of Parliament passed 1353, 1365, and 1393, aimed to prevent appeal to the pope against the power of the king, and therefore an early demonstration of independence from Rome. The statutes were opposed by English bishops.

press gang method used to recruit soldiers and sailors into the British armed forces in the 18th and early 19th centuries. In effect it was a form of kidnapping carried out by the services or their agents, often with the aid of armed men. This was similar to the practice of 'shanghaiing' sailors for duty in the merchant marine, especially in the Far East.

Preston, Battle of battle 17–19 Aug 1648 at Preston, Lancashire, in which the English defeated the Scots. The Scots invaded England under the Duke of ◊Hamilton, but were cut off from Scotland by ◊Cromwell and fled in a series of running fights. Hamilton was captured and executed.

Prestonpans, Battle of battle 1745 in which Prince ◊Charles Edward Stuart's Jacobite forces defeated the English. It took place near the town of Prestonpans in Lothian region, E Scotland.

pretender claimant to a throne. In British history, the term is widely used to describe the Old Pretender (◊James Edward Stuart) and the Young Pretender (◊Charles Edward Stuart).

Pride's purge the removal of about 100 Royalists and Presbyterians of the English House of Commons from Parliament by a detachment of soldiers led by Col Thomas Pride (died 1658) in 1648. They were accused of negotiating with Charles I and were seen as unreliable by the army. The remaining members were termed the ◊Rump and voted in favour of the king's trial.

priest's hole hiding place, in private homes, for Catholic priests in the 16th–17th centuries when there were penal laws against them in Britain. Many still exist, for example at Speke Hall, near Liverpool.

prime minister or *premier* head of a parliamentary government, usually the leader of the largest party. In countries with an executive president, the prime minister is of lesser standing, whereas in those with dual executives, such as France, power is shared with the president.

The first prime minister in Britain is usually considered to have been Robert ◊Walpole, but the office was not officially recognized until 1905. In some countries, such as Australia, a distinction is drawn between the prime minister of the whole country and the premier of an individual state.

prince royal or noble title. In Rome and medieval Italy it was used as the title of certain officials, for example, *princeps senatus* (Latin 'leader of the Senate'). The title was granted to the king's sons in 15th-century France, and in England from Henry VII's time.

prime ministers of Britain

Sir Robert Walpole	(Whig)	1721
Earl of Wilmington	(Whig)	1742
Henry Pelham	(Whig)	1743
Duke of Newcastle	(Whig)	1754
Duke of Devonshire	(Whig)	1756
Duke of Newcastle	(Whig)	1757
Earl of Bute	(Tory)	1762
George Grenville	(Whig)	1763
Marquess of Rockingham	(Whig)	1765
Duke of Grafton	(Whig)	1766
Lord North	(Tory)	1770
Marquess of Rockingham	(Whig)	1782
Earl of Shelburne	(Whig)	1782
Duke of Portland	(Coalition)	1783
William Pitt	(Tory)	1783
Henry Addington	(Tory)	1801
William Pitt	(Tory)	1804
Lord Grenville	(Whig)	1806
Duke of Portland	(Tory)	1807
Spencer Perceval	(Tory)	1809
Earl of Liverpool	(Tory)	1812
George Canning	(Tory)	1827
Viscount Goderich	(Tory)	1827
Duke of Wellington	(Tory)	1828
Earl Grey	(Whig)	1830
Viscount Melbourne	(Whig)	1834
Duke of Wellington	(Tory)	1834
Sir Robert Peel	(Tory)	1834
Viscount Melbourne	(Whig)	1835
Sir Robert Peel	(Tory)	1841
Lord J Russell	(Whig)	1846
Earl of Derby	(Tory)	1852
Earl of Aberdeen	(Peelite)	1852
Viscount Palmerston	(Liberal)	1855
Earl of Derby	(Conservative)	1858
Viscount Palmerston	(Liberal)	1859

Earl J Russell	(Liberal)	1865
Earl of Derby	(Conservative)	1866
Benjamin Disraeli	(Conservative)	1868
W E Gladstone	(Liberal)	1886
Benjamin Disraeli	(Conservative)	1874
W E Gladstone	(Liberal)	1880
Marquess of Salisbury	(Conservative)	1885
W E Gladstone	(Liberal)	1886
Marquess of Salisbury	(Conservative)	1886
W E Gladstone	(Liberal)	1892
Earl of Rosebery	(Liberal)	1894
Marquess of Salisbury	(Conservative)	1895
Arthur Balfour	(Conservative)	1902
Sir H Campbell-Bannerman	(Liberal)	1905
H H Asquith	(Liberal)	1908
H H Asquith	(Coalition)	1915
D Lloyd George	(Coalition)	1916
A Bonar Law	(Conservative)	1922
Stanley Baldwin	(Conservative)	1923
Ramsay MacDonald	(Labour)	1924
Stanley Baldwin	(Conservative)	1924
Ramsay MacDonald	(Labour)	1929
Ramsay MacDonald	(National)	1931
Stanley Baldwin	(National)	1935
N Chamberlain	(National)	1937
Sir Winston Churchill	(Coalition)	1940
Clement Attlee	(Labour)	1945
Sir Winston Churchill	(Conservative)	1951
Sir Anthony Eden	(Conservative)	1955
Harold Macmillan	(Conservative)	1957
Sir Alec Douglas-Home	(Conservative)	1963
Harold Wilson	(Labour)	1964
Edward Heath	(Conservative)	1970
Harold Wilson	(Labour)	1974
James Callaghan	(Labour)	1976
Margaret Thatcher	(Conservative)	1979
John Major	(Conservative)	1990

Princes in the Tower popular name for King ◊Edward V and his younger brother Richard, Duke of York (1472–1483). They are said to have been murdered in the Tower of London by order of their uncle, the Duke of Gloucester, so that he could succeed to the throne as ◊Richard III.

Princess Royal title borne only by the eldest daughter of the British sovereign, granted by royal declaration. It was first borne by Mary, eldest daughter of Charles I, probably in imitation of the French court where the eldest daughter of the king was styled 'Madame Royale'. The title is currently held by Princess Anne.

Princesses Royal

c. 1642	Mary (eldest daughter of Charles I)
1727	Anne (eldest daughter of George II)
1766	Charlotte (eldest daughter of George III)
1840	Victoria (eldest daughter of Queen Victoria)
1905	Louise (eldest daughter of Edward VII)
1932	Mary (only daughter of George V)
1987	Anne (only daughter of Elizabeth II)

Prior James 1927– . British Conservative politician. He held ministerial posts from 1970. As employment secretary he curbed trade-union activity with the Employment Act 1980, and was Northern Ireland secretary 1981–84. After his resignation 1984 he became chair of the General Electric Company.

Prior Matthew 1664–1721. British poet and diplomat. He was associated under the Whigs with the negotiation of the treaty of Ryswick 1697 ending the war with France and under the Tories with that of Utrecht 1714 ('Matt's Peace') ending the War of the Spanish Succession, but on the Whigs' return to power he was imprisoned by the government leader Walpole 1715–17. His gift as a poet was for light occasional verses.

privatization policy or process of selling or transferring state-owned or public assets and services (notably nationalized industries) to private investors. Privatization of services involves the government contracting private firms to supply services previously supplied by public authorities.

Privy Council council composed originally of the chief royal officials of the Norman kings in Britain; under the Tudors and early Stuarts it became the chief governing body. It was replaced from 1688 by the ◊cabinet, originally a committee of the council, and the council itself now retains only formal powers in issuing royal proclamations and orders-in-council. Cabinet ministers are automatically members, and it is presided over by the Lord President of the Council.

privy purse personal expenditure of the British sovereign, which derives from his/her own resources (as distinct from the civil list, which now finances only expenses incurred in pursuance of official functions and duties). The office that deals with this expenditure is also known as the Privy Purse.

Privy Seal, Lord until 1884, the UK officer of state in charge of the royal seal to prevent its misuse. The honorary title is now held by a senior cabinet minister who has special nondepartmental duties.

Profumo John (Dennis) 1915– . British Conservative politician, secretary of state for war from 1960 to June 1963, when he resigned on the disclosure of his involvement with Christine Keeler, mistress also of a Soviet naval attaché. In 1982 Profumo became administrator of the social and educational settlement Toynbee Hall in London.

proportional representation (PR) electoral system in which distribution of party seats corresponds to their proportion of the total votes cast, and minority votes are not wasted (as opposed to a simple majority, or 'first past the post', system).

protectorate formerly in international law, a small state under the direct or indirect control of a larger one. The 20th-century equivalent was a trust territory. In English history the rule of Oliver and Richard ◊Cromwell 1653–59 is referred to as *the Protectorate*.

Provisions of Oxford provisions issued by Henry III of England 1258 under pressure from Simon de Montfort and the baronial opposition. They provided for the establishment of a baronial council to run the government, carry out reforms, and keep a check on royal power.

Provisions of Westminster reforms issued by the parliament that met at Westminster 13 Oct 1259. They were forced on ◊Henry III by his rebellious barons, and forbade the king to grant lands, castles, or offices of state to foreigners. These provisions were a further step following the more radical ◊Provisions of Oxford 1258.

Prynne William 1600–1669. English Puritan. He published in 1632 Histriomastix, a work attacking stage plays; it contained aspersions on the Queen, Henrietta Maria, for which he was pilloried and lost his ears. In 1637 he was again pilloried and branded for an attack on the bishops. He opposed the execution of Charles I, and actively supported the Restoration.

Public Health Acts 1848, 1872, 1875 in the UK, legislation enacted by Parliament to deal with squalor and disease and to establish a code of sanitary law. The first act, in 1848, established a central board of health with three members who were responsible to Parliament to impose local boards of health in districts where the death rate was above the national average and to make provision for other local boards of health to be established by petition. The 1872 act made it obligatory for every local authority to appoint a medical officer of health. The 1875 act consolidated previous acts and provided a comprehensive code for public health.

Pym Francis 1922– . British Conservative politician. He was defence secretary 1979–81, and succeeded Lord Carrington as foreign minister 1982, but was dismissed in the post-election reshuffle 1983.

Pym John 1584–1643. English Parliamentarian, largely responsible for the ◊petition of right 1628. As leader of the Puritan opposition in the ◊Long Parliament from 1640, he moved the impeachment of Charles I's advisers the Earl of Strafford and William Laud, drew up the ◊Grand Remonstrance, and was the chief of five members of Parliament Charles I wanted arrested 1642. The five hid themselves and then emerged triumphant when the king left London.

Quaker popular name, originally derogatory, for a member of the Society of ◊Friends.

Quatre Bras, Battle of battle fought 16 June 1815 during the Napoleonic Wars, in which the British commander Wellington defeated French forces under Marshal Ney. It is named after a hamlet in Brabant, Belgium, 32 km/20 mi SE of Brussels.

Queensberry John Sholto Douglas, 8th Marquess of Queensberry 1844–1900. British patron of boxing. In 1867 he formulated the *Queensberry Rules*, which form the basis of today's boxing rules.

R

race-relations acts UK acts of Parliament 1965, 1968, and 1976 to combat discrimination. The Race Relations Act 1976 prohibits discrimination on the grounds of colour, race, nationality, or ethnic origin. Indirect as well as direct discrimination is prohibited in the provision of goods, services, facilities, employment, accommodation, and advertisements. The Commission for Racial Equality was set up under the act to investigate complaints of discrimination.

Radical in Britain, supporter of parliamentary reform before the Reform Bill 1832. As a group the Radicals later became the progressive wing of the Liberal Party. During the 1860s (led by Cobden, Bright, and J S Mill) they campaigned for extension of the franchise, free trade, and ◊laissez faire◊, but after 1870, under the leadership of Joseph Chamberlain and Charles Dilke, they adopted a republican and semi-socialist programme. With the growth of ◊socialism in the later 19th century, Radicalism ceased to exist as an organized movement.

radical one who favours extensive and rapid changes to the status quo of society. The term is popularly associated with those on the left wing of politics but may also describe extreme right-wing critics. In Australia, it was particularly used to describe militant left-wing critics of society in the 1960s.

Raffles Thomas Stamford 1781–1826. British colonial administrator, born in Jamaica. He served in the British ◊East India Company, took part in the capture of Java from the Dutch 1811, and while governor of Sumatra 1818–23 was responsible for the acquisition and founding of Singapore 1819.

Raglan FitzRoy James Henry Somerset, 1st Baron Raglan 1788–1855. English general. He took part in the Peninsular War under

Wellington, and lost his right arm at Waterloo. He commanded the British forces in the Crimean War from 1854. The *raglan sleeve*, cut right up to the neckline with no shoulder seam, is named after him.

Rahere died 1144. Minstrel and favourite of Henry I of England. In 1123, having recovered from malaria while on a pilgrimage to Rome, he founded St Bartholomew's priory and St Bartholomew's hospital in London.

Raleigh or *Ralegh* Walter c. 1552–1618. English adventurer. He made colonizing and exploring voyages to North America 1584–87 and South America 1595, and naval attacks on Spanish ports. His aggressive actions against Spanish interests brought him into conflict with the pacific James I. He was imprisoned for treason 1603–16 and executed on his return from an unsuccessful final expedition to South America.

Raleigh was knighted 1584, and made several attempts 1584–87 to establish a colony in 'Virginia' (now North Carolina, USA). In 1595 he led an expedition to South America (described in his Discoverie of Guiana 1596) and distinguished himself in expeditions against Spain in Cádiz 1596 and the Azores 1597. After James *i*'s accession 1603 he was condemned to death on a charge of conspiracy, but was reprieved and imprisoned in the Tower of London, where he wrote his unfinished History of the World. Released 1616 to lead a gold-seeking expedition to the Orinoco River in South America, which failed disastrously, he was beheaded on his return under his former sentence.

rationing restricted allowance of provisions or other supplies in time of war or shortage. Food rationing was introduced in Germany and Britain during World War I. During World War II food rationing, organized by the government, began in Britain in 1940. Each person was issued with a ration book of coupons. Bacon, butter, and sugar were restricted, followed by other goods, including sweets, petrol, clothing, soap, and furniture. Some people tried to buy extra on the black market. In 1946 the world wheat shortage led to bread rationing. All food rationing finally ended in Britain in 1954. During the Suez Crisis of 1956, petrol rationing was reintroduced in Britain.

Rebecca Riots disturbances in SW Wales 1842–44. They were primarily a protest against toll charges on public roads, but were also a symptom of general unrest following the ◊Poor Law Amendment Act 1834, which made obtaining poor relief much harder. The rioters, many disguised as women, destroyed the tollhouses and gates. Each leader was known as 'Rebecca' and followers were 'her daughters'. They took their name from the biblical prophecy that the seed of Rebekah would 'possess the gate of those which hate them' (Genesis 24.60).

Redmond John Edward 1856–1918. Irish politician, Parnell's successor as leader of the Nationalist Party 1890–1916. The 1910 elections saw him holding the balance of power in the House of Commons, and he secured the introduction of a ◊Home Rule bill, which was opposed by Protestant Ulster.

reeve in Anglo-Saxon England, an official charged with the administration of a shire or burgh, fulfilling functions similar to those of the later sheriff. After the Norman Conquest, the term tended to be restricted to the person elected by the villeins to oversee the work of the manor and to communicate with the manorial lord.

Reform Acts UK acts of Parliament 1832, 1867, and 1884 that extended voting rights and redistributed parliamentary seats; also known as ◊Representation of the People Acts. (See also ◊parliament).

The 1832 act abolished pocket and ◊rotten boroughs, which had formed unrepresentative constituencies, redistributed seats on a more equitable basis in the counties, and formed some new boroughs. The franchise was extended to male householders in property worth £10 a year or more in the boroughs and to owners of freehold property worth £2 a year, £10 copyholders, or £50 leaseholders in the counties. The

Reform Acts: growth of the electorate in 19th-century Britain

year	UK voters	approximate percentage of population enfranchised
1831	515,920	2%
1833	809,374	3%
1866	1,367,845	5%
1869	2,445,847	8%
1883	3,155,143	9%
1886	5,674,964	16%

1867 act redistributed seats from corrupt and small boroughs to the counties and large urban areas. It also extended the franchise in boroughs to adult male heads of households, and in counties to males who owned, or held on long leases, land worth £5 a year, or who occupied land worth £12 on which they paid poor rates. The 1884 act extended the franchise to male agricultural labourers.

Reformation religious and political movement in 16th-century Europe to reform the Roman Catholic church, which led to the establishment of Protestant churches. Anticipated from the 12th century by the Waldenses, Lollards, and Hussites, it was set off by German priest Martin Luther 1517, and became effective when the absolute monarchies gave it support by challenging the political power of the papacy and confiscating church wealth.

Regency in Britain, the years 1811–20 during which ◊George IV (then Prince of Wales) acted as regent for his father ◊George III.

regicide person who kills a monarch. In British history, there were the forty-nine signatories on the instrument of execution for Charles I of England in 1649, together with the two executioners (who were anonymous). After the Restoration in 1660, 29 of these men were put on trial and ten were sentenced to death.

Representation of the People Acts series of UK acts of Parliament from 1867 that extended voting rights, creating universal suffrage in 1928. The 1867 and 1884 acts are known as the second and third ◊Reform Acts.

The 1918 act gave the vote to men over the age of 21 and women over the age of 30, and the 1928 act extended the vote to women over the age of 21. Certain people had the right to more than one vote; this was abolished by the 1948 act. The 1969 act reduced the minimum age of voting to 18.

Restoration in English history, the period when the monarchy, in the person of Charles II, was re-established after the English Civil War and the fall of the ◊Protectorate 1660.

Reynolds Albert 1933–   . Irish politician, prime minister from 1992. He joined Fianna Fáil 1977, and held various government posts including minister for industry and commerce 1987–88 and minister of finance 1989–92. He became prime minister when Charles ◊Haughey was forced to resign Jan 1992, but his government was defeated on a vote of confidence Nov 1992. Subsequent elections gave no party an overall majority but, after prolonged negotiations, Reynolds succeeded in forming a Fianna Fáil–Labour coalition.

Rice-Davies Mandy (Marilyn) 1944– . English model. She achieved notoriety in 1963 following the revelations of the affair between her friend Christine ◊Keeler and war minister John ◊Profumo, and his subsequent resignation.

Richard three kings of England:

Richard (I) the Lion-Heart (French *Coeur-de-Lion*) 1157–1199. King of England from 1189, who spent all but six months of his reign abroad. He was the third son of Henry II, against whom he twice rebelled. In the third ◊Crusade 1191–92 he won victories at Cyprus, Acre, and Arsuf (against Saladin), but failed to recover Jerusalem. While returning overland he was captured by the Duke of Austria, who handed him over to the emperor Henry VI, and he was held prisoner until a large ransom was raised. He then returned briefly to England, where his brother John I had been ruling in his stead. His later years were spent in warfare in France, where he was killed.

Richard II 1367–1400. King of England from 1377, effectively from 1389, son of Edward the Black Prince. He reigned in conflict with Parliament; they executed some of his associates 1388, and he executed some of the opposing barons 1397, whereupon he made himself absolute. Two years later, forced to abdicate in favour of ◊Henry IV, he was jailed and probably assassinated.

Richard III 1452–1485. King of England from 1483. The son of Richard, Duke of York, he was created Duke of Gloucester by his brother Edward IV, and distinguished himself in the Wars of the ◊Roses. On Edward's death 1483 he became protector to his nephew Edward V, and soon secured the crown for himself on the plea that Edward IV's sons were illegitimate. He proved a capable ruler, but the suspicion that he had murdered Edward V and his brother undermined his popularity. In 1485 Henry, Earl of Richmond (later ◊Henry VII), raised a rebellion, and Richard III was defeated and killed at ◊Bosworth.

Ridgeway, the grassy track dating from prehistoric times that runs along the Berkshire Downs in S England from White Horse Hill to near Streatley.

Ridley Nicholas c. 1500–1555. English Protestant bishop. He became chaplain to Henry VIII 1541, and bishop of London 1550. He took an active part in the ◊Reformation and supported Lady Jane Grey's claim to the throne. After Mary's accession he was arrested and burned as a heretic.

Riot Act in the UK, act of Parliament passed 1714 to suppress the ◊Jacobite disorders. If three or more persons assembled unlawfully to the disturbance of the public peace, a magistrate could read a proclamation ordering them to disperse ('reading the Riot Act'), after which they might be dispersed by force. It was superseded by the Public Order Act 1986, which was instituted in response to several inner-city riots in the early 1980s, and greatly extends police powers to control marches and demonstrations by rerouting them, restricting their size and duration, or by making arrests. Under the act a person is guilty of riot if in a crowd of 12 or more, threatening violence; the maximum sentence is ten years' imprisonment.

Rizzio David 1533–1566. Italian adventurer at the court of Mary Queen of Scots. After her marriage to ◊Darnley, Rizzio's influence over her incited her husband's jealousy, and he was murdered by Darnley and his friends.

Robert three kings of Scotland:

Robert (I) the Bruce 1274–1329. King of Scotland from 1306, and grandson of Robert de ◊Bruce. He shared in the national uprising led by William ◊Wallace, and, after Wallace's execution 1305, rose once more against Edward I of England, and was crowned at Scone 1306. He defeated Edward II at ◊Bannockburn 1314. In 1328 the treaty of Northampton recognized Scotland's independence and Robert as king.

Robert II 1316–1390. King of Scotland from 1371. He was the son of Walter (1293–1326), steward of Scotland, who married Marjory, daughter of Robert the Bruce. He was the first king of the house of Stuart.

Robert III c. 1340–1406. King of Scotland from 1390, son of Robert II. He was unable to control the nobles, and the government fell largely into the hands of his brother, Robert, Duke of Albany (c. 1340–1420).

Roberts Bartholomew 1682–1722. British merchant-navy captain who joined his captors when taken by pirates in 1718. He became the most financially successful of all the sea rovers until surprised and killed in battle by the British navy.

Robertson William 1721–1793. Scottish historian who wrote a history of Scotland in the reigns of Mary and James VI (1759), and one of the reign of the emperor Charles V (1769).

Robin Hood in English legend, an outlaw and champion of the poor against the rich, said to have lived in Sherwood Forest, Nottinghamshire, during the reign of Richard I (1189–99). He feuded with the sheriff of Nottingham, accompanied by Maid Marian and a band of followers known as his 'merry men'. He appears in ballads from the 13th century, but his first datable appearance is in Langland's *Piers Plowman* in the late 14th century.

Robinson Mary 1944– . Irish Labour politician, president from 1990. She became a professor of law at 25. A strong supporter of women's rights, she has campaigned for the liberalization of Ireland's laws prohibiting divorce and abortion.

Rob Roy nickname of Robert MacGregor 1671–1734. Scottish Highland ◊Jacobite outlaw. After losing his estates, he lived by cattle theft and extortion. Captured, he was sentenced to transportation but pardoned 1727. He is a central character in Walter Scott's historical novel Rob Roy 1817.

Robsart Amy c. 1532–1560. wife of Robert Dudley, the Earl of ◊Leicester.

Rockingham Charles Watson Wentworth, 2nd Marquess of Rockingham 1730–1782. British Whig politician, prime minister 1765–66 and 1782 (when he died in office); he supported the American claim to independence.

Rodney George Brydges Rodney, Baron Rodney 1718–1792. British admiral. In 1762 he captured Martinique, St Lucia, and Grenada from the French. In 1780 he relieved Gibraltar by defeating a Spanish squadron off Cape St Vincent. In 1782 he crushed the French fleet under Count de Grasse off Dominica, for which he was raised to the peerage.

Roger of Salisbury English cleric and politician. He was appointed chancellor under ◊Henry II 1100 and bishop of Salisbury 1101. He was next in power to the king and ruled in his absence, introducing many reforms. On Henry's death 1135 he went over to ◊Stephen. His greed and acquisition of castles angered the barons, who removed him from office and forced him to surrender the castles 1139.

Roman Britain period in British history from the mid-1st century BC to the mid-4th century AD. England was rapidly Romanized, but north of York fewer remains of Roman civilization have been found. Roman towns include London, York, Chester, St Albans, Colchester, Lincoln, Gloucester, and Bath. The most enduring mark of the occupation was the system of military roads radiating from London.

Full Roman contact with Britain began with Caesar's invasions of 55 and 54 BC, but the actual conquest was not begun until AD 43. After several unsuccessful attempts to conquer Scotland, the northern frontier was fixed at ◊Hadrian's Wall. During the 4th century Britain was raided by the Saxons, Picts, and Scots. The Roman armies were withdrawn 407 but there were partial reoccupations 417–c. 427 and c. 450.

Rosebery Archibald Philip Primrose, 5th Earl of Rosebery 1847–1929. British Liberal politician. He was foreign secretary 1886 and 1892–94, when he succeeded Gladstone as prime minister, but his government survived less than a year. After 1896 his imperialist views gradually placed him further from the mainstream of the Liberal Party.

Roses, Wars of the civil wars in England 1455–85 between the houses of ◊Lancaster (badge, red rose) and ◊York (badge, white rose), both of whom claimed the throne through descent from the sons of Edward III. As a result of ◊Henry VI's lapse into insanity 1453, Richard, Duke of York, was installed as protector of the realm. Upon his recovery, Henry forced York to take up arms in self-defence.
1455 Opened with battle of St Albans 22 May, a Yorkist victory.
1459–61 War renewed. Richard, Duke of York, killed in 1460, but his son ◊Edward IV, having been proclaimed king, confirmed his position by a victory at Towton 29 March 1461.
1470 ◊Warwick (who had helped Edward to the throne) allied instead

with Henry VI's queen, ◊Margaret of Anjou; Henry VI restored to the throne.

1471 Edward returned, defeated Warwick at Barnet 14 April and Margaret at Tewkesbury 4 May, her son killed, and her forces destroyed. Henry VI was murdered in the Tower of London.

1485 Yorkist regime ended with the defeat of ◊Richard III by the future ◊Henry VII at ◊Bosworth 22 Aug.

The name Wars of the Roses was given in the 19th century by novelist Walter Scott.

rotten borough English parliamentary constituency, before the Great Reform Act 1832, that returned members to Parliament in spite of having small numbers of electors. Such a borough could easily be manipulated by those with sufficient money or influence.

Roundhead member of the Parliamentary party during the English Civil War 1640–60, opposing the royalist Cavaliers. The term referred to the short hair then worn only by men of the lower classes.

Roundway Down, Battle of battle 13 July 1643 at Roundway Down, 3 km/2 mi north of Devizes, Wiltshire, between Royalist troops under Lord Wilmot and Parliamentarians under Sir William Waller. The Parliamentarians were defeated, losing all their cannon and much ammunition.

royal commission in the UK and Canada, a group of people appointed by the government (nominally by the sovereign) to investigate a matter of public concern and make recommendations on any actions to be taken in connection with it, including changes in the law. In cases where agreement on recommendations cannot be reached, a minority report can be submitted by dissenters.

royal household personal staff of a sovereign. In Britain the chief officers are the Lord Chamberlain, the Lord Steward, and the Master of the Horse. The other principal members of the royal family also maintain their own households.

royal prerogative powers, immunities, and privileges recognized in common law as belonging to the crown. Most prerogative acts in the UK are now performed by the government on behalf of the crown. The royal prerogative belongs to the Queen as a person as well as to the

institution called the crown, and the award of some honours and digni-
ties remain her personal choice. As by prerogative 'the king can do no
wrong', the monarch is immune from prosecution.

rule of law doctrine that no individual, however powerful, is above
the law. The principle had a significant influence on attempts to restrain
the arbitrary use of power by rulers and on the growth of legally
enforceable human rights in many Western countries. It is often used as
a justification for separating legislative from judicial power.

Rump, the English parliament formed between Dec 1648 and Nov
1653 after ◊Pride's purge of the ◊Long Parliament to ensure a majority
in favour of trying Charles I. It was dismissed 1653 by Cromwell, who
replaced it with the ◊Barebones Parliament.

Runciman Walter, 1st Viscount 1870–1949. British Liberal politician. He entered Parliament in 1899 and held various ministerial offices
between 1908 and 1939. In Aug 1938 he undertook an abortive mission
to Czechoslovakia to persuade the Czech government to make concessions to Nazi Germany.

Runnymede meadow on the south bank of the river Thames near
Egham, Surrey, England, where on 15 June 1215 King John put his seal
to the ◊Magna Carta.

Rupert Prince 1619–1682. English Royalist general and admiral, born
in Prague, son of the Elector Palatine Frederick V and James I's daughter Elizabeth. Defeated by Cromwell at ◊Marston Moor and ◊Naseby in
the Civil War, he commanded a privateering fleet 1649–52, until routed
by Admiral Robert Blake, and, returning after the Restoration, was a
distinguished admiral in the Dutch Wars. He founded the ◊Hudson's
Bay Company.

Russell John, 1st Earl Russell 1792–1878. British Liberal politician,
son of the 6th Duke of Bedford. He entered the House of Commons
1813 and supported Catholic emancipation and the Reform Bill. He
held cabinet posts 1830–41, became prime minister 1846–52, and was
again a cabinet minister until becoming prime minister again 1865–66.
He retired after the defeat of his Reform Bill 1866.

Russell Lord William 1639–1683. British Whig politician. Son of the
1st Duke of Bedford, he was among the founders of the Whig Party,

and actively supported attempts in Parliament to exclude the Roman Catholic James II from succeeding to the throne. In 1683 he was accused, on dubious evidence, of complicity in the ◊Rye House Plot to murder Charles II, and was executed.

Rye House Plot conspiracy 1683 by English Whig extremists against Charles II for his Roman Catholic leanings. They intended to murder Charles and his brother James, Duke of York, at Rye House, Hoddesdon, Hertfordshire, but the plot was betrayed. The Duke of ◊Monmouth was involved, and alleged conspirators, including Lord William ◊Russell and Algernon Sidney (1622-1683), were executed for complicity.

S

Sackville Thomas, 1st Earl of Dorset 1536–1608. English poet. He collaborated with Thomas Norton on *Gorboduc* 1561, written in blank verse, one of the earliest English tragedies.

St Albans, Battle of first battle in the English Wars of the ◊Roses, on 22 May 1455 at St Albans, Hertfordshire; a victory for the house of York.

St James's Palace palace in Pall Mall, London, a royal residence 1698–1837.

St Michael and St George British orders of ◊knighthood.

Salisbury Robert Cecil, 1st Earl of Salisbury. Title conferred on Robert ◊Cecil, secretary of state to Elizabeth I of England.

Salisbury Robert Arthur Talbot Gascoyne-Cecil, 3rd Marquess of Salisbury 1830–1903. British Conservative politician. He entered the Commons 1853 and succeeded to his title 1868. As foreign secretary 1878–80, he took part in the Congress of Berlin, and as prime minister 1885–86, 1886–92, and 1895–1902 gave his main attention to foreign policy, remaining also as foreign secretary for most of this time.

Salisbury Robert Arthur James Gascoyne-Cecil, 5th Marquess of Salisbury 1893–1972. British Conservative politician. He was Dominions secretary 1940-42 and 1943-45, colonial secretary 1942, Lord Privy Seal 1942-43 and 1951-52, and Lord President of the Council 1952-57.

Sandringham House private residence of the British sovereign, built 1863 by the Prince of Wales (afterwards Edward VII) 1869–1971.

Sandwich John Montagu, 4th Earl of Sandwich 1718–1792. British politician. He was an inept First Lord of the Admiralty 1771–82 during the American Revolution, and his corrupt practices were blamed for the British navy's inadequacies.

The Sandwich Islands (Hawaii) were named after him, as are sandwiches, which he invented so that he could eat without leaving the gaming table.

Sandys Duncan Edwin Sandys, Baron Duncan-Sandys 1908–1987. British Conservative politician. As minister for Commonwealth relations 1960-64, he negotiated the independence of Malaysia 1963. He was created a life peer in 1974.

Saxe-Coburg-Gotha Saxon duchy. Albert, the Prince Consort of Britain's Queen Victoria, was a son of the 1st Duke, Ernest I (1784–1844), who was succeeded by Albert's elder brother, Ernest II (1818–1893). It remained the name of the British royal house until 1917, when it was changed to Windsor.

Saxon member of a Germanic tribe inhabiting the Danish peninsula and northern Germany. The Saxons migrated from their homelands, under pressure from the Franks, and spread into various parts of Europe, including Britain. They also undertook piracy in the North Sea and English Channel.

Scapa Flow expanse of sea in the Orkney Islands, Scotland, until 1957 a base of the Royal Navy. It was the main base of the Grand Fleet during World War I and in 1919 was the scene of the scuttling of 71 surrendered German warships.

Scargill Arthur 1938– . British trade-union leader. Elected president of the National Union of Miners (NUM) 1981, he embarked on a collision course with the Conservative government of Margaret Thatcher. The damaging strike of 1984–85 split the miners' movement.

Scilly, Isles of or *Scilly Isles/Islands*, or *Scillies* group of 140 islands and islets lying 40 km/25 mi SW of Land's End, England; administered by the Duchy of Cornwall; area 16 sq km/6.3 sq mi; population (1981) 1,850. The five inhabited islands are *St Mary's*, the largest, on which is Hugh Town, capital of the Scillies; *Tresco*, the second largest, with subtropical gardens; *St Martin's*, noted for beautiful shells; *St Agnes*; and *Bryher*.

Scone site of ancient palace where most of the Scottish kings were crowned on the Stone of Destiny (now in the Coronation Chair at Westminster, London). The village of Scone is in Tayside, Scotland, N of Perth.

Scotland the northernmost part of Britain, formerly an independent country, now part of the UK
area 78,470 sq km/30,297 sq mi
capital Edinburgh
towns Glasgow, Dundee, Aberdeen
features the Highlands in the N (with the ◊Grampian Mountains); central Lowlands, including valleys of the Clyde and Forth, with most of the country's population and industries; Southern Uplands (including the ◊Lammermuir Hills); and islands of the Orkneys, Shetlands, and Western Isles; the world's greatest concentration of nuclear weapons are at the UK and US bases on the Clyde, near Glasgow; 8,000-year-old pinewood forests once covered 1,500,000 hectares/3,706,500 acres, now reduced to 12,500 hectares/30,900 acres
industry electronics, marine and aircraft engines, oil, natural gas, chemicals, textiles, clothing, printing, paper, food processing, tourism
currency pound sterling
population (1991) 4,998,567
languages English; Scots, a lowland dialect (derived from Northumbrian Anglo-Saxon); Gaelic spoken by 1.4%, mainly in the Highlands
religions Presbyterian (Church of Scotland), Roman Catholic
famous people Robert Bruce, Walter Scott, Robert Burns, Robert Louis Stevenson, Adam Smith
government Scotland sends 72 members to the UK Parliament at Westminster. Local government is on similar lines to that of England, but there is a differing legal system (see ◊Scottish law).

There is a movement for an independent or devolved Scottish assembly.

SDLP abbreviation for ◊*Social Democratic Labour Party* (Northern Ireland).

SDP abbreviation for ◊*Social Democratic Party*.

Scotland: history

3,000 BC	Neolithic settlements include Beaker People and Skara Brae on Orkney.
1st millenium BC	Picts reached Scotland from mainland Europe.
1st century AD	More than 400 brochs, thick-walled circular towers, built in far N regions.
79–84	Roman invasion by Julius Agricola; defeat of Caledonians at Mons Graupius, E Scotland.
122–128	Hadrian's Wall built to keep the northern tribes out of England.
c. 142	Antonine Wall from Forth to the Clyde, a stone and turf wall, built by Roman general Lollius Urbicus as a forward defence.
c. 185	Antonine Wall abandoned.
297	First reference to Picts in Latin documents.
c. 500	The Scots, Gaelic-speaking Irish immigrants, led by Fergus, son of Erc, settled in Kingdom of Dalriada (modern Argyll), with capital at Dunadd.
563	St Columba founded the monastery on Iona and began conversion of Picts to Christianity.
9th century	Norsemen conquered Orkney, Shetland, Western Isles, and much of Highlands.
c. 843	Unification of Picts, Scots, Britons, and Angles under Kenneth I MacAlpine.
1018	At Battle of Carham Malcolm II defeated Northumbrian army, bringing Lothian under Scottish rule.
1034	Duncan became king of United Scotland.
1040	Duncan murdered by Macbeth.
1069	Malcolm III (Ceann Mor) married English Princess Margaret, who introduced several reforms to the Scottish church.
1263	Battle of Largs: defeat of Scots by Norwegian king Haakon.
1295	First treaty between Scotland and France (the 'Auld Alliance').
1296	Edward I of England invaded and declared himself King of Scotland.
1297	William Wallace and Andrew Moray defeated English at Battle of Stirling Bridge.
1314	Robert the Bruce defeated English under Edward II at Battle of Bannockburn.
1326	Parliament at Cambuskenneth the first to be attended by nobles, clergy, and burghs.
1328	Scottish independence under Robert the Bruce recognised by England.
1371	Robert II, first Stuart king, crowned.
1513	Scots defeated by English (and King James IV killed) at Battle of Flodden.

1542	Mary Queen of Scots succeeded to throne when less than a week old.
1544	Henry VII laid waste to Edinburgh and the Borders (the 'Rough Wooing').
1557	The First Covenant signed, pledging break with Rome.
1559	John Knox returned permanently to Scotland, to participate in shift of Scottish church to Protestantism.
1567	Mary forced to abdicate and the following year fled to England.
1603	Crowns of England and Scotland united under James VI who became James I of England.
1638	National Covenant condemned Charles I's changes in church ritual; Scottish rebellion.
1643	Solemn League and Covenant: Scottish Covenanters ally with English Parliament against Charles I.
1651	Cromwell invaded Scotland and defeated Scots at Dunbar and Inverkeithing.
1689	At Killiecrankie, Jacobite forces under Graham of Claverhouse, Viscount Dundee, defeated William of Orange's army, but Dundee mortally wounded.
1692	Massacre of Glencoe: William of Orange ordered MacDonalds of Glencoe murdered in their sleep.
1707	Act of Union united Scottish and English parliaments.
1715	The 'Fifteen': Jacobite rebellion in support of James Edward Stuart, 'James VII'.
1745	The 'Fortyfive': Charles Edward Stuart landed in Scotland and marched as far south as Derby before turning back.
1746	Jacobites defeated at Battle of Culloden by English forces under Duke of Cumberland.
1767	Creation of Edinburgh New Town, planned by James Craig (1749–1795).
1843	The Disruption: 400 ministers left the Church ofScotland to form the Free Church of Scotland.
1886	Crofters Act provided security of tenure forcrofters.
1888	James Keir Hardie founded Scottish Labour Party.
1926	Secretary for Scotland became British cabinet post.
1928	National Party of Scotland formed (became Scottish National Party 1934).
1970s	Aberdeen the centre of North Sea oil development.
1975	Scottish counties replaced by nine regions and three island areas.
1979	Referendum rejected proposal for directly elected Scottish assembly.
1989	Local rates replaced by 'poll tax' despite wide opposition.
1990	350,000 warrants issued by March for nonpayment of poll tax.

Scotland: kings and queens

(from the unification of Scotland to the union of the crowns of Scotland and England)

Celtic kings Malcolm II	1005
Duncan I	1034
Macbeth	1040
Malcolm III Canmore	1057
Donald Ban (restored)	1095
Edgar	1097
Alexander I	1107
David I	1124
Malcolm IV	1153
William the Lion	1165
Alexander II	1214
Alexander III	1249
Margaret of Norway	1286–90
English domination John Baliol	1292–96
annexed to England	1296–1306
House of Bruce	
Robert I Bruce	1306
David II	1329
House of Stuart	
Robert II	1371
Robert III	1390
James I	1406
James II	1437
James III	1460
James IV	1488
James V	1513
Mary	1542
James VI	1567
Union of crowns	1603

seal mark or impression made in a block of wax to authenticate letters and documents. Seals were used in ancient China and are still used in China, Korea, and Japan.

In medieval England, the *great seal* of the nation was kept by the chancellor. The *privy seal* of the monarch was initially kept for less serious matters, but by the 14th century it had become the most important seal.

secretary of state in the UK, a title held by a number of ministers; for example, the secretary of state for foreign and commonwealth affairs.

Sedgemoor, Battle of in English history, a battle 6 July 1685 in which ◊Monmouth's rebellion was crushed by the forces of James II, on a tract of marshy land 5 km/3 mi SE of Bridgwater, Somerset.

Selden John 1584–1654. English antiquarian and opponent of Charles I's claim to the ◊divine right of kings (the doctrine that the monarch is answerable to God alone), for which he was twice imprisoned. His Table Talk 1689 consists of short essays on political and religious questions.

select committee any of several long-standing committees of the UK House of Commons, such as the Environment Committee and the Treasury and Civil Service Committee. These were intended to restore parliamentary control of the executive, improve the quality of legislation, and scrutinize public spending and the work of government departments. Select committees represent the major parliamentary reform of the 20th century, and a possible means – through their all-party membership – of avoiding the automatic repeal of one government's measures by its successor.

Selkirk Alexander 1676–1721. Scottish sailor marooned 1704–09 in the Juan Fernández Islands in the S Pacific. His story inspired Daniel Defoe to write Robinson Crusoe.

Selwyn Lloyd John, Baron 1904–1978. British Conservative politician. He was foreign secretary 1955–60 and chancellor of the Exchequer 1960–62.

Sepoy Rebellion alternative name for the ◊Indian Mutiny, a revolt of Indian soldiers against the British in India 1857–58.

Settlement, Act of in Britain, a law passed 1701 during the reign of King William III, designed to ensure a Protestant succession to the throne by excluding the Roman Catholic descendants of James II in favour of the Protestant House of Hanover. Elizabeth II still reigns under this act.

Seymour Jane c. 1509–1537. Third wife of Henry VIII, whom she married in 1536. She died soon after the birth of her son Edward VI.

shadow cabinet the chief members of the British parliamentary opposition, each of whom is responsible for commenting on the policies and performance of a government ministry.

Shaftesbury Anthony Ashley Cooper, 1st Earl of Shaftesbury 1621–1683. English politician, a supporter of the Restoration of the monarchy. He became Lord Chancellor in 1672, but went into opposition in 1673 and began to organize the ◊Whig Party. He headed the Whigs' demand for the exclusion of the future James II from the succession, secured the passing of the ◊Habeas Corpus Act 1679, then, when accused of treason 1681, fled to Holland.

Shaftesbury Anthony Ashley Cooper, 3rd Earl of Shaftesbury 1671–1713. English philosopher, author of Characteristics of Men, Manners, Opinions, and Times 1711 and other ethical speculations.

Shaftesbury Anthony Ashley Cooper, 7th Earl of Shaftesbury 1801–1885. British Tory politician. He strongly supported the Ten Hours Act of 1847 and other factory legislation, including the 1842 act forbidding the employment of women and children underground in mines. He was also associated with the movement to provide free education for the poor.

Sharp Granville 1735–1813. English philanthropist. He was prominent in the anti-slavery movement and in 1772 secured a legal decision 'that as soon as any slave sets foot on English territory he becomes free'.

Sheffield Outrages in British history, sensational reports in the national press 1866 exemplifying summary justice exercised by trade unions to secure subscriptions and obtain compliance with rules by threats, removal of tools, sabotage of equipment at work, and assaults.

Shelburne William Petty FitzMaurice, 2nd Earl of Shelburne 1737–1805. British Whig politician. He was an opponent of George III's American policy, and as prime minister in 1783, he concluded peace with the United States of America.

Sheppard Jack 1702–1724. English criminal. Born in Stepney, E London, he was an apprentice carpenter, but turned to theft and became a popular hero by escaping four times from prison. He was finally caught and hanged.

Shetland Islands islands off the N coast of Scotland, beyond the Orkneys
area 1,400 sq km/541 sq mi
towns Lerwick (administrative headquarters), on Mainland, largest of 19 inhabited islands
physical over 100 islands including Muckle Flugga (latitude 60°8 51"m6 N) the northernmost of the British Isles
products processed fish, handknits from Fair Isle and Unst, miniature ponies. Europe's largest oil port is Sullom Voe, Mainland
population (1988 est) 22,900
language dialect derived from Norse, the islands having been a Norse dependency from the 8th century until 1472.

ship money tax for support of the navy, levied on the coastal districts of England in the Middle Ages. Ship money was declared illegal by Parliament 1641.

Short Parliament the English Parliament that was summoned by Charles I on 13 April 1640 to raise funds for his war against the Scots. It was succeeded later in the year by the ◊Long Parliament.

Shovell Cloudesley c. 1650–1707. English admiral who took part, with George Rooke (1650–1709), in the capture of Gibraltar 1704. In 1707 his flagship Association was wrecked off the Isles of Scilly and he was strangled for his rings by an islander when he came ashore.

Sidmouth, Viscount title of Henry ◊Addington, British Tory prime minister 1801–04.

Sidney Algernon 1622–1683. English Republican politician, He was a cavalry officer in the Civil War on the Parliamentary side, and was wounded at the Battle of ◊Marston Moor 1644. He was elected to the ◊Long Parliament 1646, but retired from politics when ◊Cromwell dissolved the ◊Rump 1653. After the ◊Restoration he lived in exile on the Continent, but on returning to England 1677 continued to oppose the monarchy. He was arrested after the ◊Rye House Plot 1683, convicted of high treason, and executed.

Silbury Hill steep, rounded artificial mound (40 m/130 ft high) of the Bronze Age 2660 BC, in Wiltshire, near ◊Avebury, England. Excavation has shown it not to be a ◊barrow, as was previously thought.

Simnel Lambert c. 1475–c. 1535. English impostor, a joiner's son who under the influence of an Oxford priest claimed to be Prince Edward, one of the ◊Princes in the Tower. ◊Henry VII discovered the plot and released the real Edward for one day to show him to the public. Simnel had a keen following and was crowned as Edward VI in Dublin 1487. He came with forces to England to fight the royal army, and attacked it near Stoke-on-Trent 16 June 1487. He was defeated and captured, but was contemptuously pardoned. He is then said to have worked in the king's kitchen.

Simon John Allsebrook, Viscount Simon 1873–1954. British Liberal politician. He was home secretary 1915–16, but resigned over the issue of conscription. He was foreign secretary 1931–35, home secretary again 1935–37, chancellor of the Exchequer 1937–40, and lord chancellor 1940–45.

Sinn Féin Irish nationalist party founded by Arthur Griffith (1872–1922) in 1905; in 1917 Éamon ◊de Valera became its president. It is the political wing of the Irish Republican Army, and is similarly split between comparative moderates and extremists. In 1985 it gained representation in 17 out of 26 district councils in Northern Ireland.

Six Acts in British history, acts of Parliament passed 1819 by Lord Liverpool's Tory administration to curtail political radicalism in the aftermath of the ◊Peterloo massacre and during a period of agitation for reform when habeas corpus was suspended and the powers of magistrates extended.

Six Articles act introduced by Henry VIII in England in 1539 to settle disputes over dogma in the English church. The articles affirmed belief in transubstantiation, communion in one kind only, auricular confession, monastic vows, celibacy of the clergy, and private masses; those who rejected transubstantiation were to be burned at the stake. The act was repealed in 1547, replaced by 42 articles in 1551, and by an act of Thirty-Nine Articles in 1571.

SLD abbreviation for ◊*Social and Liberal Democrats*.

Slim William Joseph, 1st Viscount 1891–1970. British field marshal in World War II. He commanded the 1st Burma Corps 1942–45, stemming the Japanese invasion of India, and then forcing them out of

Burma (now Myanmar). He was governor general of Australia 1953–60.

Sluis, Battle of (or *Sluys*) 1340 naval victory for England over France which marked the beginning of the Hundred Years' War. England took control of the English Channel and seized 200 great ships from the French navy of Philip IV; there were 30,000 French casualties.

Smith Henry George Wakelyn 1787–1860. British general. He served in the Peninsular War (1808–14) and later fought in South Africa and India. He was governor of Cape Colony 1847–52. The towns of Ladysmith and Harrismith, South Africa, are named after his wife and himself respectively.

Smith John 1580–1631. English colonist. After an adventurous early life he took part in the colonization of Virginia, acting as president of the North American colony 1608–09. He explored New England in 1614, which he named, and published pamphlets on America and an autobiography. His trade with the Indians may have kept the colonists alive in the early years.

Smith John 1938–   . British Labour politician, party leader from 1992. He was secretary of state for trade 1978–79 and from 1979 held various shadow cabinet posts, culminating in shadow chancellor 1987–92.

Snowden Philip, 1st Viscount Snowden 1864–1937. British right-wing Labour politician, chancellor of the Exchequer 1924 and 1929–31. He entered the coalition National Government in 1931 as Lord Privy Seal, but resigned in 1932.

Soames Christopher, Baron Soames 1920–1987. British Conservative politician. He held ministerial posts 1958–64, was vice president of the Commission of the European Communities 1973–77 and governor of (Southern) Rhodesia in the period of its transition to independence as Zimbabwe, Dec 1979–April 1980. He was created a life peer 1978.

socage Anglo-Saxon term for the free tenure of land by the peasantry. Sokemen, holders of land by this tenure, formed the upper stratum of peasant society at the time of the ◊Domesday Book.

Social and Liberal Democrats official name for the British political party formed 1988 from the former Liberal Party and most of the Social Democratic Party. The common name for the party is the *Liberal Democrats*.

social democracy political ideology or belief in the gradual evolution of a democratic ◊socialism within existing political structures. The earliest was the German Sozialdemokratische Partei (SPD), today one of the two main German parties, created in 1875 from August Bebel's earlier German Social Democratic Workers' Party, founded 1869. Parties along the lines of the German model were founded in the last two decades of the 19th century in a number of countries, including Austria, Belgium, the Netherlands, Hungary, Poland, and Russia. The British Labour Party is in the social democratic tradition.

Social Democratic Federation (SDF) in British history, a socialist society, founded as the Democratic Federation in 1881 and renamed in 1884. It was led by H M Hyndman (1842–1921), a former conservative journalist and stockbroker who claimed Karl Marx as his inspiration without obtaining recognition from his mentor. In 1911 it became the British Socialist Party.

Social Democratic Labour Party (SDLP) Northern Irish left-wing political party, formed in 1970. It aims ultimately at Irish unification, but distances itself from the violent tactics of the Irish Republican Army (IRA), adopting a constitutional, conciliatory role. The SDLP, led by John ◊Hume, was responsible for setting up the ◊New Ireland Forum in 1983.

Social Democratic Party (SDP) British centrist political party 1981–90, formed by members of Parliament who resigned from the Labour Party. The 1983 and 1987 general elections were fought in alliance with the Liberal Party as the *Liberal/SDP Alliance*. A merger of the two parties was voted for by the SDP 1987, and the new party became the ◊Social and Liberal Democrats, leaving a rump SDP that folded 1990.

socialism movement aiming to establish a classless society by substituting public for private ownership of the means of production, distribution, and exchange. The term has been used to describe positions as widely apart as anarchism and social democracy.

In the later 19th century, socialist parties arose in most European countries and the ◊Independent Labour Party was founded in Britain. This period, when in Russia the Bolsheviks were reviving, witnessed a reaction against Marxism, typified by the ◊Fabian Society in Britain and the German Revisionists, which appealed to popular nationalism and solved economic problems by similar means of state control of the economy, but in the general interests of private capital.

Somerset Edward Seymour, 1st Duke of Somerset c. 1506–1552. English politician. Created Earl of Hertford after Henry VIII's marriage to his sister Jane, he became Duke of Somerset and protector (regent) for Edward VI in 1547. His attempt to check ◊enclosure (the transfer of land from common to private ownership) offended landowners and his moderation in religion upset the Protestants, and he was beheaded on a fake treason charge in 1552.

South African Wars two wars between the Boers (settlers of Dutch origin) and the British; essentially fought for the gold and diamonds of the Transvaal.

The *War of 1881* was triggered by the attempt of the Boers of the Transvaal to reassert the independence surrendered 1877 in return for British aid against African peoples. The British were defeated at Majuba, and the Transvaal again became independent.

The *War of 1899–1902*, also known as the *Boer War*, was preceded by the armed Jameson Raid into the Boer Transvaal; a failed attempt, inspired by the Cape Colony prime minister Rhodes, to precipitate a revolt against Kruger, the Transvaal president. The *uitlanders* (non-Boer immigrants) were still not given the vote by the Boers, negotiations failed, and the Boers invaded British territory, besieging Ladysmith, Mafeking (now Mafikeng), and Kimberley. The war ended with the Peace of Vereeniging following the Boer defeat.

British commander ◊Kitchener countered Boer guerrilla warfare by putting the noncombatants who supported them into concentration camps, where about 26,000 women and children died of sickness.

South Sea Bubble financial crisis in Britain in 1720. The South Sea Company, founded 1711, which had a monopoly of trade with South

America, offered in 1719 to take over more than half the national debt in return for further concessions. Its 100 shares rapidly rose to 1,000, and an orgy of speculation followed. When the 'bubble' burst, thousands were ruined. The discovery that cabinet ministers had been guilty of corruption led to a political crisis.

Spanish Armada fleet sent by Philip II of Spain against England in 1588. Consisting of 130 ships, it sailed from Lisbon and carried on a running fight up the Channel with the English fleet of 197 small ships under Howard of Effingham and Francis ◊Drake. The Armada anchored off Calais but fireships forced it to put to sea, and a general action followed off Gravelines. What remained of the Armada escaped around the N of Scotland and W of Ireland, suffering many losses by storm and shipwreck on the way. Only about half the original fleet returned to Spain.

Spanish Succession, War of the war 1701–14 of Britain, Austria, the Netherlands, Portugal, and Denmark (the Allies) against France, Spain, and Bavaria. It was caused by Louis XIV's acceptance of the Spanish throne on behalf of his grandson, Philip, in defiance of the Partition Treaty of 1700, under which it would have passed to Archduke Charles of Austria (later Holy Roman emperor Charles VI).

Speaker presiding officer charged with the preservation of order in the legislatures of various countries. In the UK the equivalent of the Speaker in the House of Lords is the Lord Chancellor; in the House of Commons the Speaker is elected for each parliament, usually on an agreed basis among the parties, but often holds the office for many years. The original appointment dates from 1377.

Special Areas Acts UK acts of Parliament 1936 and 1937, aimed at dealing with high unemployment in some regions of Britain. These areas, designated 'special areas', attracted government assistance in the form of loans and subsidies to generate new employment. Other measures included setting up industrial and trading estates that could be leased at subsidized rates. The acts were an early example of regional aid.

Special Branch section of the British police originally established 1883 to deal with Irish Fenian activists. All 52 police forces in Britain now have their own Special Branches. They act as the executive arm of MI5 (the British domestic ◊intelligence service) in its duty of preventing or investigating espionage, subversion, and sabotage; carry out duties at air and sea ports in respect of naturalization and immigration; and provide armed bodyguards for public figures.

Stamford Bridge, Battle of battle 25 Sept 1066 at Stamford Bridge, a crossing of the Derwent 12 km/7 mi east of York, at which ◊Harold II defeated and killed Harold Hardraada, king of Norway, and ◊Tostig, the English king's exiled brother. Harold then marched south to face the Normans at the Battle of ◊Hastings.

Stamp Act UK act of Parliament in 1765 that sought to raise enough money from the American colonies to cover the cost of their defence. The act taxed (by requiring an official stamp) all publications and legal documents published in British colonies. Refusal to use the required tax stamps and a blockade of British merchant shipping in the colonies forced repeal of the act the following year. It helped to precipitate the American Revolution.

The act provoked vandalism and looting in America, and the *Stamp Act Congress* in Oct of that year (the first intercolonial congress) declared the act unconstitutional, with the slogan 'No taxation without representation', because the colonies were not represented in the British Parliament.

Star Chamber in English history, a civil and criminal court, named after the star-shaped ceiling decoration of the room in the Palace of Westminster, London, where its first meetings were held. Created in 1487 by Henry VII, the Star Chamber comprised some 20 or 30 judges. It was abolished 1641 by the ◊Long Parliament.

The Star Chamber became notorious under Charles I for judgements favourable to the king and to Archbishop ◊Laud (for example, the branding on both cheeks of William Prynne in 1637 for seditious libel). Under the Thatcher government 1979–90 the term was revived for private ministerial meetings at which disputes between the Treasury and high-spending departments were resolved.

Statute of Westminster in the history of the British Empire, legislation enacted 1931 which gave the dominions of the British Empire complete autonomy in their conduct of external affairs. It made them self-governing states whose only allegiance was to the British crown.

Steel David 1938– . British politician, leader of the Liberal Party 1976–88. He entered into a compact with the Labour government 1977–78, and into an alliance with the Social Democratic Party (SDP) 1983. Having supported the Liberal-SDP merger (forming the ◊Social and Liberal Democrats), he resigned the leadership 1988, becoming the Party's foreign affairs spokesman.

Stephen c. 1097–1154. King of England from 1135. A grandson of William the Conqueror, he was elected king 1135, although he had previously recognized Henry I's daughter ◊Matilda as heiress to the throne. Matilda landed in England 1139, and civil war disrupted the country until 1153, when Stephen acknowledged Matilda's son, Henry II, as his own heir.

Stone Lawrence 1919– . British-born US historian best known for his work on the English aristocracy The Crisis of the Aristocracy 1558–1641 and as a participant in the debates this engendered. Later, he moved to examine the causes of the English revolution before engaging in a study of family history, The Family, Sex and Marriage in England, 1500–1800.

Stonehenge megalithic monument dating from about 2000 BC on Salisbury Plain, Wiltshire, England. It consisted originally of a circle of 30 upright stones, their tops linked by lintel stones to form a continuous circle about 30 m/100 ft across. Within the circle was a horseshoe arrangement of five trilithons (two uprights plus a lintel, set as five separate entities), and a so-called 'altar stone' – an upright pillar – on the axis of the horseshoe at the open, NE end, which faces in the direction of the rising sun. It has been suggested that it served as an observatory.

Stonehouse John (Thompson) 1925–1988. British Labour Party politician. An active member of the Co-operative Movement, he entered Parliament in 1957 and held junior posts under Harold Wilson before joining his cabinet in 1967. In 1974 he disappeared in Florida in mysterious circumstances, surfacing in Australia, amid suspicions of fraudulent dealings. Extradited to Britain, he was tried and imprisoned for embezzlement. He was released in 1979, but was unable to resume a political career.

Strafford Thomas Wentworth, 1st Earl of Strafford 1593–1641. English politician, originally an opponent of Charles I, but from 1628 on the Royalist side. He ruled despotically as Lord Deputy of Ireland 1632–39, when he returned to England as Charles's chief adviser and received an earldom. He was impeached in 1640 by Parliament, abandoned by Charles as a scapegoat, and beheaded.

Stuart Lady Arabella 1575–1615. Claimant to the English throne. She was the cousin of ◊James I and next in succession to him to both Scottish and English thrones after ◊Elizabeth I. She was the focus of the main plot to eliminate James, and was imprisoned 1609 when Elizabeth became suspicious. On her release 1610 she secretly married William Seymour, another claimant to the throne, and they were both imprisoned. She died insane in the Tower of London.

Stuart or *Stewart* royal family who inherited the Scottish throne in 1371 and the English throne in 1603, holding it until 1714, when Queen Anne died without heirs and the house of Stuart was replaced by the house of ◊Hanover.

Suez Canal artificial waterway, 160 km/100 mi long, from Port Said to Suez, linking the Mediterranean and Red seas, separating Africa from Asia, and providing the shortest eastwards sea route from Europe. It was opened 1869, nationalized 1956, blocked by Egypt during the Arab-Israeli War 1967, and not reopened until 1975.

Suez Crisis military confrontation Oct–Dec 1956 following the nationalization of the Suez Canal by President Nasser of Egypt. In an attempt to reassert international control of the canal, Israel launched an attack, after which British and French troops landed. Widespread international censure forced the withdrawal of the British and French. The crisis resulted in the resignation of British prime minister Eden.

At a London conference of maritime powers the Australian prime minister, Robert Menzies, was appointed to negotiate a settlement in Cairo. His mission was unsuccessful. The military intervention met Soviet protest and considerable domestic opposition, and the USA did not support it. British, French, and Australian relations with the USA were greatly strained during this period.

suffragette or *suffragist* woman fighting for the right to vote. In the

UK, women's suffrage bills were repeatedly introduced and defeated in Parliament between 1886 and 1911, and a militant campaign was launched 1906 by Emmeline Pankhurst and her daughters. In 1918 women were granted limited franchise; in 1928 it was extended to all women over 21. In the USA the 19th amendment to the constitution 1920 gave women the vote in federal and state elections.

Sunderland Robert Spencer, 2nd Earl of Sunderland 1640–1702. English politician, a sceptical intriguer who converted to Roman Catholicism to secure his place under James II, and then reverted with the political tide. In 1688 he fled to Holland (disguised as a woman), where he made himself invaluable to the future William III. Now a Whig, he advised the new king to adopt the system, which still prevails, of choosing the government from the dominant party in the Commons.

Sunningdale Agreement pact Dec 1973 between the UK and Irish governments, together with the Northern Ireland executive, drawn up in Sunningdaie, England. The agreement included provisions for a power- snaring executive in Northern Ireland. However, the executive lasted only five weeks before the UK government was defeated in a general election, and a general strike May 1974 brought down the Northern Ireland government. The experiment has not been repeated.

Supremacy, Acts of two UK acts of Parliament 1534 and 1559, which established Henry VIII and Elizabeth I respectively as head of the English church in place of the pope.

Surrey Henry Howard, Earl of Surrey c. 1517–1547. English courtier and poet. With Thomas ◊Wyatt, he introduced the sonnet to England and was a pioneer of blank verse. He was executed on a poorly based charge of high treason.

Swing Riots uprising of farm workers in S and E England 1830–31. Farm labourers protested at the introduction of new threshing machines, which jeopardised their livelihood. They fired ricks, smashed the machines and sent threatening letters to farmers. They invented a Captain Swing as their leader, and he became a figure of fear to the landed gentry. The riots were suppressed by the government, with 19 executions and almost 500 transportations.

syndicalism political movement in 19th-century Europe that rejected parliamentary activity in favour of direct action, culminating in a revolutionary general strike to secure worker ownership and control of industry. After 1918 syndicalism was absorbed in communism, although it continued to have an independent existence in Spain until the late 1930s.

T

Taff Vale judgement decision 1901 by the British Law lords that trade unions were liable for their members' actions, and could hence be sued for damages in the event of a strike, picketing, or boycotting an employer. It followed a strike by union members for higher wages and union recognition against the Taff Vale Railway Company. The judgement resulted in a rapid growth of union membership, and was replaced by the Trade Disputes Act 1906.

Tariff Reform League organization set up 1903 as a vehicle for the ideas of the Liberal politician Joseph ◊Chamberlain on protective tariffs. It aimed to unify the British Empire by promoting imperial preference in trade.

Taylor A(lan) J(ohn) P(ercivale) 1906–1990. English historian and television lecturer. International history lecturer at Oxford University 1953–63, he established himself as an authority on modern British and European history and did much to popularize the subject, giving the first televised history lectures. His books include The Struggle for Mastery in Europe 1848–1918 1954, The Origins of the Second World War 1961, and English History 1914–1945 1965.

Ten Hours Act 1847 British act of Parliament that restricted the working day of all workers except adult males. It was prompted by the public campaign (the 'Ten Hours Movement') set up 1831. Women and young people were restricted to a 10 1/2 hour day, with 1 1/2 hours for meals, between 6 am and 6 pm.

Test Act act of Parliament passed in England 1673, more than 100 years after similar legislation in Scotland, requiring holders of public office to renounce the doctrine of transubstantiation and take the sacrament in an Anglican church, thus excluding Catholics, Nonconformists, and non-Christians from office. Its clauses were repealed

1828–29. Scottish tests were abolished 1889. In Ireland the Test Act was introduced 1704 and English legislation on oaths of allegiance and religious declarations were made valid there 1782. All these provisions were abolished 1871.

Tewkesbury, Battle of battle 4 May 1471 at which ◊Edward IV defeated the Lancastrian forces of Queen Margaret, wife of ◊Henry VI. Henry's only son, Prince Edward (1453–1471), was killed, as were many other leading Lancastrian supporters. The battle was decisive for Edward IV, and his throne was never seriously challenged again.

thane or *thegn* Anglo-Saxon hereditary nobleman rewarded by the granting of land for service to the monarch or a lord.

Thatcher Margaret Hilda (born Roberts), Baroness Thatcher of Kesteven 1925–   . British Conservative politician, prime minister 1979–90. She was education minister 1970–74 and Conservative Party leader from 1975. In 1982 she sent British troops to recapture the Falkland Islands from Argentina. She confronted trade-union power during the miners' strike 1984–85, sold off majority stakes in many public utilities to the private sector, and reduced the influence of local government through such measures as the abolition of metropolitan councils, the control of expenditure through 'rate-capping', and the introduction of the community charge, or ◊poll tax, from 1989. In 1990 splits in the cabinet over the issues of Europe and consensus government forced her resignation. An astute Parliamentary tactician, she tolerated little disagreement, either from the opposition or from within her own party.

Thatcherism political outlook comprising a belief in the efficacy of market forces, the need for strong central government, and a conviction that self-help is preferable to reliance on the state, combined with a strong element of nationalism. The ideology is associated with Margaret Thatcher but stems from an individualist view found in Britain's 19th-century Liberal and 20th-century Conservative parties, and is no longer confined to Britain.

thegn alternative spelling of ◊thane.

Thistlewood Arthur 1770–1820. English Radical. A follower of the pamphleteer Thomas Spence (1750–1814), he was active in the Radical movement and was executed as the chief leader of the ◊Cato Street Conspiracy to murder government ministers.

Thomas Aquinas medieval philosopher.

three-day week in the UK, the policy adopted by Prime Minister Edward Heath Jan 1974 to combat an economic crisis and coal miners' strike. A shortage of electrical power led to the allocation of energy to industry for only three days each week. A general election was called Feb 1974, which the government lost.

Throckmorton Plot plot 1583 to put ◊Mary Queen of Scots on the English throne in place of ◊Elizabeth I. The plot involved the invasion of England by English Catholic exiles in Spain, led by the Frenchman Henri, duc de Guise. Its leading figure, the zealous Roman Catholic Francis Throckmorton (1554–1584), revealed details of the plot under torture and was executed.

Titanic British passenger liner, supposedly unsinkable, that struck an iceberg and sank off the Grand Banks of Newfoundland on its first voyage 14–15 April 1912; 1,513 lives were lost. In 1985 it was located by robot submarine 4 km/2.5 mi down in an ocean canyon, preserved by the cold environment. In 1987 salvage operations began.

tithe formerly, payment exacted from the inhabitants of a parish for the maintenance of the church and its incumbent; some religious groups continue the practice by giving 10% of members' incomes to charity.

Tolpuddle Martyrs six farm labourers of Tolpuddle, a village in Dorset, SW England, who were transported to Australia in 1834 after being sentenced for 'administering unlawful oaths' – as a 'union', they had threatened to withdraw their labour unless their pay was guaranteed, and had been prepared to put this in writing. They were pardoned two years later, after nationwide agitation. They returned to England and all but one migrated to Canada.

Tone (Theobald) Wolfe 1763–1798. Irish nationalist, prominent in the revolutionary society of the United Irishmen. In 1798 he accompanied the French invasion of Ireland, was captured and condemned to death, but slit his own throat in prison.

tonnage and poundage duties granted in England 1371–1787 by Parliament to the crown on imports and exports of wine and other goods. They were levied by Charles I in 1626 without parliamentary consent, provoking controversy.

Tory democracy concept attributed to the 19th-century British Conservative Party, and to the campaign of Lord Randolph ◊Churchill against Stafford Northcote in the early 1880s. The slogan was not backed up by any specific policy proposals.

Tory Party the forerunner of the British ◊Conservative Party about 1680–1830. It was the party of the squire and parson, as opposed to the Whigs (supported by the trading classes and Nonconformists). The name is still applied colloquially to the Conservative Party. In the USA a Tory was an opponent of the break with Britain in the War of American Independence 1775–83.

Tostig Anglo-Saxon ruler, the son of Earl ◊Godwin and brother of ◊Harold II. He was made Earl of Northumbria 1055 by his brother-in-law, ◊Edward the Confessor, but was outlawed and exiled because of his severity. He joined Harold Hardraada of Norway in the invasion 1066 of northern England, but they were both defeated and killed by Harold II at the Battle of ◊Stamford Bridge 1066.

Townshend Charles 1725–1767. British politician, chancellor of the Exchequer 1766–67. The *Townshend Acts*, designed to assert Britain's traditional authority over its colonies, resulted in widespread resistance. Among other things they levied taxes on imports (such as tea, glass, and paper) into the North American colonies. Opposition in the colonies to taxation without representation (see ◊Stamp Act) precipitated the American Revolution.

Townshend Charles, 2nd Viscount Townshend (known as 'Turnip' Townshend) 1674–1738. English politician and agriculturalist. He was secretary of state under George I 1714–17, when dismissed for opposing the king's foreign policy, and 1721–30, after which he retired to his farm and did valuable work in developing crop rotation and cultivating winter feeds for cattle (hence his nickname).

Toynbee Arnold 1852–1883. English economic historian who popularised the term 'industrial revolution' in his Lectures on the Industrial Revolution, published 1884.

Toynbee Arnold Joseph 1889–1975. English historian whose *A Study of History* 1934–61 was an attempt to discover the laws governing the rise and fall of civilizations.

trade union organization of workers which exists to promote and defend the interests of its members. Trade unions are particularly concerned with pay, working conditions, job security, and redundancy. Four types of trade union are often distinguished: general unions, craft unions, industrial unions, and white-collar unions.

Trades Union Congress (TUC) voluntary organization of trade unions, founded in the UK 1868, in which delegates of affiliated unions meet annually to consider matters affecting their members. In 1993 there were 69 affiliated unions, with an aggregate membership of 7.7 million.

Ten Largest Unions 1993

Amalgamated Engineering and Electrical Union (AEEU)	1,425,830
UNISON	1,400,000
Transport and General Workers' Union (TGWU)	1,126,631
GMB (formerly General, Municipal, Boilermakers and Allied Trades Union)	862,785
Manufacturing, Science and Finance Union (MSF)	604,000
Union of Shop, Distributive and Allied Workers (USDAW)	316,491
Graphical, Paper and Media Union (GPMU)	270,023
Union of Construction, Allied Trades and Technicians (UCATT)	202,000
National Association of Schoolmasters and Union of Women Teachers (NAS/UWT)	190,637
Union of Communication Workers (UCW)	182,418

British trade unions: chronology

1799	The Combination Act outlawed organizations of workers combining for the purpose of improving conditions or raising wages. The act was slightly modified 1800.
1811	Luddite machine-breaking campaign against hosiers began; it was ended by arrests and military action 1812.
1818	Weavers and spinners formed the General Union of Trades in Lancashire.
1824	The Combination Act repealed most of the restrictive legislation but an upsurge of violent activity led to a further act 1825. Trade unions could

	only bargain peacefully over working hours and conditions.
1830	The General Union of Trades became the National Association for the Protection of Labour; it collapsed 1832.
1834	Formation of the Grand National Consolidated Trade Union, which lasted only a few months. Six agricultural labourers from Tolpuddle, Dorset, were convicted of swearing illegal oaths and transported to Australia.
1842	The 'Plug Plot' (removing plugs from boilers) took on the appearance of a general strike in support of a People's Charter.
1851	The foundation of the Amalgamated Society of Engineers marked the beginning of the 'New Model Unionism' of skilled workers.
1866	The 'Sheffield outrages' (attacks on nonunion labour) led to a Royal Commission. The Hornby v. Close case cast doubt on the legal status of unions.
1867	Amendments to the Master and Servant Act gave more scope for trade unions, and the Royal Commission recommended they be given formal legal status.
1868	The first Trades Union Congress (TUC) was held in Manchester.
1871	The Trade Union Act gave unions legal recognition.
1888	Beginnings of 'new unionism' and the organization of unskilled workers.
1901	Taff Vale case re-established union liability for damage done by strikes; this was reversed by the Trade Disputes Act 1906.
1909	Osborne judgements ruled against unions using funds for political purposes; this was reversed by the Trade Union Act 1913.
1918–20	Widespread industrial unrest on return to a peacetime economy.
1926	A general strike was called by the TUC in support of the miners.
1930–34	Union membership fell as a result of economic recession. The Transport and General Workers replaced the Miners Federation as the largest single union.
1965	The Trade Disputes Act gave unions further immunities.
1969	The TUC successfully stopped the Labour government white paper *In Place of Strife*.
1971	The Conservative government passed the Industrial Relations Act, limiting union powers.
1973–74	'Winter of Discontent'. Strikes brought about electoral defeat for the Conservative government. Labour introduced the 'Social Contract'.
1980	The Conservatives introduced the Employment Act, severely restricting the powers of unions to picket or enforced closed shop; this was extended 1982.
1984	The miners' strike led to widespread confrontation and divisions within the miners' union.
1984–90	The Conservative government continued to limit the powers of trade unions through various legislative acts.

Trafalgar, Battle of battle 21 Oct 1805 in the ◊Napoleonic Wars. The British fleet under Admiral Nelson defeated a Franco-Spanish fleet; Nelson was mortally wounded. The victory laid the foundation for British naval supremacy throughout the 19th century. It is named after Cape Trafalgar, a low headland in SW Spain, near the western entrance to the Straits of Gibraltar.

trainbands in English history, a civil militia first formed in 1573 by Elizabeth I to meet the possibility of invasion. Trainbands were used by Charles I against the Scots in 1639, but their lack of training meant they were of dubious military value.

transportation punishment of sending convicted persons to overseas territories to serve their sentences. It was introduced in England towards the end of the 17th century and was abolished 1857 after many thousands had been transported, mostly to Australia. It was also used for punishment of criminals by France until 1938.

Trenchard Hugh Montague, 1st Viscount Trenchard 1873–1956. British aviator and police commissioner. He commanded the Royal Flying Corps in World War I 1915–17, and 1918–29 organized the Royal Air Force, becoming its first marshal 1927. As commissioner of the Metropolitan Police, he established the Police College at Hendon and carried out the Trenchard Reforms, which introduced more scientific methods of detection.

Truck Acts UK acts of Parliament introduced 1831, 1887, 1896, and 1940 to prevent employers misusing wage-payment systems to the detriment of their workers. The legislation made it illegal to pay wages with goods in kind or with tokens for use in shops owned by the employers.

TUC abbreviation for ◊*Trades Union Congress*.

Tudor dynasty English dynasty 1485–1603, descended from the Welsh Owen Tudor (*c.* 1400–1461), second husband of Catherine of Valois (widow of Henry V of England). Their son Edmund married Margaret Beaufort (1443–1509), the great-granddaughter of ◊John of Gaunt, and was the father of Henry VII, who became king by overthrowing Richard III 1485. The dynasty ended with the death of Elizabeth I 1603.

Turpin Dick 1706–1739. English highwayman. The son of an innkeeper, he turned to highway robbery, cattle-thieving, and smuggling, and was hanged at York.

Tyler Wat died 1381. English leader of the ♢Peasants' Revolt of 1381. He was probably born in Kent or Essex, and may have served in the French wars. After taking Canterbury, he led the peasant army to Blackheath and occupied London. At Mile End King Richard II met the rebels and promised to redress their grievances, which included the imposition of a poll tax. At a further conference at Smithfield, Tyler was murdered.

U

Ulster former kingdom in Northern Ireland, annexed by England 1461, from Jacobean times a centre of English, and later Scottish, settlement on land confiscated from its owners; divided 1921 into Northern Ireland (counties Antrim, Armagh, Down, Fermanagh, Londonderry, and Tyrone) and the Republic of Ireland (counties Cavan, Donegal, and Monaghan).

Ulster Defence Association (UDA) Northern Ireland Protestant paramilitary organization responsible for a number of sectarian killings. Fanatically loyalist, it established a paramilitary wing (the Ulster Freedom Fighters) to combat the ◊IRA on its own terms and by its own methods. No political party has acknowledged any links with the UDA.

The UDA and the UFF were both proscribed Aug 1992 as part of a government crackdown on the rising tide of Loyalist terrorism and sectarian killings.

Ulster Freedom Fighters (UFF) paramilitary wing of the ◊Ulster Defence Association.

Uniformity, Acts of two acts of Parliament in England. The first in 1559 imposed the Prayer Book on the whole English kingdom; the second in 1662 required the Prayer Book to be used in all churches, and some 2,000 ministers who refused to comply were ejected.

Union, Act of 1707 act of Parliament that brought about the union of England and Scotland; that of 1801 united England and Ireland. The latter was revoked when the Irish Free State was constituted 1922.

union flag British national flag. It is popularly called the *Union Jack*, although, strictly speaking, this applies only when it is flown on the jackstaff of a warship.

Union Movement British political group. Founded as the *New Party* by Oswald ◊Mosley and a number of Labour members of Parliament 1931, it developed into the ***British Union of Fascists*** 1932. In 1940 the organization was declared illegal and its leaders interned, but it was revived as the Union Movement 1948, characterized by racist doctrines including anti-Semitism.

United Irishmen society formed 1791 by Wolfe ◊Tone to campaign for parliamentary reform in Ireland. It later became a secret revolutionary group.

United Kingdom of Great Britain and Northern Ireland (UK)
area 244,100 sq km/94,247 sq mi
capital London
towns Birmingham, Glasgow, Leeds, Sheffield, Liverpool, Manchester, Edinburgh, Bradford, Bristol, Belfast, Newcastle-upon-Tyne, Cardiff
physical became separated from European continent about 6000 BC; rolling landscape, increasingly mountainous towards the N, with Grampian Mountains in Scotland, Pennines in N England, Cambrian Mountains in Wales; rivers include Thames, Severn, and Spey
territories Anguilla, Bermuda, British Antarctic Territory, British Indian Ocean Territory, British Virgin Islands, Cayman Islands, Falkland Islands, Gibraltar, Hong Kong (until 1997), Montserrat, Pitcairn Islands, St Helena and Dependencies (Ascension, Tristan da Cunha), Turks and Caicos Islands
environment an estimated 67% (the highest percentage in Europe) of forests have been damaged by acid rain
features milder climate than N Europe because of Gulf Stream; considerable rainfall. Nowhere more than 120 km/74.5 mi from sea; indented coastline, various small islands
head of state Elizabeth II from 1952
head of government John Major from 1990
political system liberal democracy
political parties Conservative and Unionist Party, right of centre; Labour Party, moderate left of centre; Social and Liberal Democrats, centre-left; Scottish National Party (SNP), Scottish nationalist; Plaid Cymru (Welsh Nationalist Party), Welsh nationalist; Official Ulster Unionist Party (OUP), Democratic Unionist Party (DUP), Ulster People's Unionist Party (UPUP), all Northern Ireland right of centre, in favour of remaining

United Kingdom: chronology

1707	Act of Union between England and Scotland under Queen Anne.
1721	Robert Walpole unofficially first prime minister, under George I.
1783	Loss of North American colonies that form USA; Canada retained.
1801	Act of Ireland united Britain and Ireland.
1819	Peterloo massacre: cavalry charged a meeting of supporters of parliamentary reform.
1832	Great Reform Bill became law, shifting political power from upper to middle class.
1838	Chartist working-class movement formed.
1846	Corn Laws repealed by Robert Peel.
1851	Great Exhibition in London.
1867	Second Reform Bill, extending the franchise, introduced by Disraeli and passed.
1906	Liberal victory; programme of social reform.
1911	Powers of House of Lords curbed.
1914	Irish Home Rule Bill introduced.
1914–18	World War I.
1916	Lloyd George became prime minister.
1920	Home Rule Act incorporated NE of Ireland (Ulster) into the United Kingdom of Great Britain and Northern Ireland.
1921	Ireland, except for Ulster, became a dominion (Irish Free State, later Eire, 1937).
1924	First Labour government led by Ramsay MacDonald.
1926	General Strike.
1931	Coalition government; unemployment reached 3 million.
1939	World War II began.
1940	Winston Churchill became head of coalition government.
1945	Labour government under Clement Attlee; welfare state established.
1951	Conservatives under Winston Churchill defeated Labour.
1956	Suez Crisis.
1964	Labour victory under Harold Wilson.
1970	Conservatives under Edward Heath defeated Labour.
1972	Parliament prorogued in Northern Ireland; direct rule from Westminster began.
1973	UK joined European Economic Community.
1974	Three-day week, coal strike; Wilson replaced Heath.
1976	James Callaghan replaced Wilson as prime minister.
1977	Liberal–Labour pact.

1979	Victory for Conservatives under Margaret Thatcher.
1981	Formation of Social Democratic Party (SDP). Riots occurred in inner cities.
1982	Unemployment over 3 million. Falklands War.
1983	Thatcher re-elected.
1984–85	Coal strike, the longest in British history.
1986	Abolition of metropolitan counties.
1987	Thatcher re-elected for third term.
1988	Liberals and most of SDP merged into the Social and Liberal Democrats, leaving a splinter SDP. Inflation and interest rates rose.
1989	The Green Party polled 2 million votes in the European elections.
1990	Riots as poll tax introduced in England. Troops sent to the Persian Gulf following Iraq's invasion of Kuwait. British hostages held in Iraq, later released. Britain joined European exchange rate mechanism (ERM). Thatcher replaced by John Major as Conservative leader and prime minister.
1991	British troops took part in US-led war against Iraq under United Nations umbrella. Severe economic recession and rising unemployment.
1992	Recession continued. April: Conservative Party won fourth consecutive general election, but with reduced majority. John Smith replaced Neil Kinnock as Labour leader. Sept: sterling devalued and UK withdrawn from ERM. Oct: drastic coal mine closure programme encountered massive public opposition; later reviewed. Major's popularity at unprecedentedly low rating. Nov: government motion in favour of ratification of Maastricht Treaty narrowly passed. Revelations of past arms sales to Iraq implicated senior government figures, including theprime minister.
1993	Recession continued and unemployment reached over 3 million, highest level since 1987. May: Conservatives knocked into third place in Newbury by-election; chancellor of the Exchequer replaced; Lord Justice Scott's inquiry into government implementation of sanctions on weapons exports to Iraq opens. July: Maastricht Treaty ratified by parliament; Conservatives lose Christchurch by-election. Aug: over 1 million people awaiting hospital trea ment, highest figure ever. Oct: Conservatives launch 'Back to Basics' campaign, with emphasis on self-discipline and respect for law and having strong moral undertones. It quickly ran into trouble as a series of scandals implicating Conservative MPs rocked government confidence. Dec: peace proposal for Northern Ireland, the Downing Street Declaration, issued jointly with Irish government.

part of United Kingdom; Social Democratic Labour Party (SDLP), Northern Ireland, moderate left of centre; Sinn Féin, Northern Ireland, socialist, pro- united Ireland; Green Party, ecological

exports cereals, rape, sugar beet, potatoes, meat and meat products, poultry, dairy products, electronic and telecommunications equipment, engineering equipment and scientific instruments, oil and gas, petrochemicals, pharmaceuticals, fertilizers, film and television programmes, aircraft

currency pound sterling (£)

UK population from 1801 (millions)

Year	United Kingdom	England and Wales	Scotland	Northern Ireland
1801	–	8.893	1.608	–
1811	13.368	10.165	1.806	–
1821	15.472	12.000	2.092	–
1831	17.835	13.897	2.364	–
1841	20.183	15.914	2.620	1.649
1851	22.259	17.928	2.889	1.443
1861	24.525	20.066	3.062	1.569
1871	27.431	22.712	3.360	1.359
1881	31.015	25.974	3.736	1.305
1891	34.264	29.003	4.026	1.236
1901	38.237	32.528	4.472	1.237
1911	42.082	36.070	4.761	1.251
1921	44.027	37.887	4.882	1.258
1931	46.038	39.952	4.843	1.243
1951	50.225	43.578	5.096	1.371
1961	52.709	46.105	5.179	1.425
1971	55.515	48.750	5.229	1.536
1981	55.848	49.155	5.131	1.533
1991	56.487	49.890	4.999	1.578

Estimated population of England only in earlier years:

1570	4.160
1600	4.811
1630	5.600
1670	5.773
1700	6.045
1750	6.517

population (1992) 57,561,000 (81.5% English, 9.6% Scottish, 1.9% Welsh, 2.4% Irish, 1.8% Ulster); growth rate 0.1% p.a.

religion Christian (55% Protestant, 10% Roman Catholic); Muslim, Jewish, Hindu, Sikh

life expectancy men 72, women 78 (1989)

languages English, Welsh, Gaelic

literacy 99% (1989)

GNP $1,040.5 bn (1992)

V

Valera éamon de. Irish politician; see ◊de Valera.

Vane Henry 1613–1662. English politician. In 1640 elected a member of the ◊Long Parliament, he was prominent in the impeachment of Archbishop ◊Laud and in 1643–53 was in effect the civilian head of the Parliamentary government. At the Restoration of the monarchy he was executed.

Vansittart Robert Gilbert, 1st Baron Vansittart 1881–1957. British diplomat, noted for his anti-German polemic. He was permanent under-secretary of state for foreign affairs 1930–38 and chief diplomatic adviser to the foreign secretary 1938–41.

Verney ˉˉmund 1590–1642. English courtier, knight-marshal to Charles I from 1626. He sat as a member of both the Short and the Long Parliaments and, though sympathizing with the Parliamentary position, remained true to his allegiance: he died at his post as royal standard bearer at the Battle of ◊Edgehill.

Vernon Edward 1684–1757. English admiral who captured Portobello from the Spanish in the Caribbean 1739, with a loss of only seven men.

Victoria 1819–1901. Queen of the UK from 1837, when she succeeded her uncle William IV, and empress of India from 1876. In 1840 she married Prince ◊Albert of Saxe-Coburg and Gotha. Her relations with her prime ministers ranged from the affectionate (Melbourne and Disraeli) to the stormy (Peel, Palmerston, and Gladstone). Her golden jubilee 1887 and diamond jubilee 1897 marked a waning of republican sentiment, which had developed with her withdrawal from public life on Albert's death 1861.

Only child of Edward, Duke of Kent, fourth son of George III, she was born 24 May 1819 at Kensington Palace, London. She and Albert had four sons and five daughters. After Albert's death 1861 she lived mainly in retirement. Nevertheless, she kept control of affairs, refusing the Prince of Wales (Edward VII) any active role. From 1848 she regularly visited the Scottish Highlands, where she had a house at Balmoral built to Prince Albert's designs. She died at Osborne House, her home in the Isle of Wight, 22 Jan 1901, and was buried at Windsor.

Victorian Order, Royal one of the fraternities carrying with it the rank of knight; see ◊knighthood.

Victory British battleship, 2,198 tonnes/2,164 tons, launched 1765, and now in dry dock in Portsmouth harbour, England. It was the flagship of Admiral Nelson at Trafalgar.

Viking or *Norseman* medieval Scandinavian sea warrior. They traded with and raided Europe in the 8th–11th centuries, and often settled there. In France the Vikings were given Normandy. Under Sweyn I they conquered England 1013, and his son Canute was king of England as well as Denmark and Norway. In the east they established the first Russian state and founded ◊Novgorod. They reached the Byzantine Empire in the south, and in the west sailed the seas to Ireland, Iceland, Greenland, and North America.

viscount in the UK peerage, the fourth degree of nobility, between earl and baron.

Vortigern 5th century AD. English ruler, said by ◊Bede to have invited the Saxons to Britain to repel the ◊Picts and Scots, and to have married Rowena, daughter of ◊Hengist.

vote expression of opinion by ballot, show of hands, or other means. In systems that employ direct vote, the plebiscite and referendum are fundamental mechanisms. In parliamentary elections the results can be calculated in a number of ways.

Wales (Welsh *Cymru*) Principality of; constituent part of the UK, in the W between the Bristol Channel and the Irish Sea

area 20,780 sq km/8,021 sq mi

capital Cardiff

towns Swansea, Wrexham, Newport, Carmarthen

features Snowdonia Mountains (Snowdon 1,085 m/3,561 ft, the highest point in England and Wales) in the NW and in the SE the Black Mountains, Brecon Beacons, and Black Forest ranges; rivers Severn, Wye, Usk, and Dee

exports traditional industries (coal and steel) have declined, but varied modern and high-technology ventures are being developed; Wales has the largest concentration of Japanese-owned plants in the UK. It also has the highest density of sheep in the world and a dairy industry; tourism is important

currency pound sterling

population (1991) 2,811,865

languages Welsh 19% (1991), English

religions Nonconformist Protestant denominations; Roman Catholic minority

government returns 38 members to the UK Parliament.

Wales, Church in the Welsh Anglican Church, independent from the ◊Church of England.

Wales, Prince of title conferred on the eldest son of the UK's sovereign. Prince ◊Charles was invested as 21st prince of Wales at Caernarvon 1969 by his mother, Elizabeth II.

Wallace William 1272–1305. Scottish nationalist who led a revolt against English rule 1297, won a victory at Stirling, and assumed the

Wales: history for ancient history, see also ◊Britain, ancient.

c. 400 BC	Wales occupied by Celts from central Europe.
AD 50–60	Wales became part of the Roman Empire.
c. 200	Christianity adopted.
c. 450–600	Wales became the chief Celtic stronghold in the west since the Saxons invaded and settled in S Britain. The Celtic tribes united against England.
8th century	Frontier pushed back to ◊Offa's Dyke.
9th–11th centuries	Vikings raided the coasts. At this time Wales was divided into small states organized on a clan basis, although princes such as Rhodri (844–878), Howel the Good (*c.*904–949), and Griffith ap Llewelyn (1039–1063) temporarily united the country.
11th–12th centuries	Continual pressure on Wales from the Normans across the English border was resisted, notably by ◊Llewelyn I and II.
1277	Edward I of England accepted as overlord by the Welsh.
1284	Edward I completed the conquest of Wales that had been begun by the Normans.
1294	Revolt against English rule put down by Edward I.
1350–1500	Welsh nationalist uprisings against the English; the most notable was that led by Owen Glendower.
1485	Henry Tudor, a Welshman, became Henry VII of England.
1536–43	Acts of Union united England and Wales after conquest under Henry VIII. Wales sent representatives to the English Parliament; English law was established in Wales; English became the official language.
18th century	Evangelical revival made Nonconformism a powerful factor in Welsh life. A strong coal and iron industry developed in the south.
19th century	The miners and ironworkers were militant supporters of Chartism, and Wales became a stronghold of trade unionism and socialism.
1893	University of Wales founded.
1920s–30s	Wales suffered from industrial depression; unemployment reached 21% 1937, and a considerable exodus of population took place.
post-1945	Growing nationalist movement and a revival of the language, earlier su pressed or discouraged.
1966	◊Plaid Cymru, the Welsh National Party, returned its first member to Westminster.
1979	Referendum rejected a proposal for limited home rule.
1988	Bombing campaign against estate agents selling Welsh properties to English buyers. For other history, see ◊United Kingdom.

Wales: sovereigns and princes 844–1282

844–78	Rhodri the Great
878–916	Anarawd
915–50	Hywel Dda (Hywel the Good)
950–79	Iago ab Idwal
979–85	Hywel ab Ieuaf (Hywel the Bad)
985–86	Cadwallon
986–99	Maredudd ab Owain ap Hywel Dda
999–1008	Cynan ap Hywel ab Ieuaf
1018–23	Llywelynd ap Seisyll
1023–39	Iago ab Idwal ap Meurig
1039–63	Gruffydd ap Llywelyn ap Seisyll
1063–75	Bleddyn ap Cynfyn
1075–81	Trahaern ap Caradog
1081–1137	Gruffyd ap Cynan ab Iago
1137–70	Owain Gwynedd
1170–94	Dafydd ab Owain Gwynedd
1194–1240	Llywelyn Fawr (Llywelyn the Great)
1240–46	Daffyd ap Llywelyn
1246–82	Llywellyn ap Gruffydd ap Llywelyn

English Princes of Wales 1301 to present day

1301	Edward (II)	1688	James Francis Edward (Old Pretender)
1343	Edward (the Black Prince)		
1376	Richard (II)	1714	George Augustus (II)
1399	Henry of Monmouth (V)	1729	Frederick Lewis
1454	Edward of Westminster	1751	George William Frederick (III)
1471	Edward of Westminster (V)	1762	George Augustus Frederick (IV)
1483	Edward		
1489	Arthur Tudor	1841	Albert Edward (Edward VII)
1504	Henry Tudor (VIII)	1901	George (V)
1610	Henry Stuart	1910	Edward (VII)
1616	Charles Stuart (I)	1958	Charles Philip Arthur George
c. 1638	Charles (II)		

title 'governor of Scotland'. Edward I defeated him at Falkirk 1298, and Wallace was captured and executed.

Walpole Horace, 4th Earl of Orford 1717–1797. English novelist, letter writer and politician, the son of Robert Walpole. He was a Whig member of Parliament 1741–67. He converted his house at Strawberry Hill, Twickenham (then a separate town SW of London), into a Gothic castle; his The Castle of Otranto 1764 established the genre of the Gothic, or 'romance of terror', novel. More than 4,000 of his letters have been published.

Walpole Robert, 1st Earl of Orford 1676–1745. British Whig politician, the first 'prime minister' as First Lord of the Treasury and chancellor of the Exchequer 1715–17 and 1721–42. He encouraged trade and tried to avoid foreign disputes (until forced into the War of Jenkins's Ear with Spain 1739).

Walsingham Francis c. 1530–1590. English politician who, as secretary of state from 1573, both advocated a strong anti-Spanish policy and ran the efficient government spy system that made it work.

Walter Hubert died 1205.. Archbishop of Canterbury 1193–1205. As justiciar (chief political and legal officer) 1193–98, he ruled England during Richard I's absence and introduced the offices of coroner and justice of the peace.

Walter Lucy c. 1630–1658. Mistress of ◊Charles II, whom she met while a Royalist refugee in The Hague, Netherlands, 1648; the Duke of ◊Monmouth was their son.

wapentake subdivision of a county in the ◊Danelaw, corresponding to the ◊hundred in counties outside the Danelaw.

Warbeck Perkin c. 1474–1499. Flemish pretender to the English throne. Claiming to be Richard, brother of Edward V, he led a rising against Henry VII in 1497, and was hanged after attempting to escape from the Tower of London.

Warwick Richard Neville, Earl of Warwick 1428–1471. English politician, called *the Kingmaker*. During the Wars of the ◊Roses he fought at first on the Yorkist side against the Lancastrians, and was largely responsible for placing Edward IV on the throne. Having quarrelled with him, he restored Henry VI in 1470, but was defeated and killed by Edward at Barnet, Hertfordshire.

Waterloo, Battle of battle on 18 June 1815 in which British forces commanded by Wellington defeated the French army of Emperor Napoleon near the village of Waterloo, 13 km/8 mi S of Brussels, Belgium. Napoleon found Wellington's army isolated from his allies and began a direct offensive to smash them, but the British held on until joined by the Prussians under General Blücher. Four days later Napoleon abdicated for the second and final time.

Wavell Archibald, 1st Earl 1883–1950. British field marshal in World War II. As commander in chief in the Middle East, he successfully defended Egypt against Italy July 1939. He was transferred as commander in chief in India in July 1941, and was viceroy 1943–47.

Waverley John Anderson, 1st Viscount Waverley 1882–1958. British administrator. He organized civil defence for World War II, becoming home secretary and minister for home security in 1939 (the nationally distributed *Anderson shelters*, home outdoor air-raid shelters, were named after him). He was chancellor of the Exchequer 1943–45.

Webb (Martha) Beatrice (born Potter) 1858–1943 and Sidney (James), Baron Passfield 1859–1947. English social reformers, writers, and founders of the London School of Economics (LSE) 1895. They were early members of the socialist ◊Fabian Society, and were married in 1892. They argued for social insurance in their minority report (1909) of the Poor Law Commission, and wrote many influential books, including The History of Trade Unionism 1894, English Local Government 1906–29, and Soviet Communism 1935.

welfare state political system under which the state (rather than the individual or the private sector) has responsibility for the welfare of its citizens. Services such as unemployment and sickness benefits, family allowances and income supplements, pensions, medical care, and education may be provided and financed through state insurance schemes and taxation.

Wellesley Richard Colley, Marquess of Wellesley 1760–1842. British administrator; brother of the 1st Duke of Wellington. He was governor general of India 1798–1805, and by his victories over the Marathas of

W India greatly extended the territory under British rule. He was foreign secretary 1809–12, and lord lieutenant of Ireland 1821–28 and 1833–34.

Wellington Arthur Wellesley, 1st Duke of Wellington 1769–1852. British soldier and Tory politician. As commander in the ◊Peninsular War, he expelled the French from Spain 1814. He defeated Napoleon Bonaparte at Quatre-Bras and Waterloo 1815, and was a member of the Congress of Vienna. As prime minister 1828–30, he was forced to concede Roman Catholic emancipation.

Wellington was born in Ireland, the son of an Irish peer, and sat for a time in the Irish parliament. He was knighted for his army service in India and became a national hero with his victories of 1808–14 in the Peninsular War and as general of the allies against Napoleon. At the Congress of Vienna he opposed the dismemberment of France and supported restoration of the Bourbons. As prime minister he modified the Corn Laws but became unpopular for his opposition to parliamentary reform and his lack of opposition to Catholic emancipation. He was foreign secretary 1834–35 and a member of the cabinet 1841–46. He held the office of commander in chief of the forces at various times from 1827 and for life from 1842. His home was Apsley House in London.

wergild or *wergeld* in Anglo-Saxon and Germanic law during the Middle Ages, the compensation paid by a murderer to the relatives of the victim, its value dependent on the social rank of the deceased. It originated in European tribal society as a substitute for the blood feud (essentially a form of vendetta), and was replaced by punishments imposed by courts of law during the 10th and 11th centuries.

Wessex the kingdom of the West Saxons in Britain, said to have been founded by Cerdic about AD 500, covering present-day Hampshire, Dorset, Wiltshire, Berkshire, Somerset, and Devon. In 829 Egbert established West Saxon supremacy over all England.

Whig Party in the UK, predecessor of the Liberal Party. The name was first used of rebel ◊Covenanters and then of those who wished to exclude James II from the English succession (as a Roman Catholic). They were in power continuously 1714–60 and pressed for industrial and commercial development, a vigorous foreign policy, and religious toleration. During the French Revolution, the Whigs demanded parliamentary reform in Britain, and from the passing of the Reform Bill in 1832 became known as Liberals.

White Horse any of several hill figures in England, including the one on Bratton Hill, Wiltshire, said to commemorate Alfred the Great's victory over the Danes at Ethandun 878; and the one at Uffington, Berkshire, 110 m/360 ft long, and probably a tribal totem of the early Iron Age, 1st century BC.

White Paper in the UK and some other countries, an official document that expresses government policy on an issue. It is usually preparatory to the introduction of a parliamentary bill (a proposed act of Parliament). Its name derives from its having fewer pages than a government 'blue book', and therefore needing no blue paper cover.

Wight, Isle of island and county in S England *area* 380 sq km/147 sq mi *towns* Newport (administrative headquarters), resorts: Ryde, Sandown, Shanklin, Ventnor *features* the *Needles*, a group of pointed chalk rocks up to 30 m/100 ft high in the sea to the W; the *Solent*, the sea channel between Hampshire and the island (including the anchorage of *Spithead* opposite Portsmouth, used for naval reviews); *Cowes*, venue of Regatta Week and headquarters of the Royal Yacht Squadron; Osborne House, near Cowes, a home of Queen Victoria, for whom it was built 1845; Farringford, home of the poet Alfred Tennyson, near Freshwater *products* chiefly agricultural; tourism *population* (1991) 126,600 *famous people* Thomas Arnold, Robert Hooke *history* called *Vectis* ('separate division') by the Romans, who conquered it AD 43. Charles I was imprisoned 1647–48 in Carisbrooke Castle, now ruined.

Whittington Dick (Richard) 14th–15th centuries. English cloth merchant who was mayor of London 1397–98, 1406–07, and 1419–20. According to legend, he came to London as a poor boy with his cat when he heard that the streets were paved with gold and silver. His cat first appears in a play from 1605.

Wilberforce William 1759–1833. English reformer who was instrumental in abolishing slavery in the British Empire. He entered Parliament 1780; in 1807 his bill for the abolition of the slave trade was passed, and in 1833, largely through his efforts, slavery was abolished throughout the empire.

Wild Jonathan c. 1682–1725. English criminal who organized the thieves of London and ran an office that, for a payment, returned stolen goods to their owners. He was hanged at Tyburn.

Wilkes John 1727–1797. British Radical politician, imprisoned for his political views; member of Parliament 1757–64 and from 1774. He championed parliamentary reform, religious toleration, and US independence.

Wilkinson (Cecily) Ellen 1891–1947. journalist and Labour politician. She was an early member of the Independent Labour Party and an active campaigner for women's suffrage. As a member of parliament for Jarrow in 1936, she led the ◊Jarrow Crusade of 200 unemployed shipyard workers from Jarrow to London.

William four kings of England:

William (I) the Conqueror c. 1027–1087. King of England from 1066. He was the illegitimate son of Duke Robert the Devil and succeeded his father as duke of Normandy 1035. Claiming that his relative King Edward the Confessor had bequeathed him the English throne, William invaded the country 1066, defeating ◊Harold II at Hastings, Sussex, and was crowned king of England.

He was crowned in Westminster Abbey on Christmas Day 1066. He completed the establishment of feudalism in England, compiling detailed records of land and property in the Domesday Book, and kept the barons firmly under control. He died in Rouen after a fall from his horse and is buried in Caen, France. He was succeeded by his son William II.

William (II) Rufus ('the Red') c. 1056–1100. King of England from 1087, the third son of William the Conqueror. He spent most of his reign attempting to capture Normandy from his brother ◊Robert II, duke of Normandy. His extortion of money led his barons to revolt and caused confrontation with Bishop Anselm. He was killed while hunting in the New Forest, Hampshire, and was succeeded by his brother Henry I.

William (III) of Orange 1650–1702. King of Great Britain and Ireland from 1688, the son of William II of Orange and Mary, daughter of Charles I. He was offered the English crown by the parliamentary opposition to James II. He invaded England 1688 and in 1689 became joint sovereign with his wife, ◊Mary II. He spent much of his reign campaigning, first in Ireland, where he defeated James II at the battle of the Boyne 1690, and later against the French in Flanders. He was succeeded by Mary's sister, Anne.

William IV 1765–1837. King of Great Britain and Ireland from 1830, when he succeeded his brother George IV; third son of George III. He was created duke of Clarence 1789, and married Adelaide of Saxe-Meiningen (1792–1849) 1818. During the Reform Bill crisis he secured its passage by agreeing to create new peers to overcome the hostile majority in the House of Lords. He was succeeded by Victoria.

William the Lion 1143–1214. King of Scotland from 1165. He was captured by Henry II while invading England 1174, and forced to do homage, but Richard I abandoned the English claim to suzerainty for a money payment 1189. In 1209 William was forced by King John to renounce his claim to Northumberland.

William of Malmesbury c. 1080–c. 1143. English historian and monk. He compiled the Gesta regum/Deeds of the Kings c.1120–40 and Historia novella, which together formed a history of England to 1142.

William of Wykeham c. 1323–1404. English politician, bishop of Winchester from 1367, Lord Chancellor 1367–72 and 1389–91, and founder of Winchester College (public school) 1378 and New College, Oxford 1379.

Williams Shirley 1930–   . British Social Democrat Party politician. She was Labour minister for prices and consumer protection 1974–76, and education and science 1976–79. She became a founder member of the SDP (Social Democrat Party) 1981 and its president 1982. In 1983 she lost her parliamentary seat. She is the daughter of the socialist writer Vera Brittain (1894–1970).

William the Marshall 1st Earl of Pembroke c. 1146–1219. English knight, regent of England from 1216. After supporting the dying Henry II against Richard (later Richard I), he went on a crusade to Palestine, was pardoned by Richard, and was granted an earldom 1189. On King

John's death he was appointed guardian of the future Henry III, and defeated the French under Louis VIII to enable Henry to gain the throne.

Wilson (James) Harold, Baron Wilson of Rievaulx 1916– . British Labour politician, party leader from 1963, prime minister 1964–70 and 1974–76. His premiership was dominated by the issue of UK admission to membership of the European Community, the social contract (unofficial agreement with the trade unions), and economic difficulties.

   Wilson, born in Huddersfield, West Yorkshire, was president of the Board of Trade 1947–51 (when he resigned because of social-service cuts). In 1963 he succeeded Hugh Gaitskell as Labour leader and became prime minister the following year, increasing his majority 1966. He formed a minority government Feb 1974 and achieved a majority of three Oct 1974. He resigned 1976 and was succeeded by James Callaghan. He was knighted 1976 and made a peer 1983.

Windsor Castle British royal residence in Windsor, Berkshire, founded by William the Conqueror on the site of an earlier fortress. It includes the Perpendicular Gothic St George's Chapel and the Albert Memorial Chapel, beneath which George III, George IV, and William IV are buried. In the Home Park adjoining the castle is the Royal Mausoleum where Queen Victoria and Prince Albert are buried.

Windsor, House of official name of the British royal family since 1917, adopted in place of Saxe-Coburg-Gotha. Since 1960 those descendants of Elizabeth II not entitled to the prefix HRH (His/Her Royal Highness) have borne the surname Mountbatten-Windsor.

Wingate Orde Charles 1903–1944. British soldier. In 1936 he established a reputation for unorthodox tactics in Palestine. In World War II he served in the Middle East, and later led the Chindits, the 3rd Indian Division, in guerrilla operations against the Japanese army in Burma (now Myanmar).

Witan or *Witenagemot* council of the Anglo-Saxon kings, the forerunner of Parliament, but including only royal household officials, great landowners, and top churchmen.

Wolfe James 1727–1759. British soldier who served in Canada and commanded a victorious expedition against the French general

Montcalm in Québec on the Plains of Abraham, during which both commanders were killed. The British victory established their supremacy over Canada.

Wolseley Garnet Joseph, 1st Viscount Wolseley 1833–1913. British army officer. He fought in the Crimean War 1853–56 and then commanded in both the Ashanti War 1873–74 and last part of the Zulu War 1879–80. He campaigned in Egypt, but was too late to relieve General ¢Gordon at Khartoum.

Wolsey Thomas c. 1475–1530. English cleric and politician. In Henry VIII's service from 1509, he became archbishop of York 1514, cardinal and lord chancellor 1515, and began the dissolution of the monasteries. His reluctance to further Henry's divorce from Catherine of Aragon, partly because of his ambition to be pope, led to his downfall 1529. He was charged with high treason 1530 but died before being tried.

Woodforde James 1740–1803. British cleric who held livings in Somerset and Norfolk, and whose diaries 1758–1802 form a record of rural England.

Wookey Hole natural cave near Wells, Somerset, England, in which flint implements of Old Stone Age people and bones of extinct animals have been found.

woolsack in the UK, the seat of the Lord High Chancellor in the House of Lords: it is a large square bag of wool and is a reminder of the principal source of English wealth in the Middle Ages.

Workmen's Compensation Act British legislation 1897 that conferred on workers a right to compensation for the loss of earnings resulting from an injury at work.

Wyatt Thomas c. 1503–1542. English poet. He was employed on diplomatic missions by Henry VIII, and in 1536 was imprisoned for a time in the Tower of London, suspected of having been the lover of Henry's second wife, Anne Boleyn. In 1541 Wyatt was again imprisoned on charges of treason. With the Earl of Surrey, he introduced the sonnet to England.

Wycliffe John c. 1320–1384. English religious reformer. Allying himself with the party of John of Gaunt, which was opposed to ecclesiastical influence at court, he attacked abuses in the church, maintaining that the Bible rather than the church was the supreme authority. He criticized such fundamental doctrines as priestly absolution, confession, and indulgences, and set disciples to work on translating the Bible into English.

Y

yeoman in England, a small landowner who farmed his own fields – a system that formed a bridge between the break-up of feudalism and the agricultural revolution of the 18th–19th centuries.

Yeomen of the Guard English military corps, popularly known as *Beefeaters*, the sovereign's bodyguard since the corps was founded by Henry VII 1485. Its duties are now purely ceremonial.

York English dynasty founded by Richard, Duke of York (1411–60). He claimed the throne through his descent from Lionel, Duke of Clarence (1338–1368), third son of Edward III, whereas the reigning monarch, Henry VI of the rival house of Lancaster, was descended from the fourth son. The argument was fought out in the Wars of the ◊Roses. York was killed at the Battle of Wakefield 1460, but next year his son became King Edward IV, in turn succeeded by his son Edward V and then by his brother Richard III, with whose death at Bosworth the line ended. The Lancastrian victor in that battle was crowned Henry VII and consolidated his claim by marrying Edward IV's eldest daughter, Elizabeth.

York Frederick Augustus, duke of York 1763–1827. Second son of George III. He was an unsuccessful commander in the Netherlands 1793–99 and British commander in chief 1798–1809.

Young England group of Cambridge-educated English aristocrats, newly elected to Parliament 1841, who shared a distaste for the growth of democracy and manufacturing industry in contemporary England, and who promoted instead a revived traditional church and aristocracy to preserve society. The movement faded within five years, but its spirit was captured by Benjamin ◊Disraeli, the future prime minister, in his novel Coningsby 1844.

Young Ireland Irish nationalist organization, founded 1840 by William Smith O'Brien (1803–1864), who attempted an abortive insurrection of the peasants against the British in Tipperary 1848. O'Brien was sentenced to death, but later pardoned.

Young Pretender nickname of ◊Charles Edward Stuart, claimant to the Scottish and English thrones.

Ypres, 1st Earl of title of Sir John ◊French, British field marshal.

Appendix

the (British) Commonwealth

country	capital	date joined	area in sq km	constitutional status
in Africa				
Botswana	Gaborone	1966	582,000	sovereign republic
British Indian Ocean Territory	Victoria	1965	60	Britishdependent territory
Gambia	Banjul	1965	10,700	sovereign republic
Ghana	Accra	1957	238,300	sovereign republic
Kenya	Nairobi	1963	582,600	sovereign republic
Lesotho	Maseru	1966	30,400	sovereign constitutional monarchy
Malawi	Lilongwe	1964	118,000	sovereign republic
Mauritius	Port Louis	1968	2,000	sovereign republic
Namibia	Windhoek	1990	824,000	sovereign republic
Nigeria	Abuja	1960	924,000	sovereign republic
St Helena	Jamestown	1931	100	British dependent territory
Seychelles	Victoria	1976	450	sovereign republic
Sierra Leone	Freetown	1961	73,000	sovereign republic
Swaziland	Mbabane	1968	17,400	sovereign republic
Tanzania	Dodoma	1961	945,000	sovereign republic
Uganda	Kampala	1962	236,900	sovereign republic
Zambia	Lusaka	1964	752,600	sovereign republic
Zimbabwe	Harare	1980	390,300	sovereign republic
in the Americas				
Anguilla	The Valley	1931	155	British dependent territory
Antigua and Barbuda	St John's	1981	400	sovereign constitutional monarchy *

country	capital	date joined	area in sq km	constitutional status
Bahamas	Nassau	1973	13,900	sovereign constitutional monarchy*
Barbados	Bridgetown	1966	400	sovereign constitutional monarchy*
Belize	Belmopan	1981	23,000	sovereign constitutional monarchy*
Bermuda	Hamilton	1931	54	British dependent territory
British Virgin Islands	Road Town	1931	153	British dependent territory
Canada	Ottawa	1931	9,958,400	sovereign constitutional monarchy*
Cayman Islands	Georgetown	1931	300	British dependentterritory
Dominica	Roseau	1978	700	sovereign republic
Falkland Islands	Port Stanley	1931	12,100	British dependent territory
Grenada	St George's	1974	300	sovereign constitutional monarchy*
Guyana	Georgetown	1966	215,000	sovereign republic
Jamaica	Kingston	1962	11,400	sovereign constitutional monarchy*
Montserrat	Plymouth	1931	100	British dependent territory
St Christopher–Nevis	Basseterre	1983	300	sovereign constitutional monarchy *
St Lucia	Castries	1979	600	sovereign constitutional monarchy*
St Vincent and the Grenadines	Kingstown	1979	400	sovereign constitutional monarchy *
Trinidad and Tobago	Port of Spain	1962	5,100	sovereign republic
Turks and Caicos Islands	Grand Turk	1931	400	British dependent territory

the (British) Commonwealth (cont.)

country	capital	date joined	area in sq km	constitutional status
in the Antarctic				
Australian Antarctic Territory	uninhabited	1936	5,403,000	Australian external territory
British Antarctic Territory	uninhabited	1931	390,000	British dependent territory
Falkland Islands Dependencies	uninhabited	1931	1,600	British dependent territories
Ross Dependency	uninhabited	1931	453,000	New Zealand associated territory
in Asia				
Bangladesh	Dhaka	1972	144,000	sovereign republic
Brunei	Bandar Seri Begawan	1984	5,800	sovereign monarchy
Hong Kong	Victoria	1931	1,100	British crown colony
India	Delhi	1947	3,166,800	sovereign republic
Malaysia	Kuala Lumpur	1957	329,800	sovereign constitutional monarchy
Maldives	Malé	1982	300	sovereign republic
Pakistan	Islamabad	1947†	803,900	sovereign republic
Singapore	Singapore	1965	600	sovereign republic
Sri Lanka	Colombo	1948	66,000	sovereign republic
in Australasia and the Pacific				
Australia	Canberra	1931	7,682,300	sovereign constitutional monarchy *
Cook Islands	Avarua	1931	300	New Zealand associated territory
Norfolk Island	Kingston	1931	34	Australian external territory
Kiribati	Tarawa	1979	700	sovereign republic
Nauru	Yaren	1968	21	sovereign republic

country	capital	date joined	area in sq km	constitutional status
New Zealand	Wellington	1931	268,000	sovereign constitutional monarchy *
Niue	Alofi	1931	300	New Zealand associated territory
Papua New Guinea	Port Moresby	1975	462,800	sovereign constitutional monarchy *
Pitcairn Islands	Adamstown	1931	5	British dependent territory
Solomon Islands	Honiara	1978	27,600	sovereign constitutional monarchy *
Tokelau	Nukunonu	1931	10	New Zealand associated territory
Tonga	Nuku'alofa	1970	700	sovereign monarchy
Tuvalu	Funafuti	1978	24	sovereign constitutional monarchy*
Vanuatu	Vila	1980	15,000	sovereign republic
Western Samoa	Apia	1970	2,800	sovereign republic

in Europe

country	capital	date joined	area in sq km	constitutional status
Channel Islands		1931	200	UK crown dependencies
Guernsey	St Peter Port			
Jersey	St Helier			
Cyprus	Nicosia	1961	9,000	sovereign republic
Gibraltar	Gibraltar	1931	6	British dependent territory
Malta	Valletta	1964	300	sovereign republic
Isle of Man	Douglas	1931	600	UK crown dependency
United Kingdom	London	1931	244,100	sovereign constitutional monarchy *
England	London			
Northern Ireland	Belfast			
Scotland	Edinburgh			
Wales	Cardiff			
TOTAL			33,089,900	

*Queen Elizabeth II constitutional monarch and head of state † left 1972 and rejoined 1989

English sovereigns from 900

name	accession	relationship
West Saxon Kings		
Edward the Elder	901	son of Alfred the Great
Athelstan	925	son of Edward I
Edmund	940	half brother of Athelstan
Edred	946	brother of Edmund
Edwy	955	son of Edmund
Edgar	959	brother of Edwy
Edward the Martyr	975	son of Edgar
Ethelred II	978	son of Edgar
Edmund Ironside	1016	son of Ethelred
Danish Kings		
Canute	1016	son of Sweyn
Hardicanute	1040	son of Canute
Harold I	1035	son of Canute
West Saxon Kings (restored)		
Edward the Confessor	1042	son of Ethelred II
Harold II	1066	son of Godwin
Norman Kings		
William I	1066	
William II	1087	son of William I
Henry I	1100	son of William I
Stephen	1135	son of Adela (daughter of William I)
House of Plantagenet		
Henry II	1154	son of Matilda (daughter of Henry I)
Richard I	1189	son of Henry II
John	1199	son of Henry II
Henry III	1216	son of John
Edward I	1272	son of Henry III
Edward II	1307	son of Edward I
Edward III	1327	son of Edward II
Richard II	1377	son of the Black Prince (son of Edward III)
House of Lancaster		
Henry IV	1399	son of John of Gaunt
Henry V	1413	son of Henry IV
Henry VI	1422	son of Henry V

House of York

Edward IV	1461	son of Richard, Duke of York
Edward V	1483	son of Edward IV
Richard III	1483	brother of Edward IV

House of Tudor

Henry VII	1485	son of Edmund Tudor, Earl of Richmond
Henry VIII	1509	son of Henry VII
Edward VI	1547	son of Henry VIII
Mary I	1553	daughter of Henry VIII
Elizabeth I	1558	daughter of Henry VIII

House of Stuart

James I	1603	great-grandson of Margaret (daughter of Henry VII)
Charles I	1625	son of James I

The Commonwealth
House of Stuart (restored)

Charles II	1660	son of Charles I
James II	1685	son of Charles I
William III and Mary	1689	son of Mary (daughter of Charles I)/daughter of James II
Anne	1702	daughter of James II

House of Hanover

George I	1714	son of Sophia (granddaughter of James I)
George II	1727	son of George I
George III	1760	son of Frederick (son of George II)
George IV	1820	son of George III
William IV	1830	son of George III
Victoria	1837	daughter of Edward (son of George III)

House of Saxe Coburg

Edward VII	1901	son of Victoria

House of Windsor

George V	1910	son of Edward VII
Edward VIII	1936	son of George V
George VI	1936	son of George V
Elizabeth II	1952	daughter of George VI

England: historic and modern counties

historic counties

Bedfordshire
Berkshire
Buckinghamshire
Cambridgeshire and Isle of Ely
Cheshire
Cornwall
Cumberland
Derbyshire
Devonshire
Dorset
Durham
Essex
Gloucestershire
Hampshire
Herefordshire
Hertfordshire
Huntingdonshire and Peterborough
Kent
Lancashire
Leicestershire
Lincolnshire
  Holland
  Kesteven
  Lindsey
Greater London

Norfolk
Northamptonshire
Northumberland
Nottinghamshire
Oxfordshire
Rutland
Shropshire
Somerset
Staffordshire
Suffolk
  East Suffolk
  West Suffolk
Surrey
Sussex
  East Sussex
  West Sussex
Warwickshire
Westmorland
Wight, Isle of
Wiltshire
Worcestershire
Yorkshire
  East Riding
  North Riding
  West Riding

modern counties

county	administrative headquarters	area in sq km
Avon	Bristol	1,340
Bedfordshire	Bedford	1,240
Berkshire	Reading	1,260
Buckinghamshire	Aylesbury	1,880
Cambridgeshire	Cambridge	3,410
Cheshire	Chester	2,320

Cleveland	Middlesbrough	580
Cornwall	Truro	3,550
Cumbria	Carlisle	6,810
Derbyshire	Matlock	2,630
Devon	Exeter	6,720
Dorset	Dorchester	2,650
Durham	Durham	2,440
East Sussex	Lewes	1,800
Essex	Chelmsford	3,670
Gloucestershire	Gloucester	2,640
Hampshire	Winchester	3,770
Hereford & Worcester	Worcester	3,930
Hertfordshire	Hertford	1,630
Humberside	Beverley	3,510
Isle of Wight	Newport	380
Kent	Maidstone	3,730
Lancashire	Preston	3,040
Leicestershire	Leicester	2,550
Lincolnshire	Lincoln	5,890
London, Greater		1,580
Manchester, Greater		1,290
Merseyside		65°
Norfolk	Norwich	5
Northamptonshire	Northampton	2,.
Northumberland	Morpeth	5,03°
North Yorkshire	Northallerton	8,320
Nottinghamshire	Nottingham	2,160
Oxfordshire	Oxford	2,610
Shropshire	Shrewsbury	3,490
Somerset	Taunton	3,460
South Yorkshire		1,560
Staffordshire	Stafford	2,720
Suffolk	Ipswich	3,800
Surrey	Kingston upon Thames	1,660
Tyne & Wear		540
Warwickshire	Warwick	1,980
West Midlands		900
West Sussex	Chichester	2,020
West Yorkshire		2,040
Wiltshire	Trowbridge	3,480

Scotland: historic counties and modern regions

modern regions

Borders	Dunbarton
Central	East Lothian
Dumfries and Galloway	Fife
Fife	Inverness
Grampian	Kincardine
Highland	Kinross
Lothian	Kirkcudbright
Orkney Islands	Lanark
Shetland Islands	Midlothian
Strathclyde	Moray
Tayside	Nairn
Western Isles	Orkney
historic counties	Peebles
Aberdeen	Perth
Angus (fomerly Forfar)	Renfrew
Argyll	Ross and Cromarty
Ayr	Roxburgh
Banff	Selkirk
Berwick	Stirling
Bute	Sutherland
Caithness	West Lothian
Clackmannan .	Wigtown
Dumfries	Zetland

Wales: counties

county	administrative headquarters	area in sq km
Clwyd	Mold	2,420
Dyfed	Carmarthen	5,770
Gwent	Cwmbran	1,380
Gwynedd	Caernarfon	3,870
Mid Glamorgan	Cardiff	1,020
Powys	Llandrindod Wells	5,080
South Glamorgan	Cardiff	420
West Glamorgan	Swansea	820
		20,780

Wales: historic counties

Anglesey
Brecknockshire
Caernarvonshire
Cardiganshire
Carmarthenshire
Denbighshire
Flintshire
Glamorgan
Merioneth
Monmouthshire
Montgomeryshire
Pembrokeshire
Radnorshire

Royal Family Tree: William I to Elizabeth II

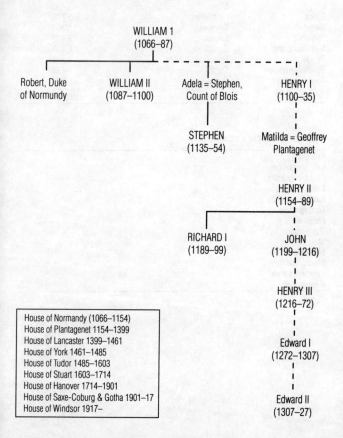

WILLIAM 1
(1066–87)

Robert, Duke
of Normundy

WILLIAM II
(1087–1100)

Adela = Stephen,
Count of Blois

HENRY I
(1100–35)

STEPHEN
(1135–54)

Matilda = Geoffrey
Plantagenet

HENRY II
(1154–89)

RICHARD I
(1189–99)

JOHN
(1199–1216)

HENRY III
(1216–72)

Edward I
(1272–1307)

Edward II
(1307–27)

House of Normandy (1066–1154)
House of Plantagenet 1154–1399
House of Lancaster 1399–1461
House of York 1461–1485
House of Tudor 1485–1603
House of Stuart 1603–1714
House of Hanover 1714–1901
House of Saxe-Coburg & Gotha 1901–17
House of Windsor 1917–

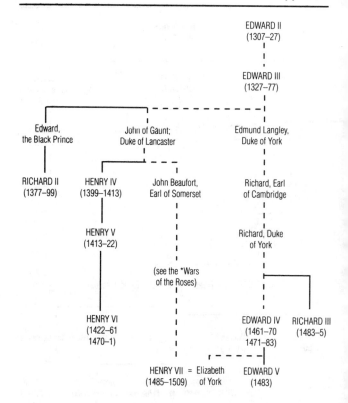

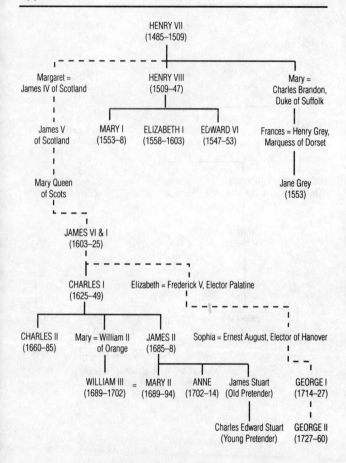

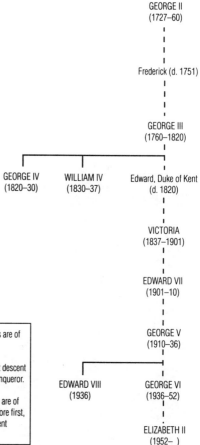

GEORGE II
(1727–60)

Frederick (d. 1751)

GEORGE III
(1760–1820)

GEORGE IV   WILLIAM IV   Edward, Duke of Kent
(1820–30)   (1830–37)   (d. 1820)

VICTORIA
(1837–1901)

EDWARD VII
(1901–10)

GEORGE V
(1910–36)

EDWARD VIII   GEORGE VI
(1936)   (1936–52)

ELIZABETH II
(1952–)

Monarchs are in capitals; the dates are of their reigns.

The − − − line traces the direct descent of Elizabeth II from William the Conqueror.

People on the same horizontal line are of the same generation and are therefore first, second or third cousins if in different branches of the family.